STATIC SOCIETY:
THE PARADOX OF LATIN AMERICA

STATIC SOCIETY:
The Paradox of Latin America

by

JOHN MANDER

LONDON
VICTOR GOLLANCZ LTD
1969

© John Mander 1969

575 00185 2

Printed in Great Britain by
The Camelot Press Ltd, London and Southampton

CONTENTS

INTRODUCTION

My PERSONAL INTEREST in Latin America began, a year
or two back, when I spent some months in Latin America
preparing a special issue of the British magazine *Encounter*.
I had no specialist knowledge of the field, and even felt, like
many Anglo-Saxons, a certain distaste for it. I had visited
Spain; but was no *aficionado*. I had been fascinated by Prescott
as a boy (with shameful precocity, I had demanded the *History
of the Conquest of Mexico* for my twelfth birthday). But, apart
from that, what did one know of Latin America? I remembered,
also from childhood, W. J. Turner's *Romance*:

> When I was but thirteen or so
> I went into a golden land
> Chimborazo, Cotopaxi
> Took me by the hand . . .
>
> I walked in a great golden dream
> To and fro from school—
> Shining Popocatepetl
> The dusty streets did rule . . .
>
> The houses, people, traffic seemed
> Thin fading dreams by day,
> Chimborazo, Cotopaxi
> They had stolen my soul away!

In reading Prescott, perhaps, one had felt a touch of the same
magic. But it was strictly an escapist interest; it belonged to
romance, not to history. It could never compete in respectability
with Latin prose.

Certainly I do not remember pursuing the interest. After
Cortes and Pizarro, the history of the continent seemed to
grow dark and confused. I did read a book on Bolivar and saw

reflected in him something of the glory of the *conquistadores*. But not until I came to read Conrad's *Nostromo* was I brought to think again of Latin America. The native literature seemed largely unknown or untranslated. Nobody at school or university ever urged me to read a book by a Latin American. (Admittedly, this was before Machado de Assis and Borges had been translated into English). I was interested in politics; but, politically, the continent seemed to have little to recommend it. There was a confused noise—it was the late 1940's—from the direction of Buenos Aires; Peron was nationalising the British railways. I, too, was anti-imperialist. But Latin American politics were not of a kind one could take seriously. Again, nobody I knew had met a Latin American or had ever been to Latin America. It seemed unlikely one would ever go there oneself. An earlier generation had uncles and cousins out in Argentina; but it was all pre-war and slightly ridiculous, like Tango Teas. For all our generation cared, Cortes and Pizarro might never have set eyes on Chimborazo or Popocatepetl. We were excited about Europe's problems, and Asia's, and Africa's. Those were serious days; one war was over; a new, cold war was about to begin. Latin America did not fit into the scheme. Her grandeurs and miseries left us unmoved.

Since then, half a generation has passed, and the picture looks different. Politically, Fidel Castro put Latin America on the map again, and gave her the reputation of a "revolutionary continent". Word got round that in the arts Latin America had something to offer: Borges, Neruda, Carpentier became something more than mere names. The new abstract painters and sculptors, the new architects of Latin America, became part of the international scene. With Leopoldo Torre Nilsson, with Buñuel's *Los Olvidados*, Latin America began to make an impression on the international film world. In response to Castro, Latin America began to enter—a little later than Asia and Africa, but not too late to share in the feast—the affluent world of international seminars, of travelling fellowships and foundation projects. The most neglected area of the under-developed world became, overnight, the most worried-over and sought-after. Several years ago, I have been told, Mr McGeorge Bundy remarked indiscreetly to some Harvard men that "second-rate subjects attract second-rate minds".

He had, it was said, Latin America in mind. The remark got around; it gave offence. Yet it was plainly correct. And it was as true of Britain as of the United States. Good students were not attracted to the subject, for a number of reasons. For one thing, there were too few opportunities to carve a career out of the subject. In the Foreign Service, Latin America was a pasture where ageing diplomats were put out to grass. Academic prospects were poor; and the chances of being sent out as a research graduate, an economic adviser or agricultural expert, were less good than in Afro-Asia. A few gallant spirits persevered; but it had the unenviable reputation of a dead-end occupation.

That has now changed. And changed suddenly and dramatically—so much so that we are entitled to be a little sceptical. For there were understandable reasons why Latin America had not appealed to the best students. Brilliant students are snobbish; and how could Latin America compete with France, Germany or Russia in the matter of learning a foreign language and spending precious years in acquiring knowledge of a different culture? This had not been the case in the days of Prescott and Ticknor, who experienced the first flush of the Romantic rediscovery of Spain. But it has been true in our own time. The Spanish language has been considered in Britain, as in the United States, an easy option—too easy, evidently, for scholars to take the trouble to learn it. The civilisation of Spain was a failed civilisation: after the *siglo de oro*, what did it have to offer? The Inquisition; the imbecile royalty of the later Habsburgs, or of Goya's Bourbons; the intellectual decay of the three centuries between Saint Theresa and Cervantes and the Generation of '98. But the famous Generation of '98—Machado and Unamuno, Baroja and Valle-Inclan—what did it amount to? Did it really offer a renaissance of the Spanish spirit, or even a Modernism comparable with that of Eliot and Proust, Yeats and Valéry, Brecht and Mayakovsky? Rightly or wrongly, most Anglo-Saxon intellectuals were unwilling to grant it the same stature. And as to Hispanic tradition, foreigners can hardly be blamed for taking what was, after all, a view taken by sophisticated Spaniards and Latin Americans themselves. Who but a Spaniard could have written Ortega y Gasset's *España Invertebrada*? Who but a Mexican, Samuel Ramos's

devastating auto-critique, *Profile of Man and Culture in Mexico*?
A neglected subject, then. But a second-rate one? This
seemed less certain. Admittedly, when one began to consult the
standard books on the subject, one's heart sank. So much easy,
hysterical journalism! So much heavy, unilluminating scholarship! It was a dispiriting experience. Part of the trouble, one
realised, was that since the days of Humboldt and Prescott
this had been an almost bookless subject. There had been great
naturalists and explorers: W. H. Hudson, Charles Darwin,
William Bates, Charles Waterton. But there had been no great
historians, no great writers—with the exception of Conrad
and of D. H. Lawrence—to open up for Anglo-Saxons this
"other America". Certainly, there was no shortage of books
with titles like "Latin America in crisis", "Whither Latin
America?", "Latin America: the turbulent continent". But
these proved disappointing: too many were journalistic write-
ups; well-informed, but surprisingly lacking in historical
perspective or even intellectual curiosity. As far as the United
States is concerned, Fidel Castro must bear the major responsibility for this mushroom growth. But the book I was looking
for—as one ignorant of the subject and anxious to be informed
—did not exist. No book conveyed what I personally was to
find interesting about Latin America, as I read myself into its
problems. Either the author must have exhausted the subject
very quickly, I reflected, or the subject the author. Was Latin
America really *so* uninteresting? In the end, I saw that carping
would do no good. If the book I was looking for did not exist, I
should have to write it myself.

This, then, is the origin of the present book. It makes no
claim to be a comprehensive survey; but neither is it purely
impressionistic. Since I had to leave out a great deal, I concentrated on those things which I found interesting and which
I missed in my own reading of the literature. Thus, I have not
attempted to go into the history and contemporary politics of
each nation in detail. That would be impractical. I have tried,
rather, to say something about those phenomena that seem
peculiar to Latin America—the Role of the Military; the rise
of left-wing-nationalist-populist parties; the Cosmopolitan-
Nativist antinomy—and to explain these peculiarities in terms
of Latin American experience. Since the purpose of my own

trip was to enlist the help of some of the intellectuals, economists, writers, and other *pensadores* of present-day Latin America, I have tended to concentrate on the reactions of such people, rather than on those of their less articulate countrymen. True, this may have led to an over-emphasis on their characteristics. I remain impenitent. An afternoon spent with Borges or Neruda, with Nicanor Parra or Carlos Fuentes, is worth many an afternoon spent visiting this government's new steel plant or that municipality's air-conditioned *crèche*. It was the *individuality* of Latin America I was looking for. The criterion by which I would like this book to be judged is whether it has caught something of that individuality. Latin America is a various continent; but it is also more consistent, for good or for ill, than people suppose. And, in the end, Latin America is not just a geographical or linguistic entity: it is an experience. To convey that experience in its fullness, of course, is not something the outsider can hope to do. But he is free to search for hints and intimations, to peer over the shoulders of those who have lived the experience. I have tried to do something of that sort in this book. I offer it as a Latin Primer, as a groundling's grammar. But also as an aperitif, an opener of the mind. And, if my own experience is any guide, this is a pump from which, once primed, others will feel inclined to slake their curiosity.

JOHN MANDER

November 1968

STATIC SOCIETY:
THE PARADOX OF LATIN AMERICA

I

MEXICO:

or Revolution and Conservatism

If anyone wishes to try the effect of strong contrast, let him come direct from the United States to this country. . . .

Travelling in New England, for example, we arrive at a small and flourishing village. We see four new churches, proclaiming four different sects; religion suited to all customers. Hard by is a tavern with a green paling, as clean and as new as the churches, and there are also various smart stores and neat dwelling-houses. . . . The whole has a cheerful, trim, and flourishing aspect. . . . Every-thing proclaims prosperity, equality, consistency; the past forgotten, the present all in all, and the future taking care of itself. No delicate attentions to posterity, who can never pay its debts. . . . Transport yourself in imagination from this New England village to that of ——, it matters not which, not far from Mexico. . . . The Indian huts, with their half-naked inmates, and little gardens full of flowers . . . at a little distance an *hacienda*, like a deserted palace, built of solid masonry, with great walls and iron-barred windows that might stand a siege. . . . There, rising in the midst of old faithful-looking trees, the church, grey and ancient, but strong as if designed for eternity; with its saints and virgins, its gold and silver and precious stones, whose value would buy up all the spare lots in the New England village. . . . Here, everything reminds us of the past; of the conquering Spaniards, who seem to build for eternities, impressing each work with their own solid, grave, and religious character. . . . It is the present that seems like a dream, a pale reflection of the past. All is decaying and growing fainter, and men seem trusting to an unknown future which they may never see. . . .

Let them beware lest half a century later, they be awak-ened from their delusion, and find the cathedral turned into a meeting house, and all painted white; the silver transformed into dollars; the Virgin's jewels sold to the highest bidder. . . . And round the whole, a nice new wooden paling, freshly done in green—and all this performed by some of the artists from the wide-awake republic farther north.

Life in Mexico: Fanny Calderon de la Barca (1843)

Mexico City

As LUCK WOULD HAVE IT, the most romantic approach to
Mexico City is also the commonest: by air from New York,
Miami, Caracas or Havana. Winging down from the Caribbean sky into the broad crater of the Valley of Mexico, lorded
over by the white-capped volcanoes of Popocatepetl and Ixtac-
cihuatl, you will experience—if your heart was ever stolen by
"shining Popocatepetl"—something of what the *conquistadores*
felt when they crossed the mountains from Vera Cruz for the
first time and came on the Aztec city of Tenochtitlan. That
first blinding vision is caught, uniquely, in the pages of Bernal
Diaz del Castillo, a young companion of Cortes. In a famous
passage of the homespun classic he wrote in Guatemala as an
old man, *The True History of the Conquest of New Spain*, Bernal
Diaz conjures back that enchantment:

> Next morning we came to a broad causeway and continued our
> march towards Itztapalapa. And when we saw all those cities
> and villages built on the water, and all the great towns on dry
> land, and that straight and level causeway leading to Mexico,
> we were astounded. These great towns and *cues* and buildings
> rising from the water, all made of stone, seemed like an enchanted
> vision from the tales of Amadis. Indeed, some of our soldiers asked
> whether it were not all a dream. It is not surprising therefore that
> I should write in this vein. It was all so wonderful that I do not
> know how to describe this first glimpse of things never heard of,
> seen, nor dreamed of before.

We need not fear, evidently, in romanticising the *conquista*,
that we are falling into historical anachronism. Cortes and his
men were fed on the romantic tales of Amadis de Gaula—
tales that, to the foreign eye, Cervantes appears to be ridiculing
in *Don Quixote*. In fact, Cervantes is not the mocker he seems to
the pragmatic Anglo-Saxon mind: he knew that Spain required
both Sancho Panza and the ingenious Don. And in these most
Spanish of exploits, the Conquests of Mexico and Peru, we
can detect the presence of both Sancho and the Don.

I shall not attempt to describe Mexico City as it is today. It has become the greatest tourist attraction in the Western Hemisphere. And not only for *yanquis*. The French, too, have a traditional *penchant* for Mexico, the tragic land of Maximilian, executed by Juarez's revolutionaries—and immortalised by Monet. It is the French who treat us to the most daring hyperboles on the subject of Mexico: both Greece and Mexico, we are told, are wild and barren and ancient in civilisation, savage and yet refined, cruel and chaotic lands where man attempts what nature has neglected, reducing to aesthetic order what would otherwise be rock and scrub and frozen lava. Nor are the French alone in their fervid *Mexicanismo*. The earliest, and most distinguished foreign observer of Mexico was the Prussian Baron Alexander von Humboldt, whose *Narrative of Travels to the Equinoctial Regions of the New World* (1799–1802), translated into English by Helen Maria Williams, is possibly the greatest book ever written by a foreigner about Latin America.

For the Germans the charm of Mexico, since the days of Humboldt, is that it is not only *Naturlandschaft*, but also *Kulturlandschaft*. It is a snobbish concept, perhaps, but a graphic one. For America is *par excellence* the continent of *Naturlandschaft*. Indeed, it was this that excited the envy of Goethe, Humboldt's friend, admirer and, in his casual way, collaborator:

> *Amerika, du hast es besser*
> *Als unser Kontinent, der alte.*
> *Du hast keine verfallenen Schlösser* . . .

Certainly, Goethe may have been mocking at those "ruined castles" out of spite for the Romantics. The Olympian of Weimar was not above that. He had employed still creakier stage machinery in his time. But for Goethe, plainly, it is *Natur* that is king in America; *Kultur* is an European importation, and possibly a discordant one. It is a theme, as we shall see, that runs like a thread through the literature of Latin America —as it does, though to lesser extent, through the literature of North America. (Let us take a decision at this point: let us use the term "America", as Latin Americans use it, to designate the entire Western hemisphere, and refer to "America" either

as the United States or as North America.) According to
German usage, North America is not a *Kulturlandschaft* at all;
it has no cathedrals, no Roman roads, no cromlechs—let alone
ruined castles. Lacking which, by European standards, it
hardly qualifies as a *Kulturlandschaft*. But what of Mexico?
Mexico has a tradition of high culture older than Northern
Europe: she cannot be denied the title of a *Kulturlandschaft*.
Yet equally, a great part of her appeal is that she is at the same
time a *Naturlandschaft* of stark, untameable beauty.

The British, of European peoples, are the least romantically
involved with Mexico. There are Lawrence's *The Plumed
Serpent* and his *Mornings in Mexico*, there are Graham Greene's
The Lawless Roads and *The Power and the Glory*; there is Malcolm
Lowry's *Under the Volcano*; there is Sybille Bedford's delightful
A Visit to Don Octavio. In the faraway 1840's, there was Fanny
Calderon de la Barca, the lively Scots girl who married a
Spanish diplomat and wrote the most entertaining, if not
the most accurate, account of life in old Mexico that we
possess. Still, none of this amounts to a romantic attachment.
It is not that Mexico is distant (she is not, after all, as distant as
India). It is rather that Britain was never involved with
Mexico as she was with Argentina and Brazil, Chile and
Uruguay—countries she helped to develop, and dominated economically for more than a century. Mexico, indeed, is one of
the few countries in the world where British influence did not
make itself felt during the nineteenth century. At few points,
therefore, do Mexican and British history impinge on one
another. For three centuries the British, and other foreigners,
were excluded by Spain. In the nineteenth century the overwhelming intellectual influence was French: the power interest
(after Santa Anna's disastrous Texan campaign of the 1840's)
that of the United States. In the twentieth century Mexico has
retreated into herself intellectually and spiritually. In terms of
economic power—whatever her leaders may say—she has become more and more a satellite of the United States.

In Buenos Aires it is impossible to enter a railway station
without being reminded of Paddington or Victoria. The banks
and post offices of Santiago and Montevideo are out of Dickens
and Arnold Bennett. But in Mexico City, Puebla or Guadala-
jara, there is nothing of this. Here all is French. The great

Paseo de la Reforma, driven through the narrow streets of the old Colonial city in Emperor Maximilian's time, reminds one of the boulevards Haussmann drove through Paris for Napoleon III (Napoleon's protégé, Maximilian, initiated the project; but it was named—such is the irony of history—after the *Reforma,* the Liberal reform movement led by Benito Juarez, who was to order his execution). The florid Art Nouveau *Museo de Bellas Artes* near the *Alameda* is ripe French nonsense from the Belle Epoque. The dominant philosophy of the time—or should it be religion?—was the *positivisme* of Comte, against whose rationalism Mexico reacted so violently in the revolutionary decade after 1910. Yet, in all this, Mexico is simply Latin America carried to an extreme. For nineteenth-century Latin America may be defined as the continent where—if one can parody Hegel—only the rational is real, and only the French is rational. A Peruvian professor assured me that, when he told his students that the ideas of the Enlightenment were of English origin, he was met with flat disbelief. The man must be joking. His students were sure that Paris, the home of literature and the fine arts, must also be the home of the Enlightenment.

Still, for all its romantic associations, Mexico City is today a characterless town. Like so many of Latin America's cities it has bartered its Colonial charm for a raffish jumble of modernistic apartment houses, cinemas and banks. It has been, in the superficial sense, "Americanised"; much of it would not seem out of place in the Middle West. Now this would be a sad outcome in any event. For Mexico City is not only the second city in Latin America—only Buenos Aires, with seven million inhabitants, is larger (Brazil's São Paulo and Rio, like Mexico City, are at the five-million mark)— Mexico City is also *Tenochtitlan,* the capital of the Aztec Empire destroyed by Cortes, the city on whose ruins the Spaniards built the first European city on the American continent. Her university, her sixteenth-century churches and palaces, are older than anything in Anglo-Saxon America. Mexico, then, is no new city; her citizens do not forget that she was once the capital of *Nueva España,* that she was ruled by a Viceroy who rivalled the grandees of the Escorial in magnificence. Something of this imperial glory can be sensed, still, on the *Zocalo,* Mexico City's central plaza, that saw both the Inquisition's *autos da fe* and the *pronunciamientos* of a dozen *caudillos*. The *Zocalo* is on the site of the great square that formed the hub of Montezuma's capital—Montezuma's palace stood where the Cathedral now stands. It is laid out on that Roman pattern that can still be traced in most Colonial cities of Spanish America: a square "*plaza mayor*" or "*plaza de armas*", surrounded by Cathedral, *ayuntamiento* or Presidential Palace and, on its flank, an arcaded *mercado* where the merchants carried on their trade—much as Bernal Diaz had seen them doing when the curious and courteous Montezuma invited them to be his guests in the city. Around this central *plaza*, a grid of narrow *calles*, placed at right angles to one another, formed—as they still form—the heart of a Latin American city.

The form is Spanish. Yet nothing could be more unlike the higgledy-piggledy, if picturesque, Moorish ground-plans of Granada, Toledo or Cordoba. And the distinction is interesting. For the Colonial ground-plan is reminiscent of an older Spain altogether—the Spain of the Romans. On the great *vega* of Granada, almost under the walls of the city, there stands today a *pueblo* which seems to prefigure these first settlements of Iberian America. It is called Santa Fe; and it was built by Ferdinand and Isabella, on the lines of a Roman *castrum*, while they waited for Granada, the last citadel of Islam in Catholic Spain, to fall to their armies. It was there in the same year of 1492, most appropriately, that Ferdinand and Isabella received the Genoese sailor, Christopher Columbus, who had set his mind on discovering a Western route to the Indies. Is it fanciful to see in Santa Fe, that encampment of militant religion, the archetype of a thousand Colonial cities planted by the Spaniards in the pagan, Indian lands of Latin America? There is something Roman in the majestic width and urbanity of Mexico's *Zocalo*. But it is the *castrum* of a Christian, crusading Rome that lies at the heart of Mexico City. Latin America may have fallen away from that vision of a Christian and Imperial Rome. But we must not forget—Latin Americans do not—that it was in this spirit that Latin America was founded by Cortes and his *conquistadores*. The Conquest of America has been called a plundering expedition. But that is a poor half-truth; had it been only that, little would have remained of the Spanish achievement. America would never have been colonised.

Yet Latin America, for all its failings, is one of the most enduring monuments to the Colonial enterprise of the European. Historically, then, Latin America has a double heritage. She is both the continuation of the Roman Empire and the last, and not the least successful, of the Crusades of Medieval Europe.

Latin America, then, is a paradoxical civilisation. One has no sooner asserted something than one feels bound to assert the opposite. Thus it is true that Latin America is in many respects a profoundly static society. The reason why Communism—contrary to common opinion—has made so poor a showing is that Latin America is *not* a revolutionary continent. The values of the traditional oligarchy are almost everywhere dominant and the new middle class seems content to align itself with these values, just as the working class and the peasantry are content to align themselves with the classes above them. There are important exceptions to this—Mexico is one —but in general Latin America is a highly deferential society. Even where there is mobility between classes, class distinctions themselves are rigid. It is not difficult to see in this recurring pattern the mould pressed on Latin America by the *conquistadores*. Especially in the "Indian" countries—in Mexico, in Guatemala, in Ecuador, Peru and Bolivia—is the persistence of this pattern apparent. The landed oligarchy are the descendants, real or imagined, of the *conquistadores*; the middle class is "poor white" or *mestizo*, the peasantry or working class are *mestizo* or pure-blooded Indian. In Mexico and Bolivia the pattern has been shaken by revolution. But it is still the case that those at the top of the scale are "white" or *mestizo*, and those at the bottom pure Indian, often with little or no knowledge of Spanish. In most countries, then, the mould imposed by the *conquistadores* still persists. In Mexico alone has the landed oligarchy been broken (at least in political terms), and a strong, self-confident middle-class asserted itself. Elsewhere, the so-called "Revolutions" of Latin America are no more than palace revolutions, involving the displacement of one military or oligarchic faction by another. They change nothing: indeed a cynic might say that this is their *raison d'être* —to make sure that nothing shall really change.

Yet here a paradox comes into play. For this conservative

society is also rooted in profoundly revolutionary aspirations. Latin America, like North America, is the Child of Revolution. In regard to North America, thanks to de Tocqueville, it is not difficult for Europeans to grasp the "revolutionary' basis of the society that was to evolve under the aegis of Andrew Jackson, Abraham Lincoln and Franklin Roosevelt. We are familiar with the idea that the United States is both a conservative and a revolutionary society. We do not always realise that Latin America is no less "American" in this respect. How should a society based on conquest and an open, insecure frontier not be adventurous and future-directed? We too easily imagine the *conquista* to be something that came to an end with the death of Cortes and Pizarro, with the establishment of Royal authority in Peru and Mexico. In point of fact the *conquista*—the "pacification" of the Indian, the opening of new lands and the conversion of their inhabitants to Christianity—is something that continued well into the second half of the nineteenth century.

Nor is it at an end today. Latin America, unlike most of the Third World, is not overpopulated. Much of it has still to be tamed and inhabited. Its minerals have still to be extracted; its rivers tapped for electric power; its jungles and forests cleared. There is, as it were, a dynamism of nature in Latin America, as in North America, which has to be reckoned with. But there is also a dynamism of social purpose, of secular and spiritual endeavour, which has never entirely disappeared. America may be a *Naturlandschaft*, but the landscape of America is also the landscape of Utopia (it is no coincidence that Thomas More's and Candide's Utopia were set in Latin America). It is this Utopian element in the Latin American that has produced Brasilia. It has also produced Neruda's great panorama of the continent in his *Canto General*; or that ideal of an "Indo-America', once dreamt by Haya de la Torre in Peru; or the *indigenista* vision of Rivera, Orozco and Siqueiros in Mexico; or, for that matter, the universalist, messianic idealism of a Fidel Castro. Latin America, as much as North America, is a New World. The fierce *conquistadores* and the friars and missionaries who followed in their wake had, as much as the New England Puritans or the Pennsylvania Quakers, an ambition to make all things new. The failures of Latin American society since Independence should not blind us to the fact that Latin America is a profoundly Utopian, a profoundly ambitious, a profoundly American society.

Mexico is often, and not always helpfully, termed a land of contradictions. It is easy to object that others are no less so: in how few countries do class conflict, race hatred and religious strife not divide brother from brother? But Latin America is especially open to such name-calling. The contradiction usually invoked—how many television documentaries are built on this formula!—is that between Latin America's rich, with their sleek cars and swimming-pools and adventurous night-lives, and the undernourished *lumpenproletariat* on the ragged fringes of her cities. I am not, in disputing this formula, denying either the facts or their implications: that Latin America displays a shocking inequality of wealth and a poorly developed social conscience. The facts of misery are bad enough; their conjunction with so much blatant luxury and waste seems almost intolerable. Latin Americans, to be sure, do not necessarily feel this. Just as their poor do not have—or do not yet have— egalitarian aspirations, their men of wealth do not have the conscience of the rich. We are shocked; and they are not. And nothing is so shocking to us than that they should be so little shocked. Still, these contradictions, however distressing, are hardly peculiar to Latin America, or to the *vecindades* of Mexico City described by Oscar Lewis in his *Children of Sanchez*.

But there are others which are. There are two in particular that seem fundamental to an understanding of Mexico: the strange contradiction between Conservatism and Revolutionism, and the "racial" antagonism that exists between the descendants of Spaniard and Indian. This is an antagonism which endures not simply between individuals of pure Spanish or Indian descent—a minority of the population—but in the minds of that majority of present-day Mexicans who have both Indian and Spanish blood in their veins. This second antagonism exists in other countries of mixed descent: in Peru, in Bolivia, in Ecuador, in Colombia, in Guatemala—and, to a lesser extent, in the "White" countries of the southern cone of South America. The simple, indeed facile, answer to this much-debated "race question" would be to say (as is too often said) that Latin America has "found the solution". As a general statement, of course, this is sentimental and silly: "racial" conflict can be as cruel in Latin America as anywhere in the world (though we must add the rider that racial conflict in Latin America seldom takes the ugly, exclusive form we are familiar with in countries settled by North Europeans). Nevertheless, in the tension produced by this double antagonism is contained the essence of Mexico's character. To understand Mexico, we must understand what Mexicans mean by Revolution; and we must understand why in the eyes of many Mexicans the original sin of Mexico is the sin committed by *La Malinche,* the daughter of an Indian prince, when she became Cortes's interpreter and mistress. *La Malinche* is the feminine Quisling of Mexican history; *malinchismo* the one unforgivable crime. To show how this works I shall discuss first Spanish contribution to Mexico's inheritance; then the Aztec; and then the complex, contradictory upshot that is the Mexico of today. We shall be engaged, to some extent, in a study in social pathology. Yet we shall find, at the end of the story, the strangest paradox of all: these conflicts have resulted in a political and social revolution that has given Mexico one of the most stable political systems that Latin America has known.

The Heritage of Spain

The traveller, in Latin America as elsewhere, expects to be told that the country he is visiting is unique. He would do well to note, further, that in Latin America nationalism is not directed solely towards the United States. There is little love lost between Venezuela and Colombia, between Ecuador and Peru, between Chile and Argentina. He must mind his tongue, then, and be careful where he praises what, and to whom. For all that, he is still likely to stumble. As he jet-hops from country to country, it is the similarities that strike him, not the contrasts. He notes that the accent with which the Uruguayans and the Argentines speak their Spanish is almost identical. Though he should not conclude from this that Uruguayans and Argentines are the same people, it will not escape him that they have much in common. He will note that the forms of Catholicism, including the forms of ecclesiastical architecture, are remarkably similar in Mexico, Colombia, or Chile. If he knows

Spain, it will not escape him that these are provincial variations
on a theme laid down by the *madre patria*: the Cathedral will
have its *coro* in the centre of the nave, opening towards the east;
echoing it, on the east wall of the chancel, will be a splendid
gilded *retablo*. The traveller will note regional differences;
but he will find the basic pattern changing remarkably little.
The baroque Cathedrals and parish churches of Spain and
Spanish America (like those of Brazil and Portugal) resemble
one another more closely than either resembles, say, the baroque
of France, Germany, or Italy. And the same is true of a hundred
points of custom, folklore, and ritual. The visitor will encounter
the same small courtesies and eccentricities, the same bureaucratic convolutions, the same tricks of expression, the same
fierce individualisms all the way from Mexico to Patagonia,
from Puerto Rico to Bolivia. Many of these things he will
recognise as having their origin in Spain, in Castile or Andalusia, Galicia or the Basque country. He will maintain, with
his host, that the country is more beautiful, more stable or more
prosperous than any of its neighbours. Politeness demands no
less. But he will note that if each Latin American country is
unique, in nothing does it resemble its neighbours more than
in its sense of uniqueness.

Certain resemblances, then, will strike even the most hurried
observer. But he may feel, apologetic for his hastiness, that his
host must be right: it is the resemblances that are superficial,
and the contrasts that are fundamental. Certainly it is as well
to be cautious in generalising. Similar customs may have
different meanings in different contexts; the apparent orthodoxy of the Guatemalan *indio* may conceal the most bizarre
Christian-pagan syncretism. Nevertheless, the traveller would
do well to stick to his original hunch: it is, by and large, the
contrasts that are superficial, and the resemblances that are
fundamental—and in a deeper sense than he may at first
imagine. To illustrate the point, let us take the case of an
imaginary *yanqui*—a young Ph.D. student, let us say, assigned
to research in Latin America. Our research graduate goes to
Peru or Colombia, eager to apply the techniques he has learnt
at college—in soil erosion, anthropology, or motivational
research—to the new territory. He meets at first with success.
Nobody, probably, has worked the field with such thoroughness

before him. Others have given general, approximate accounts; he can give facts and figures. He gets to like the country. It has that "old-world Spanish charm" he has read about. He is not merely extending his particular field of knowledge. He is also doing something to bring the benefits of American expertise to backward, undeveloped people.

Time passes. Our student returns to the United States. His thesis is completed; his associate professorship assured. He is married and has children. Years go by. He makes his second trip to Latin America—he has been granted, let us say, a sabbatical to do research on *mestizaje* among the *campesinos* of the Peruvian backlands. He is surprised to find himself beginning to dislike the subject. It is not simply the inconveniences of life south of the Rio Grande (though these had not struck him before with such force): the filth, the unpredictability, the corruption, the universal spirit of *mañanismo*. He finds he is working himself into a general rage towards the subject. But why? The rewards of research are good; indeed they get better every day. Latin America is the coming subject. What has happened is this. He has begun to see (and is he wholly wrong?) that the corruption and the dilatoriness, the *mañanismo* are not *accidental* features of the country. They are of its nature. What seemed charming on first acquaintance now simply irritates. It is not just the superficial things that are wrong; these people are acting on quite different assumptions from those he is familiar with. They do not really care about proper sanitation and accurate statistics. Their morality is casuistical, not to say jesuitical. They conform to family or racial mores; the idea of Society as the moral law-giver is unfamiliar. Very soon, he discovers he has made a mistake about Latin America. The same standards do not apply, because the same values do not operate. True, our student would not *expect* them to apply in France or Italy. But he has thought of Latin America as culturally similar to the United States. This, indeed, is the presupposition of pan-American idealism. When he wakes up to the fact that the two Americas are not only different, but perhaps fundamentally opposed, disillusionment sets in. The deeper his studies go, the more the subject repels him.

What has happened is that our student has made the voyage back through time to the age when Puritan North America abhorred all that Catholic, Counter-Reformation Spain stood for. He may not know it, but he has inherited the mantle of his Puritan ancestors—though he himself may be Boston-Irish or Chicago-Jewish by origin—and is once again fighting the Armada under Good Queen Bess. Our student is not, as it happens, an historian. He knows, of course, that the United States, and especially New England, were founded against everything that the world of the Counter-Reformation believed in. But it is easier for an historian to appreciate the ramifications of this fact than for a sociologist or an anthropologist. Our student discovers, to his bewilderment, that it is really the fundamentals of this society he dislikes, not its externals. Knowing this, he knows why there exists this strange revulsion in the United States towards Latin America. It is not difficult to be charmed by the surface aspects of life in Mexico or Guatemala or Peru. There is so much to please the visitor. The climate is splendid; the girls are beautiful; the hospitality is generous. But acquaintance does not make the *yanqui* heart grow fonder. On the contrary, he becomes scared of going too deep, for fear he may dislike it all too much. Our friend is a non-historian. There are, not surprisingly, more good sociologists and economists in the Latin American field than there are good historians. For the deeper you go historically, the more alien Latin America must appear.

Reactions of this kind, if slightly caricatured, are typical enough. And their very typicality supports our thesis that the twenty republics, though superficially different, are indeed fundamentally similar. Our emphasis, to be sure, is on the basis of Latin American culture—"culture" in the anthropological, not in the literary sense—on religion (but also on the magic that passes as religion); on the canons of Roman law (but also on the loopholes and legal fictions that govern the life of Latin American society). What the Latin may lack in case law, after all, he makes up in casuistry. Rules are never quite what they appear to be. Divorce—in an orthodox Catholic country such as Colombia—does not legally exist. (Conversely, in firmly disestablished countries like Mexico and Uruguay, it is remarkably easy.) But that is not the whole story. Where divorce is forbidden, the second family, illegitimate but universally recognised, becomes institutionalised.

Divorce does not exist; but nor, in effect, does monogamy. Nowhere does one find illegitimacy rates as high as in Latin America. Yet nowhere does less stigma seem to be attached to illegitimacy—for all Latin America's supposed Catholic piety. Rules exist; but they are made to be broken—that appears to be the Latin view. And this, of course, shocks the Anglo-Saxon. He comes to regard Latin America as corrupt, not just superficially, but from top to bottom.

For here yet another Spanish inheritance comes into play: *individualismo*. "No man is better than any other man", runs the Castilian proverb; and the saying conveys something of that rough egalitarian humanism we find in the picaresque novel, in *Lazarillo de Tormes*, or in Don Quixote, in Velazquez or Goya, and which is close to the heart of what Unamuno liked to call *castizismo*—the pure milk of the Hispanic tradition. We hear much of Spanish pride, but little of that easy, self-deprecating, deflationary quality which is equally Spanish, and which Cervantes immortalised in Sancho Panza. The truth is, Hispanic society is at bottom far more "democratic" than Anglo-Saxon; the Spaniard is too much a respecter of persons to have much respect for rank or office. But the saying has another, less cheerful face: "every man for himself". Much of the "corruption" of Latin America, so shocking to the outsider, has to be seen in this light. Man is not made for society, but society for man. A true *hombre* makes his own rules, and breaks them at will, like the swashbuckling *conquistadores* and their descendants, the *caudillos* of post-Independence Latin America. Politics is not the pragmatic horse-trading we are familiar with; it is the offering of personal loyalty to a chieftain from whose strong right arm benefits can be expected. Compared with this reckless, buccaneering *personalismo*, the "rugged individualism" of the North American must seem a spiritless thing. If the Anglo-Saxon looks on the Latin as a feckless, irresponsible creature, the Latin American looks on the *yanqui* as hidebound, inhibited and conformist.

It is not wrong, then, to see Spanish America as a unity (Portuguese America stands a little apart, certainly; but the difference between Brazil and Spanish America is not greater, say, than the difference between Argentina and Mexico. There exists also a Latin American unity). And the most obvious expression of this is also the most profound: it is the existence of a common language. The basic facts about Spanish and Portuguese are easily established; yet they are little known. Spanish, today, is the language of nearly 200 million human beings, over eighty per cent of whom live in Latin America. By the end of this century Spanish will be the language (taking Latin America's present birth-rate—the highest in the world—into account) of some 450 million human beings. This means that whereas rather more people today speak English as their mother tongue than Spanish, in a generation's time the balance will have shifted the other way. In the Western World, Spanish will have advanced from second place—it is already spoken by three times as many people as speak French or German, four times as many as speak Italian —to the first. (Portuguese will come a good third: it will be spoken by twice as many people as speak French, German or Italian.) Spanish and Portuguese will not be able to compete with English as a second language in the world at large. But they will represent by far the largest linguistic block within the European family. In the Western Hemisphere itself, Spanish- and Portuguese-speaking Americans will outnumber English-speaking by two to one (at present numbers are approximately equal). However we look at it, then, the growing importance of Spanish and Portuguese as languages is indisputable.

But has Spanish the tenacity to resist the encroachment of other languages and cultures? If Mexico City is already "Americanised", will "Americanisation" not lead to a gradual retreat from pure Castilian, giving rise to a hybrid, like the "Tex-Mex" spoken in the south-west of the United States? The answer is almost certainly no. Indeed, the tenacity of Spanish is so remarkable that it calls for examination. It is not just that Spanish is resistant to English influence: it has proved no less resistant to all the other influences that have played upon it. Two of these, at least, are of considerable importance and are of relevance to our theme: the pressure of Arabic on early Spanish during the seven centuries of Moorish occupation of Spain, and the pressure of the Indian languages of the New World on the speech of the numerically inferior *conquistadores*. The astonishing thing is that in both these cases, far from an amalgam resulting, the impact of the "foreign" language has been quite minor. Of course, there are exceptions: French influence on Spain and Iberian America in the eighteenth and nineteenth centuries brought many new words into the language. But French, being a Latin tongue, was far more assimilable than the Arabic or Amerindian languages. To be sure, Spanish has acquired new flesh, and not a little fat, in the course of its historical development. It has acquired Moorish nouns and proper names (*alcalde* and *alcazar* are familiar examples); it has acquired Indian proper names for things unknown in the Old World (hurricane and hammock, for example, in their Anglicised forms); and, later, French and English abstract nouns (e.g. *marxismo* and *psiquiatria*). But these are superficial borrowings: the bones and blood of the language remain as Latin as in the days of the Cid. Tenacity is not, perhaps a quality Anglo-Saxons associate with Latin America. But the historical tenacity of Spanish and Portuguese is remarkable, and has cultural implications easily overlooked.

For the resistance of Spanish to the encroachments of other languages, then, the evidence is strong. There is the case of the Puerto Ricans in New York, now nearly a million strong, who represent the most northerly infiltration of Spanish America into the Anglo-Saxon world. Earlier immigrants, Italians and Russian Jews, lost their native languages in the second generation. Yet these groups were far more tightly organised than the Puerto Ricans of today. Among Puerto Ricans—it is, surprisingly, a Latin American characteristic—the ties of family and religion are much less strong; there are few of the self-help associations that enabled earlier immigrants to climb the New York ladder. There are, certainly, factors to be set against this weakness: the relative closeness of Puerto Rico, and its status as a Commonwealth associated with the United States. The remarkable fact remains that the authorities issue public notices in Spanish, encourage public employees to learn Spanish, and have given the language an educational status that was never granted to Italian or Yiddish, Russian, Greek or German. It seems likely, then, that the language will survive. Yet there can be few parts of the Spanish-speaking world—not even Havana or Mexico City—that have been so harshly exposed to "Americanisation". Since the New Deal, and the coming to power of Luis Muñoz Marin in the forties, Puerto

B

Rico has benefited economically from this close association; in this respect, indeed, Puerto Rico is Mexico writ large. Puerto Rico has become something of a showcase for what enlightened Imperialism can do. Yet, despite Puerto Rico's relative cultural impoverishment—she has no strong Church, no pre-Columbian heritage, no national hero like Bolivar or San Martin or Cuba's Jose Marti—it is already clear that English is not going to displace Spanish as the national tongue, even in tough, competitive New York, where knowledge of English is essential. As in Mexico, a few words have entered the language, only to be thoroughly Hispanised: *beisbol* for baseball and (more mysteriously) *jaibol* for highball. It is a safe guess that if Spanish can withstand the assaults of English in these exposed conditions, it will not yield much ground even in superficially "Americanised" countries like Venezuela or Mexico.

The implications, surely, are interesting. No doubt it would be too simple to identify the Spanish language with Hispanic culture *tout court*. But language is one of the media through which cultural values are transmitted. And in this lies the relevance of the peculiar tenacity of Spanish to the Mexican situation. Mexico, after all, has by far the richest pre-Columbian subsoil of any country in Latin America; here, if anywhere, one would expect Hispanic culture to be modified by non-Hispanic influences. To some extent, as we shall see, this has been the case. But it is not the case that Spanish has yielded anywhere to a hybrid dialect. Indeed, the opposite has happened. The Spanish of Spain and the Spanish of Mexico and Peru and Argentina are not growing apart; they are growing together. Already, the written usage is practically identical. With the spread of mass-communications, the spoken language may follow suit. This is not the result Spanish American nationalists expected fifty years ago. There was talk at that time of a Mexican or Argentine "national language", distinct from traditional Castilian. This toughness of fibre, this resilience is not new. It is implicit in the history of "Castilian" from the time it emerged from the popular Latin of the Iberian peninsula. I have pointed out that the Arabic contribution is confined to external features of the language, the groundwork remaining Latin. The same is true of the Celtic and Germanic elements that came into the language: the former from the pre-Roman inhabitants of the country, the latter from the Vandal and Visigothic invaders who first overturned, then helped to perpetuate Roman traditions in the peninsula. These influences may be preserved in Celtic place-names; and, aptly, in Germanic words such as *guerra*, *banda* or *robar* (to sack). But that is the extent of it. Spanish is still the most Roman of the Romance languages. Indeed, it contains words that are thought to pre-date the Latin spoken in Gaul and to belong to Republican rather than to Imperial Rome.

This brief survey of the history of the Spanish language may help to explain why the Indian substratum has contributed so little to the evolution of the language. Equally, it provides further evidence for the view that English is not likely to exert more than an external influence on the language of the future (borrowings being limited to the fields of sport, science and technology). A further reason for the lack of influence of the Indian languages is to be found in the fact that most of the Indian languages of Latin America (seventy languages are spoken in modern Mexico alone) are mutually unintelligible and, indeed, linguistically unrelated. As literacy grows, and as the Indian is brought into the life of the nation, so the dominance of the Spanish language over the vernaculars will grow. In the long run, therefore, it looks as if the Indian languages were doomed (Quechua and Aymara in Peru, and Guarani in Paraguay have the best chances of survival). Yet the fact that the Spanish of Madrid, and the Spanish of Mexico, Bogota and Buenos Aires are today, from a literary point of view, almost identical must prove of more than linguistic significance. It would seem to imply that the unity of the Hispanic world, of which we hear so much, is not a mere figure of speech. The Hispanic world (and the closely related Luso-Brazilian world) possesses a unity that is potentially not inferior to the unity that exists between London, New York and Cape Town, Los Angeles, Ottawa and Sydney. The implications of this fact for the future of Latin America need not be emphasised.

Spaniard and Indian

There is no denying, then, the crucial role language has played in the evolution of present-day Latin America. For example, the existence of highly resilient, developed languages like Spanish and Portuguese ensured that the rapid political fragmentation of post-Independence Latin America was not followed by cultural fragmentation. As we have seen, the opposite was the case: language proved a homogenising and centripetal force. To put it another way: it is because Spanish and Portuguese are what they are that it is possible to speak of Latin America at all. In Latin America, language unites, and geography divides. As a geographical expression, "Latin America" signifies as much or as little as "the Middle East" or "Africa" or "Asia". But as a cultural expression—and the epithet "Latin" conveys that, doubtful as it may be in other respects—Latin America signifies something far more exact than "Africa" or "Asia". Both "pan-Africa" and "pan-Asia" are little more than political slogans: they lack cultural content. If we look for an analogy, it must be rather with the English- or Arabic-speaking world. We are dealing here, of course, with post-Columbian America; the triumph of Castilian presupposes the fire and blood of the *conquista*. Pre-Columbian America is a different case. She too was geographically divided; and it was her geography that determined her fantastic linguistic diversity. Until the rise of the Inca and Aztec empires in the fifteenth century there were few centripetal factors to counteract the disruptive force of geography. (This linguistic diversity, incidentally, does not mean that the inhabitants of pre-Columbian America had no cultural features in common. There is no doubt that they did. But though in a few cases we can explain such parallels by direct borrowing or influence, it is likely that in general they are the end-result of gradual divergence from a common norm.) Thus, while we can speak with confidence of an "Iberian-American pattern"—keeping in mind the analogy of the Arab or Hindu worlds—it is only with diffidence that we can speak of an Amerindian world. This is one of the difficulties in assessing the Indian contribution to the civilisation of Latin America. In this respect, Mexico is really Latin America in microcosm. Mexico, obviously, is a synthesis of the Hispanic and the Indian. Yet, treating her in this way, we run up against a basic difficulty in definition. We know, more or less, what we mean by Hispanic culture. It is much less clear that the concept of "Indian culture" has scientific validity.

We face here, for the first time, a difficulty with which we shall become familiar: who is the Indian, and what has he contributed to the civilisation of Latin America? There is unlikely to be a final satisfactory answer to this question. Yet, equally, the question cannot be shirked. After all, it is plain that the present-day Indians of the American continent do have a great many qualities in common. They eat maize and potatoes; they share common myths; in character they are remarkably introverted, defensive and impervious to outside influences. Now this shyness of Western civilisation is at bottom a delayed reaction to the *conquista*, and as such intelligible. But the fact that roughly similar behaviour should be found among, say, the Iroquois, the descendants of the semi-civilised Aztecs and Incas, and the savage neolithic Indians of Amazonia is striking. This behaviour is very different, after all, from the reaction of the Negro—whether North America, Caribbean or African—to Western civilisation. The social degradation of the Indian in the Americas does not compare with that of the Negro: the Negro slave was imported precisely because the Spanish crown wished to exempt its Indian subjects from slavery. Yet the Indian resists European advances wherever he can; and the Negro has seldom succeeded in doing so. Are these "racial" characteristics? What with our present racial inhibitions, we are naturally hesitant to agree. Yet the behaviour-pattern of the Negro in North or South America is not very unlike that of his distant cousin in West or South Africa. And that there is a widely-distributed archaic culture common to all the Indians of the Americas is now accepted by anthropologists. Common sense, after all, would suggest that is so. The Mongoloid physical characteristics of the American Indian are apparent, and it is certain that their ancestors crossed the Atlantic bridge from Asia into America at a comparatively late date—perhaps as late as 10,000 B.C. Divergence has taken place; but the timespan, in terms of human development, has been short. Indeed, contrary to what is often supposed, the Amerindian cultures are youthful rather than ancient.

But commonsense generalisations of this kind, while not false, do not take us very far. For beneath these surface resemblances there lies—considering the late arrival of these Asiatic colonists —a truly staggering diversity. There are no less than 123 speech-families in the Americas, each entirely independent of the other. As Cortes discovered when he first ventured into the American interior, there are adjacent valleys and villages in Mexico whose languages are mutually unintelligible. To appreciate the extraordinariness of this, we need only compare this diversity with the dominant position, in the Old World, of the great speech-families—Indo-European, Semitic, Turkish, Malay, Sino-Tibetan, Bantu. Each covers areas as vast and geographically diverse as the Americas. Yet each of these families has given rise to one or more languages of international importance, and the more developed languages are understood over huge geographical areas. Nothing like this has ever happened in the Americas. The Aztec language, Nahuatl, remained one among many tongues in the Aztec realm. The Incas in Peru insisted on Quechua as the official language of the Empire; but the local languages were not ousted. Certainly, both the Inca and Aztec Empires were still new when Pizarro and Cortes destroyed them. If left to themselves, it is argued, they would have developed into high cultures, comparable with anything in the Old World. Much of the romanticism about the Indian contribution to Latin America—what is known, in Mexico and elsewhere, as *indigenismo*—is based on speculation of this kind. The standard retort to those who argue that the major cultures of the New World had not progressed, at the time of the *conquista*, much further than Ancient Egypt or Mesopotamia (the wheel as yet undiscovered; no domestication of animals; no developed system of writing) is that their potentialities were "nipped in the bud" by Cortes and Pizarro. This is certainly the case. Nevertheless, it is well to treat the claims of the professional *indigenistas* with some scepticism.

It is no doubt a matter of taste; I confess that I am more interested in what is than in what might have been. The true quality of Aztec civilisation is another matter (we shall examine that in a moment). But if we are interested in what is, it is with the interaction of Spaniard and Indian that we must concern ourselves. Yet again we run up against a basic difficulty: looked at in one way, the problem is how the two races have managed to live together. Has racial or cultural fusion resulted? Or have the two races coexisted in a kind of voluntary *apartheid*? Since the Indian outnumbered the Spaniard in all but a few countries it would seem reasonable to assume that the influence of the Indian substratum must have been considerable. Yet, if we look at it in another way, it would seem that the dominance of Hispanic culture, language and religion over the Indian substratum has been so great as to render the Indian contribution negligible. Let me take three examples. It used to be said that the speech-patterns of Spanish-Americans, where they differed from those of Spaniards, were moulded by this Indian substratum. Or that the remarkable style of decoration evolved in Mexican churches of the 18th century—those convoluted pillars and weird geometrical patterns—was due to the modification of Hispanic models by the Indian imagination. Or, again, that the cultural wealth of Latin American countries was in proportion to the fertility of their pre-Columbian subsoil.

The attraction of these theories, especially for nationalists, is apparent. Yet their validity is questionable. Scholars doubt whether it is necessary to go beyond the tradition of the Spanish Churrigueresque in looking for the inspiration of Mexican eighteenth-century architecture. Certainly, pre-Columbian motifs are to be found; but the central inspiration of this art is Hispanic. Nor do popular theories of the life-giving properties of a pre-Hispanic subsoil stand up to examination. True, both Mexico and Peru remain, as in Colonial times, centres of cultural and even political creativity. But the most distinguished recent literature is owed to Argentina, Uruguay, and Chile; and these are territories where the Indian substratum is weak or lacking. As far as language is concerned, we have already seen that the influence of indigenous languages is confined to loan words (*cacique, maiz, huracan, tabaco, patata*); many of which have passed through Spanish into other European languages. More important, the dialectal variations within the Spanish of America can be explained in terms of the evolution of the Spanish language itself. Thus all Spanish Americans pronounce "c" as "s", rather than as "th" after the fashion of the Castilian. Mexicans pronounce the Spanish "ll" as "y" rather than as "ly" (variations technically known as the *seseo* and the *yeismo*). Are these modifications of Spanish native to the New World? Not at all. It is not necessary to go further than Andalusia to seek their explanation. Seville was for over two centuries the effective capital of the Spanish Empire. She enjoyed a monopoly of imperial trade—and many of the early settlers came either from neighbouring Extremadura (both Cortes and Pizarro were Extremadurans) or from Seville's Andalusian hinterland. Both the *seseo* and the *yeismo* are part of the normal speech of Andalusians. Evidently, the explanation of Spanish-American speech-patterns is to be sought in those of the Iberian peninsula, not in the indigenous speech-patterns of America.

There is no easy solution, therefore, to the problem of His-panic-Indian cultural interaction. Yet, if we wish to understand Latin America, we cannot evade these problems. True, there are certain countries where the Indian substratum is weak or absent: Uruguay, Argentina, Chile, Costa Rica, Cuba, Puerto Rico, the Dominican Republic. But between those countries where the "Indian question" is almost a question of national identity—Mexico, Guatemala, Peru, Ecuador, Bolivia—and the "White", European countries of the far South, there is an important intermediate group of nations where, under an apparently "Hispanic" surface, the Indian substratum not only strongly persists, but influences the national life in subtle and unexpected ways. This is particularly true of Venezuela and Colombia. But it is also true of a country like Brazil—as the great Brazilian writer Euclides da Cunha demonstrated in *Rebellion in the Backlands*. Latin America, then, is an iceberg. The Hispanic cap is what we habitually see. But deeper down, invisible to the naked eye, is something altogether different: the complex cultural phenomenon known as *mestizaje*. To get an idea of what this means it is necessary to go to a work of anthropology like Gerardo and Alicia Reichel-Dolmatoff's *The People of Aritama* or to a work of literature like *Rebellion in the Backlands*. Seen from the outside, the European-Hispanic influence must always appear dominant, indeed overwhelming. It is only when Latin-American society is studied from the inside, at the grass roots, that the mass of the iceberg comes into view.

This much is plain: generalisations about the "Indian problem" must be made with strict diffidence. They are not always so made. It is often, rashly, assumed that Latin America's Indian problem can be assimilated to the other racial problems that rack the contemporary world. Because the

Indians of Latin America are "coloured" a solidarity with the coloured peoples of Afro-Asia or North America is imputed to them which they are far from feeling. These are serious misconceptions. It is certainly not the case that Latin Americans of *mestizo* or Indian stock see the problem as Westerners or Communists would wish them to see it. Indeed, Latin Americans do not really think of the Indian problem in terms of "colour" at all. The analogy is not perfect; but it is more useful to compare the stratified society of Latin America with the Hindu caste-system. To be an *indio* in Latin America is to belong to the lowest caste. Above the pure *indio* comes the *mestizo* or *cholo*; at the top of the tree is the "white" or *criollo*. In some countries there are as many as five or six distinct "castes" based on social position and occupation and on—imagined rather than real—"racial" origin. It is usually possible to move out of an inferior caste, to "pass" as a White, by acquiring a European-type education—much as education permits the individual to escape from the bonds of caste in modern India. It is also possible, as in India, for a whole community to better its social condition, to "pass" as *mestizo* or *criollo*, if it can remove the stigma of its origins by acquiring new patterns of behaviour.

This has led enthusiastic apologists for Latin America to insist that there, and there alone, has a solution been found to the racial problem. It is an ambitious and exciting claim. That there is a degree of truth in it is evident. It would not otherwise make sense for a man to say (as Mexicans can be heard to say): "Ah, yes, my father was an Indian, but I am not." It appears to be true, again, that the strong emotions aroused by colour, particularly among people of North European origin, are not shared by most Latin Americans. It would be rash, of course, to assume that Latin Americans are altogether "colour-blind". The ancient, inbuilt social bias of Latin America—and this is as true of Mexico, where Indians are in theory emancipated, as of backward Peru—is towards the eradication of Indian traits and the substitution for them of European-Hispanic patterns of behaviour; though many rich and respected men have an unmistakably Indian physiognomy. In so far as "colour" coincides with "socially inferior" behaviour, therefore, there is most certainly discrimination against the

Indian. The paradox is that in this comparatively colour-blind society the people of colour have small chance of preserving their traditional heritage. If one thing is certain about Latin America in the next generation, it is that the emancipation of the Indian will destroy the inheritance he has guarded so jealously over the centuries.

The Aztecs

It may be useful to establish at this point what that inheritance amounts to. And it is in Mexico that the question can be put, and answered, most satisfactorily. I have said that the world of the pre-Columbian Indian—to judge by the evidence of language—was a strangely disjointed and fragmented one. An underlying pattern existed; but it was marked by divergence rather than by convergence. The American continent, at the time of the *conquista*, was remarkably empty—emptier than Africa or Asia within historical times. But if the chief cause of this fragmentation was horizontal—the vast spaces of the American continent, her jungles, rivers and *cordilleras*—there existed also a clear-cut vertical division: that between the Indians of the Plains and the Indians of the Mountains. The Plains Indians of North America, of the Amazonian jungle, and of the Argentine *pampas* had (and where they are their own masters, still have) certain characteristics in common. The *conquistadores*, like the early North Americans, found them wild and intractable. They could not be made to work; they could not be "pacified". They have therefore been wiped out, as in the greater part of North America and the Argentine, or herded into reservations. It is only within the Amazonian basin and on its margins—in southern Venezuela and Colombia, in the eastern parts of Peru and Bolivia, and in Brazil itself—that the Indian persists in his traditional savagery.

The Plains Indian is a creature apart. He is despised and feared by the Mountain Indian, much as he was in pre-Columbian times. In the literary attention he has received, he cannot compete with his mountain cousin. He belongs to the anthropologist rather than the historian. It is exaggerating only a little to say that he is today very much as he was at the time of the Conquest, and that at the time of the Conquest he was very much as he had been two millennia earlier. In the comparatively short sojourn of the *homo sapiens* in the Americas, then, he stands for historical failure: the failure of Man to overcome the American wilderness. This failure, and the fear of it, is by no means confined to the Indian; it is part of the historical experience of all American peoples, Indian, Spanish, Portuguese, and Anglo-Saxon. It is not only the North American who is obsessed with failure—on the contrary, fear of nature is perhaps the one truly unifying American experience. For the Anglo-Saxon American, no less than for the Portuguese or Spanish American, the Plains Indian stands for something the European cannot readily understand. He is mysterious and intriguing; for he is the oldest inhabitant of a comparatively youthful continent. But he is also frightening and contemptible; for he represents failure in the common enterprise.

If the Plains Indian represents failure, how far can the enterprise of the Aztecs, the Mayas, and the Incas be held to represent success? In a material sense, the question is easy to answer. The peoples of the Andes and the Mexican highlands had learnt, perhaps by the third millennium B.C., how to cultivate maize and (at first probably in South America) the potato tuber. While they never discovered the use of metals harder than bronze or copper-gold alloy, and never developed transportation by draught-animal or wheeled vehicle, they won a first and decisive victory over their environment in the discovery—or invention—of these two remarkable vegetables. With them they were no longer, like the Plains Indians, mere food-gatherers and hunters at the mercy of nature; a settled life became possible. These vegetables, then, were the material premiss of the high civilisations of the Mountain Indians. But how far does this take us? To speak of these civilisations as "high" seems to beg the question. Nor does it help to refer to them, as is sometimes done, as "semi-civilisations". The material achievements and limitations of these cultures are well understood; but in themselves these data are of limited interest. I have said that they were not, at the *conquista*, further developed than the civilisations of the Middle East two millennia before Christ. But that is not really what foreigners—let alone *indigenista* propagandists in Latin America—are most anxious to know. Material comparisons between civilisations are tedious and, in

the end, unsatisfactory. It is the *quality* of a civilisation that is of
interest to us; and this is as true of Aztec, Maya or Inca civilisation as of the civilisation of modern Latin and Anglo-Saxon
America. What, then, was the *quality* of the ancient civilisation
we know best—that of the Aztecs of the Valley of Anahuac?

We are fortunate to possess fascinating and reliable guidance
on this point. In his classical study, *The Daily Life of the Aztecs*,
Jacques Soustelle informs us (and should we not take a Frenchman's word for it?) that the Aztecs indeed deserve the title of
"civilised men":

> Such as they were, with their greatness and their weaknesses, their
> ideal of order and their cruelty, their obsession with the mystery
> of blood and death, their sensitivity to the beauty of flowers,
> birds, and gems, their strength of religious feeling—strong to
> the point of suicide, their excellent practical organisation of the
> state, their attachment to their land . . . which still did not keep
> their eyes from turning continually to the stars—with all this,
> these ancient Mexicans were civilised men.

But Soustelle does not make it easy for himself. He does not
attempt to explain away the cruelty of human sacrifice. He does
not try to balance the "positive" side of Aztec culture—that
love of flowers and birds which modern Mexicans inherit—
against what seems to us its vicious, inhuman face. He insists
that it must be seen as a whole. Yet we cannot accuse Soustelle
of historical relativism: if he insists that we see Aztec culture as
a whole, he does not insist that we judge it on its own terms.
He makes an explicit comparison with the Spaniards of the
sixteenth century. The Aztecs had an elaborate concept of
"limited war" (it was to prove their ruin); whereas the
Spaniards waged "total and ideological war". The Aztecs
practised human sacrifice; but were horrified at the methods
of the Spanish Inquisition. But, implicitly, it is against a more
absolute concept of civilisation that the Aztec achievement is
measured. I would not myself quarrel with that. It is the
comparison with civilisation as we conceive it that matters to
us, after all, not the comparison with ancient Egypt or Sumer.
And the criteria of civilisation on which Soustelle rests his case
are not, I think, unconvincing.

We have to remember that the Aztecs themselves were
acutely conscious of the distinction between civilisation and

barbarism. They knew that they came of barbarian stock, and they accepted that the earlier civilisations of the Valley of Anahuac—in particular the Toltecs—had been the bearers of a high civilisation. The Aztecs were originally, not more than two centuries before the Conquest, a warlike tribe of nomadic hunters from the northern steppes; and we know that they were still aware of their historical origins at the time of the Conquest. The fascination for us of Aztec civilisation is not only that it was the most developed in the Americas at the time of the Conquest (and thus the best documented), but that it bears historical witness to that process by which—in most cases, over many centuries—nomadic Plains Indians were transformed into settled agricultural communities. This ever-present awareness in the Aztec mind, both of the warlike qualities of their ancestors and of the civilisation of their predecessors, came to be symbolised in their two high gods: Tezcatlipoca and Quetzalcoatl.

In Tezcatlipoca, the warlike sun-god of the ancient Aztecs, we cannot help seeing the cognate of those sky-gods of the nomadic Aryans, who became the gods we know as Zeus, Jupiter, Wotan and Indra. Quetzalcoatl, on the other hand, was the god of the civilisation the Aztecs had inherited from the Toltecs. Legend had it that he had been driven from Tula of the Toltecs centuries before, but had promised to return to his people in due time (so that Cortes' expedition came to be mistaken by Montezuma for the long-awaited return of Quetzalcoatl, predicted by the astrologers for the year 1519). Quetzalcoatl was pre-eminently the god of the priests, who watched over the fortunes of the Aztec Empire. Tezcatlipoca was the god of the warriors, and of the young men learning the art of war. There were, too, a multitude of lesser gods, like Tlaloc, the rain god, whose good offices were of vital importance to all inhabitants of the Valley of Anahuac. Few of these gods were originally Aztec. But the Aztec sky-god was not of a jealous disposition. The Aztecs were one of the most syncretistic and, in this sense, most tolerant peoples history records. No sooner did the Aztecs come upon a new people with strange gods than they took steps (in this, much unlike the Spaniards of the sixteenth century) to incorporate the new deities into the traditional pantheon. We see here evidence of their political skill. By taking gods prisoner, the Aztecs ensured that both their magical potential and the loyalty of the conquered people were transferred to Tenochtitlan. For all their ferocious reputation, then, the Aztecs built up their empire as much by diplomacy as by force of arms. They owed their success to an awareness— not unlike that of the Ancient Romans—that their strength lay in balancing the simple, barbarian virtues of their ancestors against the more complex values of the civilisations they had conquered.

The Aztecs, then, were a self-conscious people: they lived their history. Their religious practices were essentially a re-enactment of it, a strategy to retain the favour of the gods who had made it possible. The notion that the Aztecs, or the other pre-Colombian people, were subject to influences from the Old World—the Norsemen being, for example, the origin of the legend of Quetzalcoatl—is not well received by modern scholars. It is far more probable that ancient America received religious and cultural influences across the Pacific. This is a disputed field; and it may be that too much of the evidence has been destroyed for us to trace out the pattern. Yet the parallels with Old World cultures, whether European or Asiatic, are often close. Even if we ignore the question of borrowings entirely, this remains true. The infusion of "barbarian vitality" into a higher, but comparatively effete culture to produce a vigorous synthesis, is a familiar story. It is the story of the Aryans in ancient India, the Dorians in Greece, the Germanic *Völkerwanderungen* after the fall of the Roman Empire. There are evident parallels in the syncretistic religions of Rome and of the Indian Aryans: here, too, the warlike sun-god of the nomads admitted the gods and godlets of agricultural peoples to his court. Again, the educational rigour and (within limits) the meritocratic mobility of Aztec society is reminiscent of classical Spartan or Roman society—though this "democratic" aspect of the Aztec polity, an inheritance from nomadic days, was probably in decline at the time of the conquest. The tendency was towards a more straightforward social stratification: Republican Rome, as it were, was turning into Imperial Rome—with an all-powerful, but elective monarchy. In some respects, again, the Aztec polity had features we associate with Oriental Despotism: the great men of the court possessed power and prestige by virtue of their office, not by right of heredity or through ownership of slaves or land.

Perhaps, as the social system grew more rigid, the Aztec ruling class would have lost its vigour, and social tensions have made themselves felt. But at the time of the Conquest this was not the case. True, the Aztecs had not in the past pursued as deliberate an imperialist policy as the Incas: theirs was less an Empire than a confederation of tributary cities (a weakness which assisted Cortes' overthrow of the Aztec power). But certain facts—the growing dominance of Tenochtitlan as the centre of administrative and trading activity, and the fact that in Montezuma's time Nahuatl was understood from the Caribbean to the Pacific coast and even as far south as Nicaragua—suggest that, had Cortes not cut short its development, something like a true empire would have come into being. There was no power in sight strong enough to resist the expansion of Aztec rule. Politically, then, there is no reason to belittle the Aztec achievement. In less years than the Romans, they had made of their rude and precarious lake-dwellings the greatest city of the Americas—a city, as the *conquistadores* agreed, to rival any in Europe for cleanliness and civic order. Like the Romans they had shown marked ability in learning from the cultures of peoples over whom they ruled. In its full development, their empire would have represented a synthesis of the achievements of the peoples of the Valley of Anahuac over many hundreds of years. In this sense the *indigenistas* are right when they protest that the cutting short of this growth was one of the great tragedies of history.

Yet, for many of us, the objections remain. Does not the cruelty of human sacrifice as practised by the Aztecs—those holocausts of 20,000 prisoners on a single state occasion—in some way cancel out the beauty of that exquisite goldwork and jewellery, of those marvellous feathered shields, of that poignant, elegiac poetry, for which the Aztecs must be honoured? Does not the inhuman ugliness—as it appears to us—of so much Aztec sculpture point to a profound inhumanity in the Aztec view of the world? Such objections may seem naïve to an age which perceives no contradiction, perhaps even a necessary connection, between art and cruelty. Equally, they may seem

naïve to a generation trained to accept, without moral preconceptions, the findings of the human biologist. Then again,
it may be said that we moderns have little reason to look down
on the Aztecs: we have not proved ourselves squeamish in the
taking of human life. Be that as it may, the horror that came
over Cortes and his captains when Montezuma led them up the
winding steps of the great temple to admire the view of Tenochtitlan, and they saw the still palpitating human hearts thrown
on the altar stone (and later they were to be Spanish hearts),
has never left the Western observer. It is this horror that makes
it hard for us to accept the Aztecs as the bearers of a high
civilisation. Allied to our horror at human sacrifice—but
this time rather a product of the modern world—is our liberal
horror of the militarism of the Aztecs. The Aztecs were un-
doubtedly a people dedicated to war; though the purpose of war
was as much the taking of prisoners for sacrifice as the acquisi-
tion of territory. Our experience of modern militarism is such,
however, that we cannot admit that a warlike society can also
be a civilised one.

The second objection, I think, is the more difficult to maintain. The tables can too easily be turned on those who see only
opposition between the warlike and the civilised society. The
truth is, there have been few periods of classical culture—
from Periclean Athens to Renaissance Italy and France under
Louis XIV—that were not also classical periods of warfare and
preparation for warfare. These societies were militaristic, not
necessarily in an expansionist sense, but in the sense that the
making of war was a central concern of the state and of those
educating the nation's youth. It is only because the British and
the American Empires have been able to treat war as a peripheral, rather than a central concern of the State—most wars
being distant frontier-wars against weak opponents—that
Anglo-Saxons are enabled to overlook this lamentable truth.
In fact, the Aztec theory and practice of war were unusually
sophisticated and humane. Only if a city still refused to pay
tribute, after a thrice-repeated diplomatic warning, did the
Aztecs levy war against her. And war was not to the death,
since the capture of the enemy's chief temple was the recognised signal for a truce, and a further round of bargaining and
negotiation. Nor were the Aztecs a militaristic society in the

sense that they exalted the military virtues to the exclusion of the softer, hedonistic virtues of the civil life. To refuse them the title of civilised men because they prized the military virtues highly would entail refusing the same title to most of the great civilisations of history.

But human sacrifice? How do we extenuate that? Soustelle remarks that every age has its own conception of what is cruel. The Romans shed more blood in their circuses, for their own amusement, and the Spaniards more in their conquest of America, than did the Aztecs before their gods. The argument, perhaps, smacks a little of *tu quoque*. But the motives that inspired these religious holocausts cannot be wholly disregarded. Thus Soustelle writes:

> Human sacrifice among the Mexicans was inspired neither by cruelty nor by hatred. It was their response . . . to the instability of a continually threatened world. . . . All the relevant descriptions, such as those that Sahagun took down from his Aztec informants, convey the impression, not of a dislike between the sacrificer and the victim nor of anything resembling a lust for blood, but of a strange fellow-feeling or rather . . . of a kind of mystical kinship.

There is little doubt that Soustelle is right. It is only possible to understand the Aztec way of thinking if we appreciate that the Aztecs were an intensely *religious* people. There is no evidence that the new security and gentler living of Montezuma's time had broken down this structure of belief and infected the ruling classes with scepticism. And the reasons for the profound, terrifying religiosity of the peoples of Mexico—human sacrifice was not an invention of the Aztecs—are not difficult to guess at. Ringed by mighty volcanoes, subject to the twin threats of drought and of thunderstorms that could bring destruction to the lake-side cities, the peoples of Anahuac inhabited an unpredictable, terrifying world. They were, in consequence, a deeply pessimistic people. But this, argues Soustelle, should increase our admiration for the courage with which they faced so implacable a destiny, promising themselves so little and denying themselves so much. It is in terms of his heroic defiance of an ill-natured universe that the Aztec's practice of human sacrifice must be understood.

If we now return to our starting point, and ask how far

Aztec civilisation does represent that victory over the American wilderness that eluded the Plains Indians, we must concede that Aztec society, and that of the other civilisations of Mexico, Guatemala and the Andes, do represent a signal triumph of man over his environment. For all that may be said of the "inhuman" world-view of the Aztecs, it is the *human* achievement of their civilisation that is most striking. Indeed, this is Soustelle's criterion of civilisation: what kind of man did the Aztecs produce? It is evident, of course, that the Aztec warrior and priest were highly disciplined: from childhood they were taught to bear pain, to honour their betters, to acquire the skills demanded by war and religion. But these qualities were not absent among the Indians of the Plains. It is not discipline alone that defines the civilised man. It is in the subtle balance between stoic indifference and heightened receptivity that civilisation consists. The Aztec pantheon is itself symbolic of this ideal: Quetzalcoatl and Tezcatlipoca preside jointly over the welfare of the Aztec nation. Politically, too, the Aztecs owed their success to a blending of qualities: on the one hand, barbarian vigour, on the other, sophisticated flexibility. What is true of the Aztecs as a people is no less true of them as individuals: they had achieved a subtle balance, whose outward expression was a cult of *mesure*. (One detects in Soustelle's concept of the "civilised man" the influence of Nietzsche; in particular, of Nietzsche's view in *The Birth of Tragedy* that Greek culture, after the age of Aeschylus and Heraclitus, lost its barbarian virtues and went into decline.) It is as much, then, for their ideals of personal behaviour, as for the sum of their cultural and political achievements, that Soustelle would grant the Aztecs the title of civilised men:

> A civilised man is primarily one who can master himself, who does not display his feelings, except when this is the accepted thing to do, and then only in the accepted manner ... what we would now call good breeding had a very great importance in the eyes of the ancient Mexicans, both as a mark of each man's quality and as a necessary factor in the social order.

The politeness of the Mexican Indian today is often remarked on. This charming primer on how to behave in a great man's house suggests that this may well be an Aztec inheritance:

"Take care how you go in, for without your noticing it you will be watched. Come respectfully, bow, and make your greeting. Do not make faces when you eat . . . if you drink water, do not make a noise, sucking it in: you are not a little dog . . . do not cough and do not spit; and take care not to dirty the clothes of any of the other guests."

The same ideal of conduct was impressed on the Emperor at the time of his election:

"It is you, lord, who for certain years are going to sustain this nation and care for it as if it were a child in a cradle. . . . Consider, lord, that from now on you are to walk upon a very high place along a narrow path that has great precipices to the right and the left. Be mild in the use of your power; show neither teeth nor claws. . . . Lord, you must also take care never to speak lightly, for that would make your person despised . . . you must now make your heart the heart of an old man, grave and severe. . . . Do not suppose, lord, that the mat and *icpalli* of kings is a place of pleasure and delight; for on the contrary, it is one of great labour, sorrow, and penance. . . ."

It is Soustelle's opinion, then, that the Aztec was a gentleman. Indeed, from Soustelle's pages, one would gather that the Aztec combined the *gravitas* of the Roman patrician with the heroic pessimism of the Greek tragedian and the exultant humanism of the man of the Renaissance. *The Daily Life of the Aztecs* is a book of great brilliance, hardly less powerful than Lévi-Strauss's classic disquisition on the world of the South American Indian, *Tristes Tropiques*. Yet Soustelle, like André Malraux, another early admirer of De Gaulle, is that dangerous thing—a French romantic with a *penchant* for German philosophy. While admiring Soustelle's evocation of the world of the Aztecs, we cannot help wondering whether something has not been left out. Why, if the Aztec world had achieved all that he claims for it, did its people show so little resilience after the Conquest? We may argue that against Spanish fanaticism and Toledo steel no resistance could have been long sustained; or that the destruction of the Aztec warrior aristocracy meant the collapse of the entire social structure. But this would seem to be truer of the Incas than of the Aztecs: the Aztec realm was composed of semi-independent cities, often with their own administration, religion, and language. It is not clear, on the face of it, that the Aztec surrender to Spanish violence was bound to lead to the total cultural collapse of the Indian world.

Is there, then, another explanation? If there is, it must necessarily be speculative. Yet the true explanation can, I think, be read between the lines of Soustelle's eloquent account. Though he does not himself develop the theme, it would seem to be implicit in his apology for the Aztecs, and not contradictory of it. The American theologian Reinhold Niebuhr once wrote that the true explanation of the superiority of the Europeans to the inhabitants of the New World was not physical, but metaphysical. The Spaniard inherited the Judaeo-Christian ontology of man as a created, finite, but free being over against nature and God. This view liberated him from the myriad magical influences with which the lives of the Aztecs (as of many ancient peoples) were hedged around. It gave him the confidence that his unique, individual soul, for all his physical frailty, was the concern of the ultimate reality in the universe. Reading the story of how Cortes and his few hundred men refused to be intimidated by the odds they faced, and went forward to destroy the Aztec power, we see that gunpowder is not the whole explanation. In the profoundest sense, the Spaniards were "knights of faith"; the Indians they fought against were not. Soustelle might not agree with this assessment; but it is not in conflict with his own view:

At bottom the ancient Mexicans had no real confidence in the future, their fragile world was perpetually at the mercy of some disaster: there were not only the natural cataclysms and the famines, but more than that, on certain nights the monstrous divinities of the west appeared at the crossroads, and there were the wizards, those dark envoys from a mysterious world, and every fifty-two years there was the great fear that fell upon all the nations of the empire when the sun set on the last day of the "century" and no man could tell whether it would ever rise again.

Perhaps then, both Niebuhr, the Protestant theologian, and Soustelle, the Nietzschean romantic, are in the right. May we not guess that the Aztec, with his pessimistic stoicism, gave way to the Spanish knight of faith for much the same reason as the empty stoicism of Rome succumbed to the faith of the early Christian? Regardless of the intrinsic truth of either system of belief, it is plain that the Christian faith offered men a security

—and, therefore, a freedom—that was absent in the Aztec scheme of things. Soustelle's interpretation is not wrong. But he is unwilling to admit that what he praises in the Aztec world view was also its greatest weakness. Yet it is here that the true explanation for that collapse of the Indian world after the *conquista*, which still haunts contemporary Mexico, is to be looked for:

> Indeed, man had but an insignificant place in the Mexican vision of the world. He was governed by predestination; neither his life nor his after-life were in his own hands, and determinism ruled every phase of his short stay on earth. He was crushed under the weight of the gods and the stars: he was the prisoner of the omnipotent signs. The very world in which he made his brief struggle was no more than an ephemeral shape, one experiment among others, and like them doomed to catastrophe. . . . The moral climate of ancient Mexico was soaked in pessimism. The poems of the great king Nezaualcoyotl are haunted by the idea of death and annihilation; and even when other poets celebrate the beauties of tropical nature one feels that the obsession is there and that "it takes them by the throat even amidst the flowers".

The Psychology of "Mestizaje"

The story of the Aztecs, and by implication of the other civilised pre-Columbian peoples, is the story of the triumph of man over his environment. But it is a precarious triumph. The competing claims of the *indigenistas* and of the apologists for Spain—and the debate is at the heart of Mexico's intellectual life—are therefore perhaps more easily reconciled than either supposes. On the one hand, it is true that the Aztec, Maya, and other cultures represented a unique human achievement. But it is also true that they were peculiarly vulnerable, not simply in military terms, but in a psychological and metaphysical sense. The Spaniards were guilty of appalling acts of vandalism; they destroyed the written records of the Aztecs, they melted down the golden treasure of the Incas. They were responsible, too, for dreadful acts of cruelty. (Though the rapid decline of the Indian population after the Conquest—from about thirty million to some six million—must be put down to disease, according to modern scholars, rather than to any deliberate

action of the *conquistadores*.) But the true reason for the collapse
of the indigenous cultures is to be sought within those cultures
themselves, in their inherent fragility and lack of resilience.
There is no doubt that the Black Legend of Spanish cruelty has
been much exaggerated, by Protestant northerners as well
as by Las Casas, the Dominican friar on whose passionate
denunciations of the Spanish they delighted to draw. (In fact,
the very existence of a Las Casas, and the pro-Indian influence
he brought to bear on the Spanish Court, speaks well for the
Spaniards of the Age of Discovery.) But the Black Legend is
not in any case sufficient to explain the disappearance of the
Indian as a creative element in the New Spain founded by the
conquerors.

The *indigenistas* are almost certainly mistaken when they
deduce from the undoubted achievements of the Aztecs and the
Mayas that their descendants are destined to make their own
contribution to the culture of modern Mexico. Mexico boasts
an Indigenous Institute, which has done fine work in recovering
Indian traditions, and is helping to "integrate" the Indian into
present-day Mexican society. This will to integrate the three
elements in Mexican society ('White', *mestizo*, and Indian) is a
legacy of the Mexican Revolution of 1910, a revolution in other
respects strangely contradictory and lacking in articulate
ideology. This revolutionary goal at least has achieved considerable success; indeed it threatens to be so successful that the
Indian may be eliminated altogether. But this relative success is
merely an aspect of that remarkable political harmony at which
Mexico has arrived after the turbulent anarchy of her first
century of Independence. *Indigenismo* remains the official
ideology of the Revolution. But, as always in Latin America,
one is sceptical as to how far ideology corresponds to, let alone
determines, political and social reality. Again, if the political
problem has been resolved with some success, the psychological
problem persists. Well-meaning friends of Mexico, in recent
years, have lavished considerable praise on Mexico's political
harmony and economic progress (her apparently steady eight
per cent growth rate is easily the most impressive and most
consistent in Latin America). They are right to do so; it is
a remarkable achievement. But what her friends—I have in
mind especially her *yanqui* neighbours—do not see is that be-

neath the political economic harmony of modern Mexico a profound psychological disharmony lingers on.

For Mexico's is a *mestizo* culture. It is not only that the majority of Mexicans today are of mixed blood. The two "minority" groups—the "pure Whites" and "pure Indians"—are today equally removed from the centres of power: the Indian through his backwardness; the White through the destruction of his landed power in the Revolution, and the rise to power of a largely *mestizo* middle class in the service of the new State. Yet it is not easy to define the term *mestizo* satisfactorily. Perhaps the greatest figure of post-Independence Mexico, the Jacobin high-priest of the *Reforma*, Benito Juarez, was a pure-blooded Zapotec Indian. Yet there is no better example of the single-minded imitation of a European model—that very Latin American phenomenon—than Juarez's struggle to rid Mexico of her reactionary, Catholic-Hispanic past. It is argued that Juarez's Indian blood is evident in the fanatical, unyielding integrity of his nature. But it makes as good sense to see him as a Mexican Robespierre. It is the Latin-Catholic nations that produce fanatical anti-clericals of this stamp. The Jacobin is first cousin to the Jesuit. A purely "racial" explanation of Juarez's character clearly will not do: though no doubt it was his membership of the lowest caste of Mexican society that awoke his sympathy for the oppressed. Juarez, then, for all his Zapotec blood, was as much a *mestizo* as the *mestizo* Porfirio Diaz, his successor, the dictator who ruled Mexico for forty years before the revolution of 1910, or as the *mestizo* "*caudillos*" of the Revolution itself (though Zapata, again, was a pure-blooded Zapotec). Plainly, then, the term *mestizo* has a cultural rather than a racial reference. It implies a complete inter-penetration of native and European beliefs and modes of behaviour, not blood-intermixture alone. For the same reason *mestizo* characteristics are to be found in Mexicans who have no Indian blood at all. Mexico is a *mestizo* culture because she is the product of a fusion between the conflicting Spanish and Indian heritages of her peoples.

What happens when different "races" meet, and interfuse, as they have been doing in Mexico over the past 450 years? Frankness in these matters is not characteristic of the modern age; least of all, perhaps, among the Liberal intelligentsia of

Anglo-Saxon nations. The nineteenth century was less mealy-mouthed. Sixty years ago, the Brazilian Euclides da Cunha could take it for granted (albeit on doubtful social-Darwinist premisses) that a mixed race must be inferior to a pure. Since da Cunha's time, we have known an Adolf Hitler, and such views are unfashionable. In reaction, it has even been suggested that the final solution to the Negro problem, in America and elsewhere, could lie in universal miscegenation. If we are to understand Mexico, and Latin America in general, we must register some protest at these Liberal assumptions. What da Cunha has to say of his native Brazil is not doctrinaire; rather it is uncomfortably commonsensical. Da Cunha points to the likelihood that a mixed race will share the defects, rather than virtues of the races of which it is composed. His grounds for this are only apparently biological. The problem, as da Cunha sees it, is psychological. The man of mixed blood lacks the security that membership either of the static Indian sub-culture or of the dominant White élite is likely to give. He aspires to civilisation yet is rejected by those who are its guardians. Rejected, he falls back into the barbarous ways of his ancestors (this is the phenomenon da Cunha describes in *Rebellion in the Backlands*). He lacks the psychological stability that only the values of a settled society can confer. He veers between extremes; he is at one moment boastful and violent, the next meek and submissive. Here, perhaps, is the root of the exaggerated masculinity, the famous *machismo*, of the Mexican? Is this the explanation of the Mexican's sudden unpredictable violence (Mexico City is credited with the highest murder rate in the world)? Of that puzzling alternation between sullen resignation and explosive *joie-de-vivre*, as in the traditional *fiesta*, that has struck all observers of Mexican life from Fanny Calderon to D. H. Lawrence and Malcolm Lowry?

To say this, I realise, is to appear deliberately provocative. It is fashionable to hold up Mexico (and Brazil) as examples to the world of how it should manage its colour problems. Now, in a political sense, this may be true. In the integrated, quasi-democratic one-party state of present-day Mexico the more obvious social tensions of *mestizaje* have been resolved. But the underlying psychological tensions remain, and no portrait of Mexico can leave these out of account. To avoid misunderstand-

ing, let me say at once that this charge of psychological disharmony is not an invention of the foreign devils. It is what
intelligent Mexicans have been saying for a generation and
more. Two books, in particular, bear witness to it: Samuel
Ramos' *Profile of Man and Culture in Mexico*, and Octavio Paz's
The Labyrinth of Solitude. Ramos's book first appeared in Spanish
in 1933. It is therefore contemporaneous with certain other
Latin American essays in self-analysis which we shall look at
later: the Brazilian Gilberto Freyre's *The Masters and the Slaves*,
and the writings of Martinez Estrada and Eudardo Mallea in
the Argentine. Octavio Paz's book is somewhat later, being
first published in Spanish in 1950. It, too, offers an analysis of
the Mexican character, though from a somewhat different
angle. Taken together, these two books represent an attempt to
define those elusive qualities of *mexicanismo* which, if they baffle
foreigners, seems no less to baffle Mexicans themselves.

The agreements and differences between these books are
therefore of considerable interest. Both, in their dissection of
the Mexican character, are critical, even harsh. But whereas
Ramos's "Adlerian" interpretation leads him to demand a
somewhat naïve Adlerian therapy, Octavo Paz reinterprets the
Mexican's introverted, sado-masochistic psychology in existentialist terms. Thus reinterpteted, it can be presented as an
attitude to life not only different from, but superior to, the brash
extrovert materialism of the North American. (Paz's position
is here close to that of a famous Latin American *pensador* of
the turn of the century, the Uruguayan Jose Enrique Rodo.
In his book *Ariel*, Rodo opposes the spiritual-artistic temperament—"Ariel"—of the Latin American to the philistine
materialism of the North American "Caliban"). About the
Mexican's traditional inferiority complex, however, both
Ramos and Paz are frank. And much of what they say is
applicable elsewhere in Latin America. Ramos writes:

> The failures of culture in our country have not been due to
> deficiencies in the culture itself, but to a vice in the system of
> application. The vice in the system is none other than the *imita-
> tion* which has been universally practised in Mexico for more than
> a century. . . . Mimesis is an unconscious phenomenon that reveals
> a peculiar characteristic of *mestizo* psychology. . . .

As examples of this mimesis, Ramos cites the political-cultural borrowings of the nineteenth century, from North American Federalism and Presidentialism to the dogmatic French *positivisme* of the nineteenth-century Liberals. What Ramos has to say of the Mexican mania for constitution-making—a logical development of the training in Roman Law of Independent Mexico's politicians—is also of wider application:

> Imitation has brought about in Mexican life a situation which has not greatly attracted the attention of historians, but which is nevertheless essential to an understanding of our immediate past. . . . When a constitution is proclaimed, for example, political reality must be appraised within its standards, but when political reality does not coincide with the constitutional precepts, it always appears to be unconstitutional. The reader should note well what we mean. If life develops in two distinct ways—one, according to the law, and the other, according to reality—*reality will inevitably be illegal.* (My italics.)

If this tendency to imitation is itself the product of an inferiority complex, its operation reinforces that complex. *Mestizaje* is a vicious circle:

> Such is the effect of the mimetic procedure already described. In their reliance on principles of European civilisation our compatriots are therefore disqualified from doing spontaneous (if not creative) work in which the Mexican spirit might sincerely speak, Perhaps the most lamentable truth of our history . . . is to be found in our ancestors' feeling that *they had not been themselves*, with all their vices and virtues, but instead had concealed reality behind a rhetorical façade from abroad. . . . (My italics.)

To conceal reality behind a mask is a well-known characteristic of the American Indian and, therefore, of the *mestizo*. But in Ramos's analysis, this mask-wearing is not a positive thing. It is contrasted, rather, with the *sincerity* that Ramos deems essential if the Mexican is to become truly himself.

"How big a dose of truth can a man endure?" asks Ramos, echoing Nietzsche. And his conclusion is plainly that the modern Mexican, unlike Soustelle's Aztec, cannot endure very much reality. But then, Ramos is asking a great deal of his fellow-countrymen, when he asks them to accept this portrait of the Mexican *pelado* (literally, "peeled one"):

The Mexican psyche is the result of reactions that strive to conceal an inferiority complex . . . the best model for study is the Mexican *pelado*. . . . His name defines him accurately. He is the kind of person who continually lays bare his soul, so that its most intimate confines are visible. . . . Life from every quarter has been hostile to him and his reaction has been black resentment. His is an explosive being with whom relationship is dangerous, for the slightest friction causes him to blow up. . . . Any exterior circumstance that might aggravate his sense of inferiority will provoke a violent reprisal, the aim of which is to subdue his depression. The result is a constant irritability that incites him to fight with others on the most insignificant pretext. . . . The *pelado's* terminology abounds in sexual allusions which reveal his phallic obsession . . . in verbal combat he attributes to his adversary an imaginary feminity, reserving for himself the masculine role. . . .

The sexual instinct, already overburdened, acquires a new, almost a political dimension.

Here then, in Ramos's view, is the explanation of that cult of *machismo* which plays so large a part in Mexican and Latin American life. It is the same psychology, no doubt, as underlies the Don Juanism of the classic Latin American playboy: Porfirio Rubirosa or Baby Pignatari. Something similar, perhaps, underlies the prodigious phallicism often imputed to, and readily accepted by, the African or American Negro. Sex is the soft underbelly of the liberal conscience: it is here that Caliban looks for revenge on his tormentor. But the Mexican's attitude to life breeds, as it feeds upon, mutual distrust. In origin this lack of trust is personal. But it too has social and political implications:

The most striking aspect of Mexican character, at first sight, is distrust. . . . His distrust is not limited to the human race; it embraces all that exists and happens. . . . What then does the Mexican live for? . . . In its totality, Mexican life gives the impression of being an unreflecting activity, entirely without plan, In Mexico each man concerns himself with immediate issues. He works for today and tomorrow but never for later on. . . . He is incapable of adventure in projects that offer only remote results. He has therefore suppressed from his life one of its most important dimensions—the future. Such are the effects of Mexican distrust.

It is a little disconcerting, perhaps, after this brilliant and

devastating self-analysis, to come upon Ramos's almost glib
solution to the problems he raises:

> We know today that the natural faculties of man are inadequate
> for acquiring self-knowledge; he must first equip himself with the
> intellectual tools devised by psychoanalysis. When, thus prepared,
> man discovers what he is, a solution to the remaining problems
> will follow automatically. Phantoms are nocturnal beings that
> vanish. They simply have to be exposed to the light of day.

Seldom, I think, has a writer so ruthlessly exposed his fellow-
countrymen's weaknesses and self-delusions. There is in Ramos's
book that spirit of radical self-examination we find in the
writings of the Spanish Generation of '98. Indeed Ramos's
study, like those of Mallea and Martinez Estrada, may be seen
as a late product of that stock-taking Hispanic intellectuals felt
to be necessary after the victory of the United States in the
Spanish-American War of 1898, and which, in Spain itself,
was so tragically cut short by the Civil War. The reasons for this
crisis of the Hispanic spirit at the turn of the twentieth century
are plain enough. Though Spain and her Empire had been in
decline since the seventeenth century, and though her Empire
itself had disintegrated, the Hispanic world remained remarkably self-contained. It was not until the twentieth century that
the implications of Spain's backwardness, and that of Latin
America, began to be felt. Where, asked a new generation, are
the Newtons and Descartes and Kants, or even the Edisons and
Pasteurs, of our Hispanic world? Where are the painters and
poets and novelists to give the world a new Don Juan or Don
Quixote, a Hispanic equivalent to the new literature coming
out of no less backward Russia?

Then there was the staggering material success of newcomers
to the industrial revolution like Germany or the United States.
At Independence, these countries had been scarcely more
industrialised than Spain or Latin America. Yet now Rodó's
Caliban threatened to overtake, indeed to overwhelm, the
Hispanic civilisation of both hemispheres. At Independence, as
the Mexican historian Daniel Cosio Villegas has argued,
Mexico was territorially larger than the United States, and
apparently better endowed with material resources. It might
well have been predicted, in 1810, that Mexico would have

grown into the greatest power in the Americas by the turn of
the century. Instead, by 1850, Mexico had lost half her territory
to a forward-thrusting United States, thanks to her own mis-
government, corruption and incompetence. The last illusions
of the Hispanic world about the material superiority of Anglo-
Saxon civilisation were to go down before Roosevelt's Rough
Riders and the activities of American Marines in the Caribbean during the first decades of this century.

We can, then, assimilate Latin America to the Iberian nations
in these respects. We know that the declared purpose of the
Liberators was to wean Latin America from the tutelage of
Spain and her Black Legend—by substituting British, French,
and North American influences for Hispanic. Yet the new
Presidential Republics quickly turned into *caudillo* dictatorships, and the hold of the traditional *criollo* oligarchy was not
broken. If the merchants and middle classes of Buenos Aires and
Mexico City forced the disestablishment of the Church in the
nineteenth century, the Liberals of Spain, after the Carlist
wars, did the same. Indeed, the post-Napoleonic parallels
between Iberia and Latin America are very close. In both
hemispheres, middle class Liberals and landed Conservatives
tended to alternate in power—with or without the assistance of
military *pronunciamientos*—and the typical twentieth-century
mass parties, Anarchist, Socialist and Communist, long remained weak. Is it significant that in Colombia, one of the most
Spanish of Latin American countries, this nineteenth-century
pattern still prevails. Once the intellectuals of the Hispanic
world woke up to their true position—their economic backwardness, their chronic political instability, the relegation of the
Hispanic culture to the fringe of European civilisation—the
reaction was explosive.

It is beyond the scope of this book to discuss the Iberian
reaction to the crisis—though it was in Spain that it was most
coherent and most articulate. Broadly, it seems that two
courses lay open to the self-critical Hispanic intellectuals of
that epoch. The Hispanic intellectuals were divided in their
loyalties, very much as the Russian intellectuals of the late
nineteenth century were divided between Slavophiles and
Westerners. Faced with the staggering wealth of Europe and
North America, the choice seemed to lie between emulation

and withdrawal. Emulation meant the deliberate assimilation of Western thought, whatever the cost to traditional values. This was the course taken by Japan and Turkey, and ultimately by Russia and China. Withdrawal meant cultivation of that spiritual essence—*casticismo*—that was the source of the nation's virtues and of its real, if temporarily obscured, superiority to other nations. The 'Westernising' reaction was not absent in Spain; and, in its *positiviste* form, was powerful in Latin America. But it was the second, defensive and, in part, obscurantist reaction that often took root in many Hispanic countries. The Castilian *casticismo* (purity) preached by Unamuno, and the *arielismo* preached by Rodo, belong to this second category. So, though it lacked a coherent ideology, does the Mexican Revolution. The notion of a Hispanic-Indian "cosmic race" evolved by Vasconcelos, Minister of Education in the twenties, and the patron of Rivera, Orozco and Siqueiros, came closest to providing such an ideology. (Vasconcelos, with Alfonso Reyes and Antonio Caso one of the leading intellectuals of the Revolutionary era, became a fiery anti-American, and an apologist for Hispanic-Catholic values.) The Revolutionary generals, of course, took precious little interest in questions of ideology. The intellectuals were always of quite marginal significance in the Mexican Revolution. And this has remained so. Octavio Paz has been Mexican ambassador to France and to India; his *Labyrinth of Solitude* is a brilliant book. But it would be a mistake to imagine that he, or the other diplomatically honoured *pensadores* of Latin America, carry much political weight.

It would be wrong, too, to present Octavio Paz as an uncritical apologist for *mexicanismo*. He is in the line of Samuel Ramos and other self-critical Hispanic intellectuals (he fought in Spain during the Civil War): their self-analysis, necessarily, is his starting point. But in Paz's evaluation of the Mexican character there is a difference of tone. He admits Ramos's case, but enters a plea for extenuation. Perhaps, he seems to be saying, there is something even in our most negative characteristics that is redeemable, that is not altogether to be despised. That he can turn the argument about in this way is due to an intellectual substitution, a substitution which is partly explained by the dates of Ramos's and Paz's books (and which is at the same time witness of the strength of European intellectual influences). Ramos's mentor, in 1933, was Alfred Adler; Octavio Paz's, in 1950, is Jean-Paul Sartre. That this switch of allegiance should bring Paz back to a Rodo-like position *vis-à-vis* the United States is perhaps not surprising. Paz, though no "anti-American" in a political sense, finds himself speaking for Latin America, not for Mexico alone:

> Some people claim that the only differences between the North Americans and ourselves are economic. That is, they are rich and we are poor, and while their legacy is Democracy, Capitalism and the Industrial Revolution, ours is the Counter-Reformation, Monopoly and Feudalism. . . . When I arrived in the United States, I was surprised above all by the self-assurance and confidence of the people, by their apparent happiness and apparent adjustment to the world around them. This satisfaction does not stifle criticism, however, and that criticism is valuable and forthright . . . but it is a criticism that accepts the existing system and never touches the roots.

North American self-criticism, then, is "reformist": it is based on an unexamined faith in the "natural goodness of life". North American protestantism has swung far from its Puritan, Manichean origins. The modern United States is as much the champion of the Pelagian heresy as were the Spanish Visigoths of the Arian. Mexico, by contrast, is the legatee of a pessimistic, "mediterranean", Indo-Hispanic view of life:

> I heard a good deal of talk about American realism and also about American ingenuousness, qualities that would seem to be mutually exclusive. To us a realist is always a pessimist. And an ingenuous person would not remain so for very long if he truly contemplated life realistically. Would it not be more accurate to say that the North American wants to *use* reality rather than to know it? In some matters—death, for example— he not only has no desire to understand it, he obviously avoids the very idea. . . . Death, on the other hand, has always been a native Mexican speciality. . . .
>
> One of the most notable traits of the Mexican's character is his willingness to contemplate horror: he is even familiar and complacent in his dealings with it. The bloody Christs in our village churches, the macabre humour in some of our newspaper headlines, our wakes, the custom of eating skull-shaped cakes and candies on the Day of the Dead, are habits inherited from the

Indians and the Spaniards and are now an inseparable part of our being. . . . Our fondness for self-destruction derives not only from our masochistic tendencies but also from a certain variety of religious emotion.

Death is a stranger to the American; to the Mexican he is an enemy, but also an intimate. Much, then, of Ramos's criticism of the Mexican character is subtly transmuted in Paz's interpretation. If the Mexican understands death better than the North American, he also understands life better than the pragmatic Anglo-Saxon. The Mexican is a born existentialist:

> The North Americans are credulous and we are believers, they love fairy tales and detective stories and we love myths and legends. The Mexican tells lies because he delights in fantasy. . . . The North American does not tell lies, but he substitutes social truth for the real truth, which is always disagreeable. We get drunk in order to confess; they get drunk in order to forget. They are optimists and we are nihilists . . . we are suspicious and they are trusting. . . . They are activists and we are quietists; we enjoy our wounds and they enjoy their inventions. They believe in hygiene, health, work, and contentment, but perhaps they have never experienced true joy, which is an intoxication, a whirlwind. In the hubbub of a *fiesta* night our voices explode into brilliant lights, and life and death mingle together, while their vitality becomes a fixed smile that denies old age and death but that changes life to motionless stone.

The potential danger, even silliness, of this line of argument is apparent from the following—though it is hardly for the modern European to preach to the Latin American on the subject of violence:

> When the Mexican kills—for revenge, pleasure, or caprice—he kills a person, a human being. Modern criminals and statesmen do not kill; they abolish. They experiment with beings who have lost their human qualities. Prisoners in the concentration camps were first degraded, changed into mere objects; then they were executed *en masse*. . . . Murder is still a relationship in Mexico, and in this sense it has the same liberating significance as the *fiesta* or the confession. Hence its drama, its poetry and—why not say it?—its grandeur. Through murder we achieve a momentary transcendence. . . .

From Anarchy to Order

In *England, Your England*, George Orwell remarks that nationalism is the strongest political force in the modern world. That
verdict was given in 1940. Little has occurred to confound
Orwell's prophecy. It is nationalism that threatens the Communist monolith; it is nationalism that threatens to break
up the Western Alliance. The revolts of the underdeveloped
world—India, Egypt, Algeria—are nationalist in inspiration.
Only in a few cases has nationalism taken on a Communist
colouring: in China, in Vietnam, in Cuba. Otherwise, Third
World nationalism has striven, and largely succeeded, in
preserving its political virginity from the assaults of East or
West. This is true of Mexico, which has contrived to keep open
diplomatic relations with Cuba, while remaining on excellent
terms with the United States. And nationalism, indeed, is the
key to Mexico. In point of time, her Revolution was the first of
the great nationalist revolutions of the twentieth century.
Though more or less contemporary with Sun Yat-sen's revolution in China and Kemal Ataturk's in Turkey, it anticipated
Lenin's revolution by seven years, and the nationalist revolutions of Mao, Nehru, Nasser, and Sukarno by half a century.
For this reason, it is of unique historical interest. For what can
be said of so many political phenomena in Latin America—
that they are little more than reflections of European ideologies
—cannot be said of the Mexican Revolution of 1910. Here was a
revolution that was not a mere barracks revolt, or an incompetent parody of Napoleon III or Robespierre. Here was a
political phenomenon truly indigenous and self-made.

For that very reason, there are few phenomena so difficult
to analyse. None of the leaders of the Mexican Revolution
acquired world stature, as did Nasser or Sukarno or Nkrumah.
Some, like the peasant leaders Zapata or Pancho Villa, retain a
romantic aura (Zapata owes his largely to Marlon Brando).
But the rest of the world does not remember Madero, or
Carranza, or Calles, or Obregon. The name of Lazaro Cardenas
is preserved chiefly because the outside world took fright at his
nationalisation of petroleum. Of the presidents who held office
in the tranquil years after 1940 even less is known. For many in

c

North America, Pancho Villa is still riding, and changes of government in Mexico are still effected by noose and halter. Yet in fact Mexico has not suffered a military rising since the 1930's; and Presidential succession is now a frictionless routine. One index of Mexico's stability is that her Presidents grow more colourless decade by decade. The President is all-powerful. Yet in few countries would the assassination of a President cause so little consternation. Mexico has cast off the incubus of *personalismo*, as she has rid herself of the curse of militarism. She has succeeded, in other words, where most of Latin America has failed. She has *institutionalised* her Revolution. To foreigners, it is a ludicrous paradox that she should be ruled by the "Institutional Revolutionary Party" (PRI). Ludicrous it may be; but, despite the recent violence, the paradox seems to work.

The significance of the Mexican Revolution, then, is non-ideological. It is a pragmatic success. And this, at first sight, is surprising. We ascribe to the Latins an inordinate liking for rhetoric and ideology; pragmatism is what Latins lack, and what Anglo-Saxons are anxious to teach them. Nor is this wholly wrong: the *Reforma* was indeed an exercise in dogmatic Jacobinism, the mirror-image of Hispanic Catholicism. But the Latin American revolutions of the twentieth century do not conform to this pattern. Even where they possess a developed ideology, they are far more pragmatic than their rhetoric suggests. In this respect Mexico's PRI is not alone; it is essentially similar to Venezuela's *Accion Democratica*, Peru's APRA, or even Peron's *Justicialismo*. These movements differ in many respects. But all are essentially nationalist movements, allied with the working class or the peasantry, often with official sponsorship from the army or a section of the bureaucracy or the bourgeoisie. More purely ideological movements, such as Communism and Fascism, have never taken root in Latin America. (We shall see whether Cuba proves an exception.) Indeed, in studying these "revolutionary" parties of the New World, it is easy to become sceptical of the view that Latin Americans are especially given to ideological dogmatism. The dogmatism may be merely verbal, and the practice at variance with the ideology. We must not forget that the Latin American world traditionally tolerates a remarkable dichotomy between word and action. Since it comes amiss from an Anglo-Saxon to say these things, let me quote what the Peruvian Francisco Garcia Calderon, whom André Siegfried (in his *Amérique Latine*) once called the "Tocqueville of Latin America", had to say about the Latin legacy of the peoples south of the Rio Grande:

> The qualities and defects of the classical spirit are revealed in American life: its tenacious idealism which underrates all attainment of the useful; its ideas of humanity, equality and universality. Its formalist cult; Latin vivacity and instability; faith in pure ideas and political dogmas. In these lands all this is found, as well as a brilliant and superficial intelligence, Jacobinism, and oratorical facility. These republics are not sheltered from any of the common weaknesses of the Latin races. The state is omnipotent, the liberal arts and professions are overdeveloped, the power of bureaucracy is disturbing. The character of the citizen is weak, inferior to his imagination and intelligence . . . dominated by exterior demands and by the tumult of politics, these men lack interior life; neither great mystics nor great poets are found among them. Against common realities they raise their exasperated individualism.

As an exercise in self-analysis this is no less devastating than Ramos's opinion. There is no pretence, *à la* Rodo, that the extravert, materialist virtues of the North Americans are balanced by a more sensitive, interior life south of the Rio Grande. If Garcia Calderon is right, Latin rhetoric is as much the enemy of spiritual inwardness as it is the enemy of pragmatic politics. Nor does the Latins' "exasperated individualism" hold much promise of success either in a practical or a psychological sense. Nevertheless, these pessimistic analyses of Ramos and Garcia Calderon must be looked at afresh in the light of the achievements of the Mexican Revolution. The first hundred years of independent Mexican history certainly abound in "exasperated individualism"; Mexico suffered, it is reckoned, a hundred "revolutions" in the first fifty years of her independence. But this has not prevented Mexico from achieving one of the most stable polities in Latin America and, indeed, in the underdeveloped world. How was it done?

The importance of the question is evident. For if Mexico has found a solution to the political anarchy that plagued her, there is a case for the "New States" that have come into being over the past twenty years to study her example. The centrifugal forces now at work in so many of these New States—militarism, tribalism, communalism—are all to be found in Mexican history. Yet they have been contained, and their centrifugality reversed. How was the tide turned? Plainly, any answer to this question must take into account the deeper reasons for the political anarchy of post-Independence Latin America. Some of these spring to the eye. Mexico and Latin America, like Spain, are at the mercy of a disruptive geography. Volcanic ranges and untamed rivers, deserts and jungles, militate against political unity. The tendency, as in Spain, is towards loyalty to the *patria chica*, towards the region rather than the nation. Thus any dissident military leader in the past was likely to find the materials of "revolution" to hand. Irreducible, except through lengthy guerrilla warfare, he could hope, by skilful manœuvring, to bring other potential dissidents to his side. The chances of success were good; the perils of failure—exile, or in ancient Aztec fashion, a careful accommodation with the civil power—seldom disastrous.

We shall examine, later, the curious mechanism of Latin America's militarism—neither as bloody nor as systematic as its European counterpart. What must be stressed is that Latin American "militarism" is a *negative* phenomenon. It is not because her armies are so strong—they are tiny by outside standards—that military intervention is common in Latin America. It is because her civil polity is so weak. In his excellent study of the subject, *The Man on Horseback*, S. E. Finer suggests that it is the "low political culture" of the New States—and the Latin American republics are merely the oldest of the New States—that creates the political vacuum into which the military are, often reluctantly, drawn. The new ex-colonial nations have at least one political experience in common: that of living under the colonial rule of metropolitan powers. This rule was usually authoritarian and bureaucratic. That is how the precedent for post-colonial authoritarianism and bureaucraticism was created. But once the authority of the metropolis had been challenged, the authority of the men who replaced it —*junta* or revolutionary council—was also open to challenge. At this point the problem of legitimacy arose. And, in the oligarchic society of the post-Independence period, there was no clear answer to it. The seat of the Viceroy had become vacant;

but why should General A. have more right to it than General
B.? The oligarchs were divided; the mass of the people were
excluded from the political process. It was this crisis of legitimacy that gave rise to the Latin American *caudillo*, from
Mexico's Santa Anna (twenty times President of Mexico) to
the Trujillos and Perons of the past generation. Where legitimacy is in doubt the law of the jungle prevails.

As in Europe, the long-term solution to the problem of
legitimacy lay in the principle of democracy. In theory, all the
Liberators of Latin America—Miranda, Bolivar, San Martin—
were democrats. In practice, however, they found their support
among the *criollo* aristocracy; and it was the interests of this
land-owning upper class that moulded post-Independence
Latin America. Only in Mexico was a break with this tradition
effected. The revolution of 1910, certainly, is not to be assimilated to any European model. But it did express the need for a
new legitimation of the basis of Mexican government. Under
Porfirio Diaz, the arch-enemy, yet in many ways the predecessor of the present régime, power had rested with the landowners
and the bourgeoisie. The Indian *campesinos* had little power:
indeed, they had probably lost ground on account of the growth
of a new landowning oligarchy, basing its power on the church
lands confiscated by Juarez. It was the aim of the peasant
armies of Zapata and Pancho Villa to restore the land of
Mexico to the tiller, that is, to the *campesino*. Beyond this, however, there was an aspiration which it is reasonable to call
democratic: the desire of the Indian and *mestizo* masses to share
in the running of the country. In its basic aims, then, the Mexican Revolution was a recapitulation of the Independence
movement a hundred years before. Its profoundest significance
was the need to give the all-powerful Presidency, and its
accompanying bureaucracy, a legitimacy it had lacked since
the days of the Viceorys. This legitimacy could only come from
the people of Mexico themselves. How it came to be realised is a
curious and instructive story.

The Revolution began as a challenge to the thirty-five-year
old dictatorship of Porfirio Diaz. Francisco Madero, its first
champion, produced the slogan, "effective suffrage, no re-
election!", the purpose of which was to prevent Diaz's auto-
matic re-election as President in 1910. Madero was a north

Mexican landowner, much given to spiritualism—hardly the commanding, charismatic figure the Revolution required. But his challenge to Diaz's monopoly of office coincided with a general upsurge of discontent: the land-hunger of the peasantry; the resentment felt by Mexicans at the "rule of the old men"; the revolt of intellectuals like Alfonso Reyes and Vasconcelos against the arid *positivisme* of official philosophy. It was not simply that Diaz and his old men were corrupt and brutal. (They had imposed a *pax porfiriana* on Mexico which benefited the country economically.) They had also been there too long. A generational change was overdue. The elections of 1910, preceding the anniversary of the 1810 rising, were shamelessly rigged. Madero was thrown into prison; Diaz was credited with millions of votes, Madero with a ludicrous 196. Then Diaz, in his over-confidence, made a crucial mistake. Madero was permitted to "escape" from prison and take refuge in the United States. There he issued his "Plan of San Luis Potosi", urging the Mexican people to revolt against Diaz's tyranny. Among those who followed Madero's call to arms were the soon-to-be-famous (or notorious) Pancho Villa, Emilio Zapata, and Venustiano Carranza. Though much of the country remained loyal, Diaz realised by May 1911 that his position was impossible. He left the country; Francisco Madero became President.

What followed, between 1911 and 1917, was as bloody as it was predictable. Mexico reverted to the age of Santa Anna. She became the prey of rival *caudillos*, each with his geographically inaccessible power-base. The obvious reason for this reversion to anarchy was Madero's weakness as President. Doubtless only a Strong Man could have controlled so explosive a situation; and Madero was ousted, and murdered, within two years, by a counter-revolutionary coup. But it may be that the anarchy that followed the *pax porfiriana* could not have been avoided. As one of Juarez's generals, Diaz had created his own legitimacy. It was a legitimacy based on personal power and patronage; it could not be transferred. The next six years, as a consequence, were among the bloodiest in Mexican history. A million Mexicans lost their lives. Madero had won according to the traditional rules. There had been no civil war as Europeans and North Americans understand it. A "plan" had been promulgated, in traditional fashion. Once it was clear that the incumbent President could no longer command the support of the civil and military authorities, he bowed to the inevitable. But with Madero's removal the game ceased to be played according to the rules. The regional *caudillos* no longer stood only for themselves; they embodied social forces that could no longer be denied expression. One enemy alone was clearly visible: the land-owning oligarchy that had profited from Diaz's régime and frustrated the Indians' land-hunger. Everywhere *haciendas* burned, and the old, *criollo* aristocracy were evicted from power. The new men were pure Indians, like Zapata, or *mestizos* from the towns and villages of Chiapas or northern Mexico. For all their confused and cruel ambitions, these were men of the people; in them the aspirations of the Mexican people had come to self-consciousness.

How was this anarchy resolved? How, within fifteen years, was the unexampled *confusionismo* of the post-1911 period not merely eliminated, but converted into the one-party system that has given Mexico a stability, and a measure of economic progress, that Diaz himself might have envied? Certainly, Mexico's one-party system owes nothing to the one-party systems of European Communism or Fascism. It was a pragmatic growth. There appear to have been three distinct phases in its maturation. In the first, the more anarchic and irresponsible leaders of the Revolution—Zapata and Pancho Villa—fell victim to a process of elimination. The remaining leaders, Carranza, de la Huerta, Calles, and Obregon, formed an alliance and promulgated the "Constitution of 1917". By the mid-twenties Carranza had been eliminated in a barracks revolt; de la Huerta likewise. The Calles–Obregon duumvirate had total power. Since the sacred revolutionary principle of "non-re-election" had to be observed, Obregon and Calles were obliged to succeed one another in the Presidency. Obregon was President from 1920–4; Calles from 1924–8.

This pattern was to be rudely shattered. Before Obregon could succeed his fellow-duumvir in 1928 he was assassinated by a religious fanatic. This unforeseeable historical accident ushered in the second phase of the Revolution. Calles, according to the principle of non-re-election, could not succeed himself. Yet Calles, with Obregon's removal, was the chief source of revolutionary power. To resolve the dilemma, the followers of

Calles and Obregon created a political cartel, the National Revolutionary Party, the ancestor of the PRI. The origin of Mexico's one-party system was, therefore, accidental; and it is here that comparison with the Communist and Fascist systems is instructive. In Soviet history it has been through control of the Party that the "strong man"—Stalin or Khrushchev—has come to power. The pre-existent party has been a necessary instrument in the manipulation of power. In Mexico, the process was reversed. The all-powerful Calles was compelled to create a monolithic party, since he could not succeed himself, in order to impose his puppet President on the country. In Mexico, therefore, the all-powerful party was the product of Calles's frustration, and of the curious legalism of the Hispano-American mind. The strong man created the party, not the party the strong man.

This second stage in the founding of the Revolutionary Party was decisive. But it required a further step to transform this loose alliance of revolutionary chieftains into a monolithic party. This third stage was inaugurated by Calles himself, who did much to whittle away the power of the regional *caudillos* in the years after 1928. But the crucial step was the result of a miscalculation by Calles, who had grown more and more remote from Mexican actuality. In 1934 he put forward the name of a popular general, Lazaro Cardenas, as Presidential candidate, on the assumption that he would prove another compliant puppet. He was sadly mistaken. Cardenas appealed to the country over the heads of the newly-rich revolutionary generals, demanding a renewal of the revolutionary enterprise. Elected on a massive popular vote, Cardenas proceeded to reorganise the Revolutionary Party on lines of which Calles disapproved— a dispute which finally led to the elimination of Calles from the political scene. The essence of Cardenas's reorganisation of the Party was the substitution of "functional", non-regional unities —military, labour, agrarian, and "popular"—for the regional power-bases of the Revolutionary chieftains.

This "institutionalising" of the Revolutionary Party had profound consequences. The new centralising tendency eliminated those centrifugal forces that had sprung up in the wake of the Revolution, and which were the traditional curse of Mexico. Politics became a matter of horse-dealing between the various "sectors" of the Revolutionary Party (one sector supporting the other in one state in return for equivalent favours in another). Though Cardenas himself had much of the *caudillo* in his make-up, he had created a bureaucratic party in which all national interests—with exception of the Church and big business—were represented. Yet the Party he created, though it gave lip-service to the Constitution of 1917, was essentially non-ideological. It deftly destroyed its opponents by adopting their ideology (this was the fate of the Communists and other left-wing groups). Even in religious matters it was a good deal more tolerant than its inherited ideology let it appear; and its successors have proved more tolerant still. The Party came to embody a national consensus which few challenged. Not because it ruled by political terror, but because the Party was sufficiently inclusive to allow of sectional interests being fought out within the organisation itself. If an analogy is sought, it should be with India's Congress Party rather than with the Communist Parties of Russia or China. Where the Leninist parties drew strength from their exclusiveness, the Indian and Mexican parties drew strength from their inclusiveness, their ability to embody a genuine national consensus.

We must be careful not to idealise this solution. If there is a degree of internal democracy in the PRI—in Lenin's "democratic-centralist" sense—there is a sad lack of free criticism in the press and the other organs of public communication. In this respect, Mexico is a less "free" country than many others in Latin America where, if little actually gets done, there is no lack of free discussion as to what might be done. Still, political liberty is a relative thing. Mexico's government does not throw her opponents into concentration camps; but then she is not seriously worried by the opposition she meets at the polls. The chief evils of the system are those inseparable from any semi-monopoly system of government. One-party control of news, information and patronage must lead to a situation where opposition, even if permitted in theory, becomes etiolated and ineffectual. A complementary danger is that, far from a "strong man" emerging to dominate party and state, the typical President may be the good bureaucrat, the machine-man who knows how to express the will of the party, while offending none of its rival factions or competing interests.

Stability, then, has been bought at a price. In much of Latin America the danger is that the *personalismo* of some general or *caudillo* may frustrate democratic development. In Mexico there exists the opposite danger: that the system may produce a procession of colourless bureaucrats who, trimmers by nature and training, evade decisions at which a Calles or a Cardenas would not have blanched. The negative side of Mexico's stability, paradoxically, is that she may be destined to suffer from weak government—and that, in consequence, a new generation may demand a greater "activism" which, in turn, may lead to further brutal governmental suppression. Nevertheless, Mexico's "stability" remains an achievement. How far other Latin American, or Asian or African countries, are in a position to learn from it is certainly questionable. But it seems that in any geographically divided and racially heterogeneous country a one-party "coalition of interests" is likely to provide a more permanent basis for government than either one-party ideological rule or one-man dictatorship. Mexico's experience is perhaps unrepeatable. But the statesmen of the Third World might ponder how those apparently irreconcilable conflicts —between Spaniard and Aztec, Centralist and Federalist, Liberal and Conservative—that rent Mexico for over a century found, if only for a period, an unexpected resolution.

2

GUATEMALA:
or The Character of the Conqueror

The discovery of America was a disaster for Spain, and possibly for Europe as well. It was a pity that things did not happen otherwise. America should have been discovered by the English, which is what might have happened if Ferdinand and Isabella had locked up Columbus in the lunatic asylum where he belonged. That formidable reservoir of human energy which went west and mastered a continent in a generation should have invaded the southern shores of the Mediterranean, from Tangiers to the Bosphorus. The Spanish-American nations would today be Spanish-African; the whole of America would be an English-speaking continent; and France, free in Europe, would have spread her culture from Paris to Moscow in peace.

Latin America between the Eagle and the Bear:
Salvador de Madariaga (1962)

How many Americas?

MEXICO IS THE MOST ANCIENT, the most dynamic, and the most populous of the Spanish American republics. She has not forgotten that she once bore the proud title of *Nueva España*. Nor has she forgotten the wealth and sophistication of her pre-Hispanic civilisation. Yet Mexico is not really typical of Latin America; in several respects she stands apart from her sister republics and forms a civilisation of her own. She lacks, for one thing, the Messianic strain: she has no Bolivar, no San Martin, no Jose Marti. She keeps her heroes to herself; her history, unlike that of most of Latin America, is self-contained. The Mexican Revolution has accentuated these characteristics. Its very success has cut Mexico off from those *criollo*-ruled, predominantly Indian societies like Peru, Ecuador or Guatemala, where "national integration" is still a pious watchword. Guatemala, then, is Mexico *avant le déluge*; it is Mexico as she might be if the 1910 Revolution had not taken place. Theoretically, Mexico should be a model to Guatemala and the rest of Latin America. But in practice the very nationalism of her Revolution has made it an unrepeatable experience. Yet if Mexico is not "typical", what country is? Argentina and Uruguay, with their boundless *pampas*, their European orientation, their "White" populations? Cuba and Brazil, with their semi-Negro populations, their ardent, volatile *tropicalismo*? Bolivia and Peru with their Quechua- or Aymara-speaking Indian *campesinos* on the high Andean plateau? The differences seem as great as the similarities. Perhaps, after all, there is no typical Latin American country; despite the unity that common political cultural and ecclesiastical traditions have imposed on the republics.

Still, bearing in mind that all such divisions are arbitrary, Latin America can be usefully subdivided into five main regions, each with certain common characteristics. The first subdivision, the Mexican, we have examined in some detail: this is an Indian-*mestizo*, non-Negro, partly sub-tropical, partly highland territory, rich in pre-Columbian history, traditionally turbulent, though latterly remarkably quiescent. Against this relative racial harmony, there stand those countries where the Indian-*criollo* dichotomy is still virtually absolute: Ecuador, Peru, and the republics of Central America (with the exception of Panama and Costa Rica). Like Mexico, these too are highland countries, rich in pre-Columbian traditions. They differ from Mexico in that each is still ruled by a dominant *criollo* oligarchy. While the short-term prospects for these countries point to stability (Bolivia experienced a Mexican-type revolution in 1952, but has since faltered), the long-term prospects point to social and radical conflict on the Mexican model, unless the Indian masses can be drawn into the life of the nation by non-violent methods. The third subdivision is the easiest to distinguish, having become traditional: it comprises the "White" countries of the Southern Cone, Argentina, Chile and Uruguay. To this group one might add, for neatness's sake, not only "White" Costa Rica, but the predominantly European southern and central regions of Brazil, including the cities of Rio de Janeiro and São Paulo. The countries of this group are largely non-Indian and non-Negro, poor in pre-Columbian remains, and equally poor in Hispanic-Colonial traditions. But we may note that while flat, featureless, culturally-impoverished Argentina is a late-developer, she is also one of the most *American* of the Latin nations. It was there that the *gaucho*, the counterpart of the American cowboy, came into being. It was there that the great themes of American literature—the conquest of the wilderness by man and of man by the wilderness—found their most eloquent expression: in Sarmiento's *Facundo*, in W. H. Hudson's *Purple Land*, in Guiraldes's *Don Segundo Sombra*.

The fourth, and fifth, subdivisions are less neatly distinguishable. Nor, for all the furore to which they have recently given rise, are they comparable in importance to those we have just discussed. Thus we can distinguish a "Caribbean" group, characterised by a tropical climate, a substantial Negro population, the almost total lack of an Indian substratum, together with a certain thinness of "Latin" subsoil. Cuba, Haiti, Santo Domingo, and Puerto Rico belong to this group; as do Panama, the narrow coastal fringes of Venezuela, Colombia and Peru and—most importantly—the huge, tropical, Negro-dominated coastal fringe of north-eastern Brazil. The fifth, and final, subdivision would comprise the predominantly "White" highlands of Colombia and Venezuela. Many people do not think of these countries as a group at all. But they have certain characteristics in common, often neglected by the foreign observer. Like the Southern Cone, this is an area where, despite a powerful Indian and *mestizo* minority, the European *criollo* element remains the norm. If the archetypal hero of Mexico is the Zapotec Indian Juarez, the heroes of the Southern Cone and of this northern Andean region remain the *criollo* Liberators San Martin and Simon Bolivar. It is in these regions, then, as in Brazil and Peru, that the "messianic" spirit is most strongly developed. It is significant that neither the "Indian" countries of Central America or the Andes, nor the Negro countries of the Caribbean or the Atlantic littoral, have produced figures (with the exception of Toussaint Louverture and Jose Marti) of comparable significance.

None of these categories should be taken too strictly. But they help to define the very different components that go to make up Latin America. I have stressed the unity that Latin America possesses in virtue of its Luso-Hispanic inheritance. I am not contradicting that assertion in pointing to these regional variations. It is rather that what is true of the whole is expressed more clearly, more concentratedly, in the parts. Latin America is a complex theme; it must be studied in its variations as well as in its sum. Certain of these variations we have considered in the case of Mexico: the ancient Spanish-Indian antithesis and its partial, latter-day resolution; the peculiar psychology of *mestizaje*; that American-Utopian spirit coexisting with a nihilistic pessimism that has as much a Spanish as an Aztec origin. It is in Mexico that the psychology of *mestizaje* is most developed; in Brazil and Argentina that the aspirations and the tragedies of Americanism are most apparent. We shall return to these themes in due course.

The Negro element in Latin American culture, on the other hand, is less important than some Anglo-Saxon commentators, obsessed with the Negro problem at home, would have us think. I did not go to Cuba: it is therefore, perhaps, rash to put forward the view that she and her revolution have suffered from over-exposure. But this must be said: if, in the age of Columbus and Cortes, Latin America began in Havana, Santo Domingo,

and the Antilles, she does not begin there today. It is not difficult to wax sentimental over the Caribbean—not difficult, that
is, for the outsider. But we should get the thing into perspective.
Historically, the Caribbean islands—British, Spanish and
French—are no more than the flotsam and jetsam bobbing in
the wake of the Spanish galleons and the slavers and clippers of
Liverpool. Picturesque as they are, the West Indies are the
detritus of Empire, heirs to a broken-backed culture. This is not
to deny the charm of the Caribbean peoples, or their creativity
in certain fields. There is Afro-Cuban music, and there is the
literature in French and English that has come out of the
Caribbean over the past generation. But the pessimistic conclusions of a book like Mr V. S. Naipaul's *The Middle Passage*
must be taken to heart. The West Indies are the product of
their history; and, in the light of that history, the widespread
fears that Castro's Cuba could become the focus of a continent-
wide revolution in Latin America do not carry much conviction. The "Caribbean" group of cultures is peripheral to Latin
America; and has been so in effect since Cortes and Pizarro
conquered the American mainland. (The great sugar boom of
the seventeenth and eighteenth centuries, of course, made the
Creole planters richer than their counterparts on the mainland.
But most of the money went into the pockets of Englishmen,
Frenchmen, and Dutchmen, not into the coffers of Spain.) The
evidence suggests, then, that the Indian substratum, though not
easy to define, is of an importance that cannot be exaggerated,
but that the Negro contribution—except in Brazil—is marginal.

Antigua

Guatemala is Indian country *par excellence*. Yet her Indians,
heirs to the great Mayan civilisations, though in the majority,
and probably purer in blood than in most regions of Mexico,
remain elusive. Guatemala, I have said, is a Mexico *avant le
déluge*; to travel there is to travel backwards in time. Even in an
age of space-travel, however, time-travel has not lost its charms.
Where, then, and what is Guatemala? There is a giant model
relief map in a park in Guatemala City to help the traveller sort
out her physiognomy. She lies between the Caribbean and the
Pacific; but the sea is not her element. Like Mexico, she is a

corrugated reticulum of volcanic fissures and soaring *cordilleras*, of landlocked lakes and raging torrents. Driving straight into her hinterland, on arrival from Mexico City (not wishing to spend more time than necessary in the characterless, small-town metropolis that is modern Guatemala City), I realised that one at least of the truisms about Latin America is true: she is superbly beautiful. In our travels we latter-day Anglo-Saxons are incurable Puritans. We cannot admire Rio's skyline for the squalid *favelas* nestling between her sugar-loaf hills. Mexico City, if we are not careful, will be spoilt for us by Oscar Lewis's *The Children of Sanchez*. We do not like to be told that Latin America is beautiful, for unlike Latin America's masters we suffer from the conscience of the rich. True, sociologists assure us that these slums are rather signs of economic progress and social mobility than of hopeless poverty. Yet the Puritan in us—so absurd to the Catholic-bred Latin American—is not easily kept down. We eat our dinners no less heartily; but Lazarus gives us bad dreams at night.

From Guatemala City airport one climbs quickly to 7,000 feet. At once, one is astonished at the richness of soil and vegetation, arriving from the parched, Old Castilian bleakness of the Valley of Anahuac. In Cortes' time, the Valley had moisture-conserving forests around the great lakes. Now both forests and lakes are gone, and the landscape resembles—as the drier land must always have resembled—the *meseta* of Spain. Bernal Diaz, in his *True History*, compared the landscape on the famous march to Tenochtitlan with that of "my beloved Medina del Campo". Here, the Spanish preference met with the Indian: both chose the temperate uplands in preference to the lush, tropical *tierra caliente* of the coast. Yet the Spaniards were not averse to lushness when they found it, as in Guatemala, in combination with a tolerable climate. (Spanish hatred of nature is proverbial. It was left to Humboldt and Bates, to Darwin and Hudson, to explore that superabundant *naturaleza* of America, for which the Spaniards had an almost theological distaste.) But once the quest for gold was disappointed, as in Guatemala, there was no alternative: the Conquerors had to fall back on America's human treasure, the labour of the Indian. It was on this wealth that Central America, of which Antigua was the Colonial capital, subsisted in the centuries of Colonial rule. Yet fertile as is this well-watered, volcanic soil by nature, it remains astonishing how little wealth the Spaniards knew how to extract from it. As one drives into the mountains, the near-tropical luxuriousness of the valleys gives way to the neat coffee plantations that girdle the volcanic slopes. These coffee plantations— three-quarters of Guatemala's exports depend on them—were largely developed, in the sixties of the last century, by German immigrants. As in Argentina and Brazil, it took foreign eyes to see the potential wealth of the American *naturaleza*. Above 5,000 feet coffee yields to wheat and to the ancient, traditional subsistence crops of maize and beans: wheat for the *criollo*, maize and beans for the *indio*. Higher still, the mountain slopes are covered with oak and beech and, close to the summit, with pine. If much of Central and Northern Mexico resembles the Castilian *meseta*, Pacific Guatemala resembles the rain-washed landscapes of *La Montaña* and the Basque country, those mountain fastnesses from which the feudal chieftains went forth to reconquer Spain from the Moors.

My purpose was to visit Antigua. That indispensable guide for all travellers in Latin America, *The South American Handbook*, says it is a must. And so it is. Antigua, as its name implies, is the "Old" capital of Central America. It was once a city of 80,000 souls, larger than many European capitals. Bernal Diaz had a house here; it was in Guatemala that he wrote his memoirs of the *conquista* in old age. With its university, its monasteries, churches and town houses, Antigua is the most perfectly preserved specimen of the Spanish Colonial town. Around the central square, the *Plaza Mayor*, where bullfights and markets were held, stand the Cathedral (to the east); the elaborate eighteenth century Palace of the Captains General (to the south); the Municipal Palace (to the north); and, to the west, a *mercado* or arcade of small shops. Antigua, too, has the geometrical castrum-plan of Ferdinand and Isabella's Santa Fe. She, too, is a secular citadel of the Roman faith. But the fascination of Antigua is that she is a fossil. She was destroyed by an earthquake in 1773, and the capital removed to Guatemala City by order of Charles III. Most of the buildings were ruined; many still lie in ruins. But there is none of that deadening post-Colonial, or commercial-modernistic architecture that has spoilt the charm of Mexico's Puebla or of Lima, the City of the Kings.

Antigua is a good place to meditate on the virtues and vices
of the Conquerors; to balance their piety and civic enterprise
against their short-sighted lust for gain. That they "exploited"
the Indians whom the King of Spain had committed to their
charge under the *encomendero* system is for sure. Still, we must
beware of anachronism; all conquering peoples have been
exploiters. To blacken the name of Spanish Colonial civilisation
on that account comes ill from Anglo-Saxons. The early Spanish
Americans, unlike the Anglo-Saxons in North America and
Australia, did not indulge in deliberate genocide. It is easy to
exaggerate the bloodshed of the *conquista*; just as it is easy to
exaggerate the bloodshed of Latin American revolutions. To be
fair, we should set against the millions of Indians (we know
neither the exact figures, nor the exact causes) who died in the
century following the *conquista*, the attempts of Church and
Crown—following Las Casas's lead—to prevent enslavement of
the Indian and the destruction of his culture. Nor should we
forget the centuries of peace under the *pax hispanica* that shielded
Latin Americans—*criollo* and Indian alike—from the barbari-
ties of the European scene. Only in the late nineteenth century
War of Paraguay, for example, do we find anything comparable
to the religious wars of seventeenth-century Europe. There have
been civil wars in Latin America; but none as bloody as that
fought by Lincoln in the United States. From all the evidence,
the *pax hispanica* Cortes and Alvarado brought to these regions
was an improvement on what went before. It brought greater
stability, or at least stability over a longer period, than did the
pax britannica.

Yet it was a fragile and fragmentary achievement. **Fragmentary** because the descendants of the Mayas, in many respects
the most advanced of all pre-Columbian peoples, were not
integrated into the civilisation the Spaniards brought. **Fragile,**
because the order the Spaniards brought was threatened no less
by natural catastrophe than by the inertly hostile Indian masses
over whom they ruled. We have seen that the hazards of life
on the Mexican plateau deeply influenced the cosmology and
the religion of the Aztecs. What is true of the Aztecs is true
of the Meso-American and Andean civilisations, and colours the
Indian's outlook today. It is hazardous to argue from geology to
metaphysics; but it is a fact that the regions inhabited by the

advanced Mountain Indians were those worst plagued by natural catastrophes. That this basic geological condition of his life should have affected the mentality of the civilised Indian—whether in Mexico, Guatemala or Cuzco—is a reasonable assumption. May we not assume that the Spaniards, who chose the same volcanic region for their cities, inherited the curse? Near Antigua lie the ruins of another city which suggest that this may indeed have been their experience: nature, hostile on the baked plains of Castile, was to prove no less hostile in the New World. But in the New World that theme has a different ring. In Castile, nature may be shunned or shrugged off; in America it demands to be conquered. That this second *conquista* should have failed, comparatively speaking, in Latin America, and should have succeeded in Anglo-Saxon America beyond the wildest imaginings of her pioneers, is something the Latin cannot easily forgive.

Guatemala's first capital was not Antigua, but a now almost deserted *pueblo*, Ciudad Vieja, three miles by road from the city. The situation is as solitary and romantic as one could wish. A handsome pink-and-red church still stands, absurdly large for the handful of *indios* who buy and sell in its shadow. The remains of the Governor's Palace can still be made out. But for those who like their America romantic (and I am one of their number) there is more. My car reached Ciudad Vieja at seven in the evening. Sombre against a flaming sunset, two volcanoes loom over the ruined city, Agua and Fuego; a more operatic backdrop cannot be imagined. Agua and Fuego are well-named. From the former, one night in the year 1541, a torrent of water swept down on this first settlement of the Spaniards in Central America and destroyed the city. Among the drowned was the widow of that Pedro de Alvarado whose famous leap during the *noche triste*—that disastrous forced retreat of Cortes' from Tenochtitlan after Montezuma had been murdered by his own people—had made history among the *conquistadores*. Later, Alvarado became the Conqueror of Guatemala and, after the conquest, her first Governor. When he died, his widow, Doña Beatriz de la Cueva, succeeded to the governorship. Then she, too, fell victim to those fierce twin elements of the New World's *naturaleza*—fire and water—against which the taming of the Indian had been child's play. In a convent in Antigua there is preserved a portrait of Doña Beatriz. It bears the inscription *"La sin ventura"*: she who had no luck. Is it sentimental to see in that epithet the whole pathos of the *conquista*? For what brought the *conquistadores* to this land but *ventura*, the pursuit of fortune?

The *"Conquistadores"*

There is no cause to be sentimental about the *conquistadores*: they were not sentimental about themselves. They were, literally, soldiers of fortune. Like all Spaniards, they were gamblers. And, being Spaniards, they were able to endure fortune's whims with that stoicism which Unamuno—with Seneca, the Spanish-Roman from Cordoba in mind—saw as the essence of *casticismo*. It is not easy for us, at this distance, to see the *conquistadores* for what they were. Spain quickly came down in the world. Gallant *Diego* became the puffed-up, ridiculous "dago" of English slang; or Don Amado, the fantastical Spaniard. *Don Quixote* has not helped either. It has been taken too literally, without benefit of irony. Yet Don Quixote is no more the typical Spaniard than Dr Faustus is the typical German. True, Cervantes's eye saw a dichotomy in the Spanish nature. Like Goethe, he saw an alternation between fanatic idealism and earthy materialism in the national character. Still, it is rather a dichotomy in human nature that is the subject of Goethe and Cervantes; and it is this, if *Don Quixote* and *Faust* are great books, that is the criterion of their greatness. This does not mean that Faust and Don Quixote are not profoundly national in inspiration. Who would dispute that the expeditions of Cortes and Pizarro were *quixotic* enterprises? Still, if the *conquistadores* had not had something of Sancho Panza in their character, the *conquista* would have remained an aspiration. The *conquistadores* may have read their Amadis de Gaula; but they were not content to tilt at windmills in the wastes of La Mancha.

What kind of men were the *conquistadores*? The question is not idle. It is necessary to know what these men were like if we want to understand Latin America; just as it is necessary to know what the Puritans were like to understand Anglo-Saxon America. The Black Legend of Spain paints these men as thugs and robbers; it finds no room for the Knightly Crusaders of

Spanish apologists. Modern Mexico has seen to it that no statue of Cortes stands on Mexican soil; Cortes is the national enemy, the ravisher of Tenochtitlan. Yet we know that Cortes was no Genghis Khan. On the contrary, there is good evidence that the Indians looked up to him as their hero and protector. Nor is there much doubt that his policies, as Mexico's first ruler, were prudent and sagacious. In trying to appreciate the character of the Conqueror, then, we must beware as much of the Black Legend as of the White. These men were not simply lily-white crusaders, or brutal marauders, or adventurers in search of gold. True, they were capable at times of behaving in each of these characters. But to reduce their behaviour to a single character is to fail to see them for the complex beings they were. It is also to accept uncritically those prejudices about the character of the Spaniard that lie embedded in three centuries of Anglo-Saxon culture.

The most attractive self-portrait of a *conquistador* that we possess is in Bernal Diaz's *True History*. It is a self-portrait *malgré lui*. Diaz wrote, as he thought, merely to set the record straight. He had a poor opinion of earlier chroniclers, like Gomara; after all, he had been there himself. Yet what emerges from his book, from his unemphatic, modest, often rather clumsy style tells us more about the character of the Conquest than Prescott himself. Here is no fantastical Spaniard, full of sound and fury, bragging of sexual or martial conquest. Here is the Spain of *The Spanish Bawd*, of *Lazarillo de Tormes*, of the *Life of Saint Theresa*. This is a salty, vigorous, realistic Spain, a Spain that has not yet undergone that bewildering sea-change of the Baroque, of *Gongorismo*—all that distastefully overblown rhetoric in literature and in art that accompanied Spain's decline and must seem to the Anglo-Saxon the bane of so much modern Spanish, Spanish-American and Brazilian culture. This is a Spain, by contrast, very sympathetic to the Anglo-Saxon; for it has many of the qualities—clarity, realism, humour—characteristic of the Anglo-Saxon temperament. The true successor to the sharp-tongued, picaresque novel of sixteenth-century Spain is the novel of eighteenth-century England: *Tom Jones* and *Lazarillo de Tormes* are two of a pair. Bernal Diaz may not have been such a lively dog—though a spark of youthful devilry glints in the writing of his old age. But why did Bernal Diaz and his friends come to the New World in the first place? As Cortes sees it, in a speech Bernal Diaz puts into his mouth, there is no great mystery in that (with habitual cunning, Cortes is in the act of putting down an incipient rebellion):

> Feeling that Narvaez's followers would not willingly assist us in the relief of Alvarado's garrison, Cortes implored them to forget their hostility. . . . Since they had come to seek their fortunes, he told them, and were in a country where they could serve both God and his Majesty and enrich themselves, now was their chance. He was so persuasive in fact that everyone of them offered to come with us. But if they had known the Mexicans' strength, not one of them would have volunteered.

Bernal Diaz is a good Christian and a Catholic. But he trusts, when in doubt, the evidence of his senses. Referring to a battle described by Gomara, the historian of the Conquest, he remarks somewhat scornfully:

> Francisco de Morla arrived on a dapple-grey horse in advance of Cortes and the rest of the cavalry, and the blessed apostles St James and St Peter appeared. I say that all our deeds and victories were the work of our Lord Jesus Christ, and that in this battle there were so many Indians to every one of us that the dust they made would have blinded us, had not God in his unfailing mercy come to our aid. It may be, as Gomara says, that the glorious apostles did appear and that I, a sinner, was not worthy to see them. . . . But if so, since there were more than four hundred soldiers in our company, as well as Cortes himself and many other gentlemen, the miracle would have been discussed and evidence taken. . . .

Bernal Diaz's famous description of the Spaniards' first sight of Tenochtitlan I have already quoted: it is moving, not for its fine rhetoric, but for its inarticulateness, its naïve wonder, its modest refusal to attempt a description of "things never heard of, seen, nor dreamed of before". Yet Bernal Diaz does not conceal his pride in the achievements of the *conquistadores*. He knew what it meant to have taken part in one of the most extraordinary expeditions the world had ever seen. But it is a pride so sure of itself that it has no need to brag:

> Those readers who are interested by this history must wonder at the great deeds we did in those days. First in destroying our ships: then in having the temerity to seize the great Montezuma in his

own city and inside his very palace. . . . Now that I am old, I often pause to consider the heroic actions of that time. I seem to see them present before my eyes; and I believe that we performed them not of our own volition, but of the will of God. For what soldiers in the world, numbering only four hundred, would have dared to enter a city as strong as Mexico, which is larger than Venice and more than four thousand five hundred miles away from our own Castile? There is much to ponder on, and not in the matter-of-fact way in which I have presented it. . . .

Some readers, perhaps, will find this matter-of-factness, this plainness, un-Spanish. But it is not difficult to show that it forms part of the Spanish inheritance. If we are looking for clues as to the Spanish character at the time of the *conquista*, we must look to the past rather than to the future. We must bear in mind that the *conquista* was a recapitulation of that centuries-long *reconquista* ended at Granada in the same year Columbus discovered America. It is not fanciful, therefore, to look to the great epic of the *reconquista*, the *Poema de mio Cid*, for clues as to the character of the *conquistador*. Indeed, what Gerald Brenan says of that poem (in his *Literature of the Spanish People*) could almost have been written of the *conquista* as Bernal Diaz describes it:

> We note that there is no question . . . of any crusade. The Cid's motive is to win *averes*, that is, lands and money. He is a good Christian and when he takes Valencia he sets up a French bishop, but he does not interfere with his subject's religion. He has friends and allies among the Moors and in fact, though the poet glosses over this, was in the pay of the Arab Emir of Saragossa. But if the religious feeling displayed in the poem is moderate, the social feeling is strong. . . . The Cid came from the class of simple *caballeros*, men who possessed a *solar* or small manor and a good horse—and he had risen by his own exertions to being an *infanzon*, which was the name given to a leader who employed *caballeros* under him. . . . He was thus the type of self-made man, and the point of the story is the triumph of this man with his natural courage and ability.

This reads like a description of the archetypal *conquistador*, the impoverished *hidalgo* from Castile or Extremadura who triumphs through "his own natural courage and ability". Further, the style of the *Poema de mio Cid*, as described by Brenan, brings to mind the style of Bernal Diaz's *True History*:

The whole tone of the poem is sober and realistic. The Cid is a man like any other, only more doughty and capable, and he acts from the natural human desire to make money, settle down with his wife, and marry his daughters well. One might say, like any modern business man. But money and position were in those days won not by trade, but by fighting, and therefore the Cid has the code of honour that is normally found in all countries among men who risk their lives. Yet this code is not exaggerated, as it was in feudal courts, or, in later times, among noblemen who carried swords which they did not use. . . . *The Poema de mio Cid* is thus not only a perfect expression of the dry, bare, soberly realistic imagination of the peoples of the *meseta* and the moral and juristic sense of the Castilians: it also foreshadows the picaresque novels and drama of the *Siglo de Oro*.

Brenan anticipates the objection that these qualities may be thought "un-Spanish":

> The *Poem of the Cid* . . . shows us a society which is healthy and self-assured. It is rude, because it is the society of a frontier people engaged in continual warfare. But it possesses an old culture or habit of life whose roots go back uninterruptedly to Roman times. We see this in the sobriety and lack of emphasis of the description, but also in the prudence and self-restraint displayed by the principal actors. There is an adjustment of means to end shown by the Cid and his companions that is far from according with our idea of the Spanish—still less of the Castilian—character.

Is it that the Anglo-Saxon misunderstands the character of the Castilian? Or did Castile herself change? Is it rather that the qualities found in Castile in the centuries between the age of the Cid did not survive the "marvellous but fatal intoxication known as the Golden Age and the prolixity that followed it"? In comparing the *Poema de mio Cid* with its French predecessor, the *Chanson de Roland*, Mr Brenan makes the point that it is the French epic, not the Spanish, that exhibits a fanatical crusading spirit:

> These men from the north were more passionately and romantically religious than the men who lived south of the Pyrenees. They therefore looked on these wars as holy wars undertaken against the enemies of Christ, whereas the Spaniards, who knew the Moslems and respected them, thought of them chiefly as wars for

booty or for the reconquest of their land. . . . The *Chanson de Roland* is hagiography of the crudest kind and presupposes an audience of fanatical pilgrims or crusaders who are ready to believe anything.

Again, it is the Spanish epic, not the French, that is the more democratic, the more tolerant and the more socially mature:

This is reflected in the poem. Not only are its themes political, but the comments that the poet makes are mostly political too. Take the well-known line that sums up the injustice and folly of the King in letting himself be persuaded by the nobles to banish the Cid:

> *Dios que buen vasallo, si oviese buen senor!*
> God, what a good vassal, if only he had a good lord!

And contrast it with that famous speech of Roland's in which, after declaring that the only duty of a vassal is to suffer great heat and great cold for his lord, he ends with the pronouncement:

> *Paiens ont tort e Chriestiens ont droit!*
> Pagans are wrong and Christians are right!

A pronouncement which, of course, gives him a good conscience in killing them all.

Pagans are wrong and Christians are right! A Spanish concept, surely, not a French? Yet, according to Mr Brenan, not at all. Granted that we may trace a historical link from the Visigothic chieftains who conquered Spain in the fifth century, and the *caballeros* of the age of the Cid, down to the land-hungry *hidalgos* who followed Cortes and who reappear as the lawless *caudillos* of the post-Independence period, we must adjust our view of Latin America accordingly. The Spaniard, and the Spanish American, is credited with a fierce ideological and religious fanaticism. How else do we explain the fearful atrocities of the Carlist wars, of the Mexican Revolution, of the Spanish Civil War? But this may be a misconception. It was the French who launched the modern world on its career of ideological warfare. The atrocities of the Carlists or of Pancho Villa, of Peron or Trujillo, are not to be denied. But these atrocities, if we look more carefully, proceed less from ideological motives than from that ferocious *personalismo* which is the degenerate form of the *hidalgo*'s pride and independence of spirit. Nor is the

point academic. We have seen that all attempts to interpret the
Mexican Revolution in terms of European ideology fall down.
The same is true of the politics of the greater part of Spanish
America, in the nineteenth century as today. Brenan's two
quotations can tell us more about the politics of Spanish
America than a dozen theses. Spanish Americans do not so
easily accept the black-and-white fanaticism implied in the
sentiment: "Christians are right and Pagans are wrong!" In
their quest for the just leader—a quest that can degenerate,
admittedly, into time-serving prostration before a ferocious
caudillo—they are more liable to say with the anonymous author
of the *Poema de mio Cid*: "God what a good vassal, if only he had
a good lord!" Like the Cid, the Spaniard and the Spanish
American have something in them of the freebooter, but something also of the Crusader. But at bottom it is the crusade for
secular, not for supernatural justice that is the spring of their
actions.

3

PANAMA:
or Why Don't They Love Us As We Deserve?

'The Costaguana Government shall play its hand for all it's worth—and don't you forget it, Mr Gould. Now, what is Costaguana? It is the bottomless pit of 10 per cent loans and other fool investments. European capital had been flung into it with both hands for years. Not ours, though. We in this country know just about enough to keep indoors when it rains. We can sit and watch. Of course, some day we shall step in. We are bound to. But there's no hurry. Time itself has got to wait on the greatest country in the whole of God's Universe. We shall be giving the word for everything: industry, trade, law, journalism, art, politics, and religion, from Cape Horn clear over to Smith's Sound, and beyond, too, if anything worth taking hold of turns up at the North Pole. And then we shall have the leisure to take in hand the outlying islands and continents of the earth. We shall run the world's business whether the world likes it or not. The world can't help it—and neither can we, I guess.'

Nostromo: Joseph Conrad (1905)

Panama City

WHAT IS THERE TO SEE in Panama? Not much, I fear, for the landscape-lover, not much for these in pursuit of the *folclorico*. But enough for the politically-inclined tourist to need to spend a night there en route for Caracas. Here, after all, he may expect to see the Latin-*gringo* confrontation in the raw. Elsewhere, in Guatemala not least, he will have heard dark whispers of the machinations of the Pentagon, the CIA, and the United Fruit Company. And with reason: the events of 1954, when the CIA assisted in the removal of the Arbenz government, are not forgotten. All Latin America, since the Bay of Pigs, and especially since the Dominican intervention, is alive with such rumours. There is a new demonology with which Latin Americans torture themselves: nothing, anywhere, can happen without the foreknowledge, advice and consent of the CIA. That this paranoid notion should have taken hold is more than unfortunate. It is a theory that paralyses thought and action. While reflecting to some degree the past experience of Latin with *gringo*, it makes the future appear blacker than it need. Springing from an old-fashioned fatalism, it breeds a new-fashioned fatalism. Yet what Latin Americans need is a world-view that stresses the openness of the future and the potentialities of their continent. To blame the US for all the backwardness, corruption and violence of Latin America is ludicrous. Latin America's troubles are rooted in the four and a half centuries of her own history, and the United States could do little about them if she chose. The truth is, the United States is the universal scapegoat; if she did not exist, she would have to be invented.

However, let anyone inclined to play apologist for the *gringos* spend a day in Panama. In Guatemala and elsewhere, *imperialismo* has a finger in the pie; but there is little to be seen on the surface. Here, in Panama, it is out in the open. Panama is America's Suez: if it is unadorned *gringo* imperialism you are looking for, you will find it here. And, indeed, it looks the part.

In the Mexican highlands and in Guatemala, you are never uncomfortably aware of climate: altitude cancels latitude. But in Panama City, a few degrees from the Equator, at sea level, climate is with you all the time. The Spaniards liked to build on high ground, which is why much of Latin America is not, as the image prescribes, hot and humid and tropical, but equable and invigorating. (So much for those ingenious theories about the influence of climate on character.) But Panama is like something out of *Nostromo*. And, indeed, it was Conrad's impressions of Colombia's Caribbean coastline—Panama was part of Colombia till Teddy Roosevelt seduced it away with the lure of a canal across the isthmus—that provided the *donnée* for the greatest novel ever written about Latin America in English.

One notices, to start with, that the racial mixture has changed. Panama has almost no Indians. The native tribes were as wild as the Plains Indians when the Spaniards arrived, and their descendants have been absorbed or exterminated or driven inland. The street-traders and the dock-workers in the narrow, evil-smelling streets of the Old City are Negro or Mulatto. The small retail shops are owned—a reminder of Suez or Gibraltar—by East Indians, Chinese or Lebanese. The sombre expressionless Indian face has vanished. Further north, the blank taciturnity of the Indian, caught by D. H. Lawrence in *Mornings in Mexico*, is strangely frightening: the trauma of the *conquista* invests those numb features. Here, suddenly, all that is gone. This is a people gay, gesticulatory, improvident. The high country is behind us; this is Caribbean America. No earnestness here: life is exotic, languorous, feckless. The beauty of the Indian or *mestiza* woman, of which we hear a good deal, is something of a myth—at least in my brief observation. (As good liberals, have we come to believe that racial intermixture must automatically be good, not only politically, but aesthetically? The old-fashioned view could be nearer the truth.) In Panama, certainly, the number of pretty, provocatively-dressed girls, and of handsome, lounging young men, hits the eye. The Negro strain is dominant; the Negro's natural *tropicalismo* redeems something of the squalor of this international slum.

Certainly, nothing could be more striking than the contrast with the "racial problem" a few hundred miles to the north. Both races still live on the margin of society. But the Negro, imported to build the canal, is open—pathetically open—to the forces of our civilisation (what he is permitted to get of it). The Indian, almost everywhere, is withdrawn, politely hostile. The Caribbean Negro is extravert; he appears to have nothing to hide. But the Indian: who knows what he is thinking? In romantic mood, we may imagine that he knows of the lost treasure of the Aztecs, that he is brooding on the might-have-beens of pre-Columbian civilisation. Perhaps the *indigenistas* are right; perhaps, after all, something can be rescued from the long dream. Or is it that the Indian is frozen into an attitude, that what he hugs to himself is something that no longer exists? Is it, perhaps, that he has nothing to hide?

Up on the hill, in their spotless concrete redoubts, live the *gringos*. They have big houses, big allowances, a big white hospital, schools and cinemas, their own television station and the ubiquitous PX. The *gringos* occupy the high ground: they have a fine view of the bay. Their spacious lawns are mown by black labour from below; their exotic tropical shrubs pruned by an army of black gardeners. They are the masters; they live well. In January 1964 there was a famous riot here. American schoolboys refused to let the Panamanian flag fly alongside Old Glory in the Canal Zone. The city went mad. Students exchanged shots with the police. President Johnson was in hourly touch. Order was soon restored; a number of lives were lost. Since then, the two flags fly peaceably side by side. The situation, it seems, was handled with more tact than the Dominican crisis a year later. Concessions were made, a reappraisal promised. Hints were dropped in Washington to the effect that a sea-level canal (Teddy Roosevelt's canal has numerous locks and will soon be too small), if and when it is built, could well be built through Nicaragua or Colombia and not through Panama.

Which would settle Panama's hash. For Panama has done well over the past fifty years as the *rentier* of her own canal. True, the *gringos* could have done more for Panama. But then, a colonial power, just because it is apparently all-powerful, can never do enough. Nevertheless, a great deal has been done: we have only to imagine what health, hygiene and standard of living would be like without the *gringo* presence. Yet Panama is profoundly dissatisfied. She feels her impotence; and the affluent *gringo* on the high ground is a constant irritation. Where does the fault lie? With that cheap, liquid treasure flowing through one's country, the inducement to explore other sources of wealth is not great. If it is true that Panama shows us that the Latin-*gringo* clash in the raw, then it is true of both parties. The Americans are not more insolent than the British once were in similar circumstances. They are, possibly, less discreet, less aware of their responsibilities to "lesser breeds". ("Take up the white man's burden": Kipling's exhortation, we forget, was addressed to the Saxons of North America.) Part of the truth, ironically, may be that the Americans have not been imperialist enough. Could this be why they earn only hatred and suspicion in Latin America; while the British in India, now the pains of the Independence struggle are forgotten, are looked on with not wholly deserved tolerance and gratitude? Certainly, the curse of the unequal relationship affects both sides. The mixture of subservience, fecklessness, and explosive resentment—even if it were confined to a lunatic fringe, and it is plainly not—is an unattractive thing. History, one reflects, has played some ill tricks on Panama since Balboa the *conquistador* strode into her billows with drawn sword and claimed the Pacific Ocean for the King of Castile. (Keats's vision of Stout Cortes "silent upon a peak in Darien" belongs, I fear, to that tradition of romantic imprecision Latin America appears to foster.) Nevertheless, Panama should get her accounting right. She has done better out of Teddy Roosevelt's canal than she did out of the treasure of Peru which was landed here, transported on mule-back along the *camino real* to the other side of the isthmus, only to be plundered by English buccaneers from Jamaica like Henry Morgan. Still, she has paid a price.

Anti-Americanism

But Panama, you may say, is not typical. Like Puerto Rico, and at various periods Haiti, Cuba, and Nicaragua, she has experienced *el imperialismo yanqui* directly. More typical—or so Latin Americans will tell you—is that indirect control

Conrad analyses with such subtlety in *Nostromo*. (*Nostromo*
records, among other things, the passing of commercial
supremacy from Britain to the US at the turn of the century.)
Be that as it may, we shall find Panama's attitudes repeated up
and down the continent: in this respect she is typical enough. I
start from the premiss that any discussion of Latin-*gringo*
relations is worthless unless it is prepared to be frank. Let us,
then, be frank. The distaste felt for the United States throughout Latin America is no myth. Nor is it due to some misunderstanding, which a subtler diplomacy might eliminate. We are
told that Latin Americans hate the United States and all its
works. But hatred is both too strong and too weak a word. In
the last resort, the United States is not hated for what she does,
but for what she is. I had met the kind of distaste Latin
Americans feel for their northern neighbour only once before:
that was in Eastern Europe, and the object was not the United
States, but Germany. Such a comparison must be wounding
and odious. Some will find it altogether too strong. When,
after all, did the *yanquis* gas six million Indians, or set up a
Treblinka or an Auschwitz? The Mexicans, certainly, have not
forgiven the United States for stealing half their territory in
the 1840's. The Caribbean countries have not forgotten the
activities of the US Marines between the war of 1898 and
Franklin Roosevelt's Good Neighbour policy of the 1930's.
But the American, however ugly, is no Jew-baiting *Gauleiter*.

Yet it is not, in the end, a question of the degree of atrocity.
Here the United States would emerge from any comparison
with her fellow-imperialists very favourably. National enmity
is an elusive and ambivalent emotion. Nevertheless, a distinction
can be drawn between necessary and contingent enmity.
Mere contingent enmity—between Britain and France, say,
or Chile and Argentina—is something that is perhaps necessary,
psychologically or politically, to the survival of either party.
But the enmity Eastern Europe feels towards Germany is a
different matter. For many East European states enmity to
Germany is a *sine qua non* of their national existence: they
hate the Germans, not because the Germans are exceptionally
wicked (though they have proved themselves capable of
exceptional wickedness), but because the Germans are especially
strong. True, much of that hatred is now directed against the

Russians. But for the Russians too, until recently, Germany was the necessary enemy; the bogy, yet at the same time the admired competitor. The historical reasons for these enmities are clear and by no means entirely irrational. As the nations of Eastern Europe grow in strength and confidence it is likely that anti-Germanism will decline. But anti-Germanism in Eastern Europe, like anti-Americanism in Latin America, will not disappear until the unequal relationship that produced it in the first place has disappeared. We cling to our enemies until we feel strong enough to discard them.

America, then, is hated for what she is, not for what she does. But opinions differ as to what she is. Fundamentally, the trouble is that she is too strong, economically and militarily; and that the gap between her strength and that of Latin America has widened, not decreased, since the turn of the century. Since this disparity will continue to grow, it is likely that whatever America does or leaves undone, the anti-Americanism of the Latins will increase. This does not mean that Latin America will "go Communist": that is improbable for other reasons. The growth of anti-Americanism will not be without political effect. But it will feed left-wing nationalism of the type of Venezuela's *Accion Democratica*, or Chile's Christian Democracy, or even Mexico's PRI or Argentina's *Peronismo*, I think, rather than benefit Soviet- or Chinese-orientated Communism.

North Americans, in other words, will have to accept the brickbats they receive with good grace. What they must not expect is that they can buy exemption through generous aid programmes. Not only can one not buy friends, but one must not expect the hand that holds out the dollar not to be bitten. As yet, Americans are altogether too tender-minded; they have not acquired the tough hide of European imperialists, British, French or Dutch. I do not suggest a return to Teddy Roosevelt: that was tried by President Johnson, with unfortunate results, in the Dominican Republic. What is needed is something more difficult: a steely indifference to abuse such as would try the patience of a saint—let alone the greatest power the world has seen—combined with a sharp sensitivity to the real needs of the undeveloped world. That is, the US must be prepared to do the right thing regardless of short-term reaction. It is a good deal to

ask. But, in asking it, the world is not asking America for a
Utopian foreign policy. She is only asking that Americans see
frankly what they are up against in Latin America and the
Third World. Americans have worried in the past that other
nations do not think her "mature". Here is a test: the United
States will be mature when she has learnt to guard against the
alternating optimism and pessimism that have bedevilled her
Latin American policy in the past.

What is she up against? Not simply, to be sure, the natural
resentment of her economic hegemony. Not simply, in the
political field, the fear of further intervention on the Guatemalan or Dominican model. She is up against the fact that
Latin Americans resent, while admiring, the North American
way of life, and that nothing she can do will alter this. It is
important to be clear why this should be so. It would be easy to
say, as many Americans do say, that this distaste for everything
norteamericano is motivated by a cultural inferiority complex.
The North American success story is not the result of luck, we
are told, or even of hard work: it is the product of certain
virtues, certain behaviour patterns, implanted in the North
American by his ancestors. Latin America, it is argued, lacks
these virtues. Despite her potential wealth, despite the fact that
the Spaniards had conquered, explored and settled three-
quarters of the continent while the English at Jamestown and
Massachusetts Bay were still nibbling at its outer fringes, Latin
America has not made the grade. No wonder, then, that Latin
Americans are uncomfortably conscious of the "inferior" Iberian
civilisation they have inherited. No wonder they react by
affecting to despise the "materialistic" values of a society that
has left them behind in the race. Already, half a century ago,
Rodo had expressed the Latin American resentment of this
fact by playing off *gringo* "Caliban" against Latin "Ariel".
Nowadays, we might not put it in such romantic-literary terms;
we live in the age of development ideology. But the Latins,
striving to emulate the North American success story (for that
is what "development" is taken to mean) has made matters
worse. The more Latin Americans become aware of their
relative backwardness—and their population explosion may
soon lead to a fall in living standards—the more will their
sense of inferiority grow. If this is true, the next fifty years

of Latin-*gringo* relations could well be worse than the last.

What I have just given, of course, is a *gringo* assessment of the situation. This is Prospero's view: Caliban—aware of his brutishness, but striving for acceptance in the best circles—is suffering from an inferiority complex. And it is the worse because, like Thurber's patient, the poor fellow really *is* inferior; he has Doctor Prospero at hand to whisper it in his ear, until every statistic is a fresh wound, every proffered dollar a fresh insult. In calling it a *gringo* view I am not implying that it is untrue. I am implying that it may be true only within certain terms of reference, and that these terms of reference should be open to criticism. I shall define in a moment what these terms of reference are. The point, I think, is that Americans are not always aware of their own presuppositions. I have tried to show, though an imaginary example, that the American student may find it peculiarly hard to penetrate beneath the surface of Latin American life; when he does so, it is only to find that its assumptions are distasteful. But, of course, most Americans have neither the desire nor the opportunity to penetrate that deep. They are vaguely aware of the resistance Latin America offers to their assumptions about the good life. But they take Prospero's view that all tiresome Caliban wants is to be more like Prospero. They do not cry: *vive la différence!* The *"différence"* is regarded as unimportant, or as a fact, as troublesome as it is obsolete, to be eliminated as quickly as possible.

It is at this point that any critique of North American attitudes should start. For the North American, by not cherishing *la différence*, finds it hard to appreciate the values of a society unlike his own. Let me give some *yanqui* reactions to Latin America I came across on my journey. I have already quoted Mr McGeorge Bundy's remark about Latin American studies —that "second-rate subjects attract second-rate minds". There is more than a dash of Harvard arrogance in this; but it is by no means untypical of academic and intellectual attitudes. Take, for example, my friend Mr Irving Kristol, the very model of a New York intellectual. Mr Kristol wished my journey well. He had often regretted, he said, that he knew no Spanish; but he imagined it was the kind of language one could pick up in a week or two's intensive cramming. Like Mr Bundy's wounding aside, it was an off-the-cuff remark. But I was amused to discover, some days later, that it had a most respectable ancestry:

> About this Time, understanding the way for our communications with the *Spanish Indies* opens more and more, I sett myself to learn the *Spanish language*. The Lord wonderfully prospered me in this Undertaking. . . . Accordingly I composed a little Body of the *Protestant* Religion, in certain articles, back'd with irresistible Sentences of Scripture. This I turn'd into the Spanish Tongue; and am now printing it with a Design to send it all the ways that I can, into the several parts of *Spanish America*; as not knowing, how great a matter a little Fire may kindle, or whether the time for our Lord Jesus Christ to have glorious Churches in *America* be not at hand.

Thus Cotton Mather, in seventeenth-century New England. Neither Cotton Mather's nor Mr Irving Kristol's comments show, I fear, much respect for "Spanish civilisation". But this is a view so common that it may be called traditional. Mr Edmund Wilson, for example, has written

> I have been bored by Hispanophiles. . . . I have made a point of learning no Spanish and I have never got through *Don Quixote*. I have never visited Spain or any other Hispanic country.

This is one traditional view. But there is another, ostensibly far from patronising, but in fact not much less so. This view makes a virtue of Latin America's "primitiveness" and uses it as a stick to beat the United States. Take this passage from a book famous in the thirties, Stuart Chase's *Mexico*:

> Middletown is essentially practical, Tepotzlan essentially mystical in its mental processes. Yet in coming to terms with one's environment, Tepotzlan has exhibited, I think, the superior commonsense. Middletown has its due quota of neurotic and mentally unbalanced individuals. In Tepotzlan a Freudian complex is unthinkable. The men of the South are craftsmen—they can put their hands to almost anything, fashion it, repair it, recreate it. Their popular arts, weaving, pottery, glass work, basketry, are as authentic and delightful as any the modern or the ancient world has seen.

Let me add one last item to this brief anthology of *yanqui* attitudes. It comes from a Texan cowboy (James Emmet

McCauley in *A Stove-Up Cowboy's Story*). Its provenance
suggests that *yanqui* incomprehension of the Latin is not
confined to literary intellectuals. "The work was hard,"
McCauley writes of his Texan youth in the eighties, "but
there was always grub and mescal liquor at night, and down
Mexico way there were bullfights—though it did look like a
man was getting tolerable low to fight a duel with a bull when
he could easy get out of it."

Pragmatism, surely, can go no further. It took a Hemingway
to bring home the mysteries of the *corrida* to Anglo-Saxons;
and, even now, they are not convinced. As Stuart Chase put it:
"Middletown is essentially practical, Tepotzlan mystical in
its mental processes." Yet we must look at this notion of the
pragmatical Yankee more closely. A pragmatic approach,
presumably, is an approach that takes things as they are.
But is this what the *yanqui* does when confronted with an
unfamiliar culture? Surely not. He assumes that other cultures
are, or are becoming, more or less similar to his own; and that
the same formulas apply. A technique for combating soil
erosion in Iowa is equally valid in Pakistan and Colombia. At
this level, the *yanqui* may be right—though he may be ignoring
the technological gap that makes what can be done in Iowa
virtually impossible to get done in Pakistan and Colombia. But
at the political level the analogy may not work at all. In the
bright morning of the Alliance for Progress, after the elimination of Trujillo, Washington decided that what the Dominican
Republic needed was rapid mass education. How else could
Juan Bosch build a viable democracy after thirty years of
political demagoguery? There was sense and idealism in
the reasoning. But there was a serious mistake in the timing.
Nobody considered that, even assuming mass education
necessarily creates a democratic mentality (a doubtful proposition when we consider Germany or Argentina), this was not a
process that could show results in under a decade. What
Bosch really needed, as it turned out, was the kind of support
from the US that would have enabled him to purge the corrupt
military and police forces left behind by Trujillo. Lacking this,
Bosch's reformism never got off the ground.

The point, to put it another way, is that North America's
is a universalist culture. Like the Frenchman, but unlike the

Englishman, the *yanqui* does not think of his civilisation as something peculiar to himself. He thinks of it as a universal achievement, an achievement in which other nations may (and no doubt should) wish to participate. The Frenchman respects *la différence*. American universalism does not: its premisses are progressivist, and it sees other civilisations as stages on the road to its own. Now it may be objected that this, though possibly the view of Middletown, is hardly that of your Washington or New York sophisticate. For all their lack of relish for things Hispanic, it is obviously not the world-view of Mr Irving Kristol or Mr Edmund Wilson. But were we so sure that it was not, in some degree, the view of President Lyndon Johnson? Politicians may be as sophisticated as you like; but they are apt to be sensitive to public opinion. It is not surprising, then, that something like this popular view should be found underlying an otherwise very sophisticated hypothesis.

The hypothesis I have in mind is Professor Rostow's theory of the stages of economic growth. The elements of this theory are well-known. It is suggested that, for each country, a roughly similar pattern of economic growth can be traced. There is a "pre-industrial phase"; an "early industrial phase" which, once the point of "take-off" has been achieved, becomes the "mature economy" we are familiar with in North America, Europe and Japan. To some extent these changes are even "quantifiable". The lapse of time between the beginnings of industrialisation and the point of "take-off" is of the order of forty years. But every society has its foot on a rung of this Jacob's ladder. It is an unspoken assumption of the theory that the American economy, being the most "mature", stands at the apex. Though Professor Rostow would no doubt discount any intention to go beyond the economic in these speculations, the provenance of these ideas is evident. What we have here is an elaboration of the idea of progress that has been current, indeed dominant, in the Western world for over a century and a half. But the idea of progress is at bottom a secularisation of the Judaeo-Christian notion that history, far from being cyclical (as both Aztecs and Greeks thought), moves towards a predestined goal. Marxism itself represents a secularisation, through Hegel and Proudhon, of this Judaeo-Christian view. The Marxist and the Rostovian hypotheses are therefore cousins beneath the skin. They are cognate projects for the redemption of a secularised humanity.

I am not competent to discuss the economic implications of Mr Rostow's theory. But it is in any case the political and cultural implications that concern us. There is surely no doubt that Rostow's hypothesis is very close, for all its technical phraseology, to the popular American view. The component elements are there. America is the most favoured nation, because she is the most prosperous and advanced (Calvinist terminology is hard to avoid). Other nations are also on the road to salvation, having achieved "take-off" (grace); and they may hope, through perseverance-in-grace, to arrive at the same state. Still other nations are backward and undeveloped: but these are not outside the scheme of salvation. They must wait their turn and, by evidence of good works, earn a place on the ladder. I do not, as I say, wish to challenge the economic validity of the argument. But what can be criticised are the hidden implications for North America, as for Latin America, of the implied theory of history. As regards North America, it gives theoretical foundation to the popular view that other countries are, or ought to be, or are becoming more and more like the United States. It discourages curiosity as to the differences that exist between cultures. Worse, it appears to rule out the possibility that other cultures may be striving for goals *different* from those American society proposes for itself. Yet a pluralism of human aims is surely as plausible, considering the diversity of human history, as this universalism of the North Americans. In practice, again, this theory discourages the student—let alone the international planner or administrator—from studying the *specific* characteristics of the culture he is working in. That such an approach makes life easier for the planner is true. But though it saves bother, it encourages glibness and superficiality. On the Washington cocktail circuit it was said, maliciously, that Asians were full of praise for Professor Rostow's thesis—with the reservation that it applied more exactly to Africa and Latin America than to Asia. Latin Americans replied that, well as the theory might suit Africa and Asia, it suited Latin America not at all.

No doubt this is evil-minded gossip. Still, the fact remains that the Rostow thesis, or something like it, is widely believed among Latin Americans, Africans, and Asians. And the implications of the historical theory that underlies it are far more deleterious for the underdeveloped peoples than for their advanced neighbours. Indeed, the uncritical acceptance of this theory by the intelligentsia of the underdeveloped countries is surely one of the intellectual disasters of our time. By accepting "economic development" as the sole criterion of historical maturity they undermine the values of their own society. They ensure that the next generation will be ridden by an inferiority complex more harrowing than the one they themselves have to bear. This is a strange paradox: for all their anti-Americanism, Latin Americans have swallowed uncritically what is a *yanqui* theory *par excellence*. Yet this act of intellectual suicide is not likely to bring any comfort to its originators. For this most *yanqui* of theories is also the theory most likely to generate hatred of the country whose *weltanschauung* it expresses.

4

VENEZUELA:
or Who's Afraid of the Big Red Wolf?

I was sitting in Mike's Place, Fidel
    waiting for someone else to act
      like a good Liberal
I hadn't quite finished reading Camus' *Rebel*
so I couldn't quite recognise you, Fidel
    walking up and down your island
        when they came for you, Fidel
     "My Country or Death" you told them
Well you've got your little death, Fidel
      like old Honest Abe
      one of your boyhood heroes
    who also had his little Civil War
and was a different kind of Liberator
     (since no one was shot in his war)
     and also was murdered
in the course of human events

     Fidel . . . Fidel . . .
    your coffin passes by
thru lanes and streets you never knew
     thru day and night Fidel
While lilacs last in the dooryard bloom Fidel
     your futile trip is done
     yet is not done and
     is not futile
I give you my sprig of laurel.

One Thousand Fearful Words for Fidel Castro:
    Lawrence Ferlinghetti (1961)

Caracas

CARACAS HAS A BAD REPUTATION. Venezuelans are not liked by their fellow Latin Americans. Why should this be? There must be some reason for so universal a sentiment. And, indeed, there is. Caracas is brash, bustling, and successful; she is a boom town, and she lets you know it. In her thrustfulness and lack of piety she is almost *yanqui*. The oil gushes; and the white skyscrapers rise sheer against a green Andean backcloth, making of Caracas the most beautiful modern city in all Latin America. Compared with today's Caracas, Santiago, Buenos Aires and Montevideo, the boom-towns of fifty years ago, look rickety, down-at-heel, shabby-genteel. Compared with Caracas, Mexico City is an awkward amalgam of the Spanish Baroque, the Parisian Belle Epoque and the *yanqui* Middle West. The Caracas of Colonial times, the Caracas where Bolivar was born, survives only in the back streets. Relatively poor until the oil boom of the nineteen-twenties, Caracas has few of those stranded Victorian monsters that give other cities of the New World their disconcertingly old-world air. Caracas is uncompromisingly modern. Her architecture, and her plastic arts, seem to express her will to modernity.

The world has heard about Oscar Niemeyer's Brasilia, or about Le Corbusier's Education Ministry in Rio. But the fine architecture to be found elsewhere in Latin America tends to be overlooked. In Mexico, for example, there are Felix Candela's works: elegant, curvaceous, parabolic structures of wafer-thin concrete—or so it seems—that may turn out to be churches or petrol stations or luxury restaurants for the tourist. Then, in Venezuela, there is the work of Villanueva, in particular the University City of Caracas (a state within a state, and the centre of leftist agitation in the city; one hall of residence is known anachronistically as "Stalingrad"). Villanueva's University Hall, with its murals by Lèger, its forest of slender concrete columns (walking among them is like walking through the Mosque at Cordoba), and its ingenious use of work by the local school

of kinetic artists, is as exciting as any post-war building I
have seen. It is surely no accident that in recent years Caracas
has produced talented experimental artists like de Soto and
Cruz-Diez. It is as if, against the foreigner's accusation of
brashness, she were making a virtue of her freedom from
conventional pieties and inhibitions.

Brash, then, but not philistine. At the moment, in the arts,
Venezuela ranks with the best in Latin America. And, in saying
this, one is not "making allowances". Painting and sculpture
in Latin America are no longer provincial. A generation ago
this was not the case. After a nineteenth century that was pre-
occupied—whether in philosophy, art, literature, or constitution-making—with keeping up with Europe, the new century
brought a "nativist" reaction, a demand for a return to *criollo*
values. This was the Latin version of the demand for the Great
American Novel. Prose epics were written about the down-
trodden, Peruvian Indian, the exploited Bolivian tin-miner, the
dying race of Argentine *gauchos*. Painting followed the same
trend, with Rivera, Orozco, and Siqueiros in Mexico, with
Portinari in Brazil. The ideas of the Mexican Revolution sprang,
like the Peruvian Haya de la Torre's dream of Indo-America,
from the same source. At that time, Venezuela herself was
hardly in the race. She had her oil and her Bolivar, the greatest
pensador of the Independence struggle, Andres Bello, and the
novelist Romulo Gallegos; otherwise she was innocent of high
culture. The *indigenistas* of that age insisted that it was in those
countries with a rich pre-Columbian heritage that new art
forms, indigenous to the Americas, would arise. Today the
fallacy is apparent. Borges and Neruda alone make nonsense
of the theory; for neither of these writers—the greatest Latin
America has produced in this century—can be said to owe anything to a pre-Columbian heritage.

Today, the younger artists make no bones about it: in their
view the notion was pernicious, and has done untold harm.
Listen, for example, to what Jose Luis Cuevas, the young
Mexican painter, has to say about the self-conscious "nativism"
of that generation. Possibly, the younger generation has
swung too far in the opposite direction. But Cuevas's is a
damning indictment of an entire mystique. It is, therefore, by
implication an apologia for what younger artists are doing

(Juan is a Mexican boy who would like to become a painter):

> Juan had no access to books on the art of other countries either
> in school or in the public library, much less in the Palace of
> Fine Arts. Nor were there any museums in which he could see
> foreign art of the present or the past. When there was an exhibi-
> tion of some artist who was not Mexican or who refused to follow
> the style that he had been taught to believe was the only one,
> Juan's friends told him that it was not worth seeing, because it
> pertained to an exhausted, degenerate culture. . . . On one
> occasion a friend told him about a certain Hitler, who pro-
> nounced the same things about a blond race that talked from the
> oesophagus. But Hitler was wrong; if he had known the Mexican
> race, with its dark skin, straight blue-black hair, almond eyes and
> labial speech, he would have changed his doctrine. The superior
> race was to be found in Tenochtitlan and environs. . . .

This is fighting talk. Nor is there any mistaking the inner logic
that, in Cuevas's view, limited the cultural and political mani-
festations of "nativism", though it is rather the implications for
art that concern us here.

> But one day in a bookstore on the Alameda Juan saw an art
> magazine containing things very different from his own work.
> Some of them were unintelligible to him and others struck him
> as absurd. But all of them fascinated him. "So there are artists
> in other countries, too" he said to himself, "not just here in
> Mexico." He went back to the bookstore several times and began
> to see meaning in what had at first been mere puzzles. . . . After
> a number of visits he no longer felt any desire to continue work-
> ing in the style he had been taught. The new ideas had begun to
> intrude among the local themes he was treating, and his work was
> being dominated and vitalised by other concepts.

Cuevas, whose speciality is a kind of satirical-surrealist art out
of Kafka and Goya, is an idiosyncratic fellow. He would not
wish to be seen as the leader of a generation, or even as especially representative. In his art, indeed, he is far from
representative. He is far more rooted in the Hispanic, and even
the Mexican tradition (he greatly admires the nineteenth-
century Mexican satirist Posada), than his Op Art, surrealist, or
abstract-expressionist contemporaries in Venezuela, Brazil or
Argentina. Yet his *Cuevas on Cuevas* is in many ways the standard
biography of the young Latin American artist. What we are

seeing in the reaction of this generation against its elders is the swing of the pendulum from provincial nativism towards a new internationalism. In the nineteenth century, Latin America's openness to European culture was a handicap; it led to the apeing of European models. Today that is no longer the case. Art itself has become international, in style, subject-matter and (not least) marketability, to a degree unimaginable in the past. In embracing an international style, therefore, the artist is no longer apeing Paris or New York. Or, if he is, the same must be said of most of his fellow-artists in the world today. Where art is truly cosmopolitan, the bogy of provincialism disappears. What has happened is that the artists of Latin America, after the "nativist" reaction of the early twentieth century, have returned to the mainstream. But they have returned to the mainstream at a time when there is not only no viable alternative, but no reason why Latin Americans—any more, say, than Britons, Japanese, or Germans—should feel that their native vocabulary of feeling cannot be expressed in the newly available alphabet.

We touch here on one of the perennial themes of Latin American life: whether in politics, fashion, or art. How, when opposing extremes exert so great an attraction, to find a happy mean, a way of expressing native values that will be valid in a wider context? This problem faces any Latin American artist or writer; and, to some degree, any person engaged in intellectual activity. Nor is there any ready solution. Still, if the extremes are unfruitful, a certain degree of tension between them seems to be unavoidable, and may even be beneficial. Mr Philip Rahv, in a famous essay, has divided North American writers into "Palefaces" and "Redskins"; Henry James belonging to the former species, Mark Twain to the latter. It is a distinction that makes good sense in the Latin American context: Borges and Machado de Assis are Palefaces; Neruda and da Cunha Redskins. Yet Borges, for all his cosmopolitanism, is very much a citizen of Buenos Aires. And Neruda's Whitmanesque Americanism does not make him any the less a citizen of the world, or a great poet of the Spanish language. The problem, certainly, is not unique to Latin America. It is the problem of any local culture that is aware of the distance that separates it from the creative centre of the larger culture of which it is a part, and which is yet determined to preserve its individuality. In this sense it is one of the key problems of our time. In this, as in much else, Latin America's experience over the past century and a half prefigures the experience of much of the Third World today. The passing of colonialism does not, we know, put an end to the dilemma. Indeed, there is no short-term panacea. Perhaps only the achievement of individual artists, local in inspiration, but international in resonance, can overcome this sense of cultural deprivation. That is why the achievements of a Borges, a Neruda, a Niemeyer—or even the young Op-Artists of Caracas—have an importance that is not to be measured by aesthetic criteria alone.

Province and Metropolis

The problem has been aggravated for Latin Americans in a special way. Until Independence the centre of their civilisation lay necessarily in Madrid or in Lisbon, much as London re-mained the centre for Anglo-Saxon America. True, in both cases, new-fangled rationalist, democratic influences out of France had gained ground, and had modified the inherited pattern. But there any resemblance ceases. Great Britain, certainly during the first century of North American Inde-pendence (and in some respects until the present day), retained her cultural authority after her political authority was gone. Not so with Spain and Portugal. For a century before Inde-pendence the Iberian countries had been in a condition of cultural sterility and political impotence. The revolt against the *madre patria* brought with it, therefore, a turning away from Hispanic culture. In part, of course, this was because Hispanic culture was bound up with clerical obscurantism and political autocracy. But Hispanic culture was rejected also because of its manifest inferiority—for example, in the natural sciences and in most branches of scholarship—to the cultures of Britain and France. This, I believe, is the true origin of that rage for the new—in art, in science, in politics—that has been a feature of Latin American life since Independence. The new, in Latin America, means the non-Hispanic.

There exists also, of course, a pride in the Hispanic heritage. But it is highly ambivalent: while praising the virtues of *hispanidad*, Latin Americans are uncomfortably aware of its vices. It was in Caracas, I remember, that I talked (only shortly before his death) with Señor Mariano Picon-Salas, one of the most distinguished historians of the Colonial Age. I asked him, perhaps impertinently, how he would define the virtues of *hispanidad*. He smiled, and replied that he would put the emphasis on the tradition of *individualismo*, so intimately linked with the Spanish sense of honour. For here might be found the basis for that love of liberty and sense of mutual respect apparently lacking in the tradition of Latin America. (Señor Picon-Salas, at the time of his death, was in charge of an ambitious cultural diffusion programme, reminiscent of Vasconcelos's schemes in the Mexico of the 1920's, and sponsored by the *Accion Democratica* government.) Yes: but could one not argue that this very *individualismo*, with its contempt for Anglo-Saxon "public-spiritedness", was one of the chief reasons for Spanish America's political instability? Had not Bolivar, himself a Venezuelan, written from exile:

> There is no good faith in America, nor amongst the nations of America. Treaties are scraps of paper; Constitutions mere printed matter; elections, battles; and life a torment. . . . All those who have laboured for the freedom of America have ploughed the sea.

Bolivar had remarked disgustedly that Venezuela was a "barracks": had not Venezuelan history borne out the predictions of the Liberator? I remember Señor Picon-Salas's melancholy ironic smile at this too-predictable Anglo-Saxon objection: "Ah, yes, our notorious *ingobernabilidad*! It's a contradiction, I confess. It is our *pride* to be ungovernable. But that has not, alas, made us democrats. The opposite of an autocrat is not a democrat, but an anarchist. And our *individualismo* makes us into the latter rather than into the former."

The new is non-Hispanic. And the non-Hispanic, in nine cases out of ten, is French. True, many of the ideas coming out of France are not new; and not all of them are French. But it does not matter. What matters is that Paris is the channel through which the intellectual currents of the Old World reach the New; and that this often gives France a prestige beyond her intellectual deserts. (In technology, and many of

the natural and human sciences, after all, Europe has long
lost her lead to the United States; younger Latin Americans
are perfectly aware of this.) I quoted, earlier, the Peruvian
professor who remarked that his pupils, if asked where the
Englightenment had originated, would infallibly answer:
"France!" I recall a similar conversation with an *Accion
Democratica* intellectual. The *Accion Democratica* is the moderate
Social Democratic Party which succeeded, under Romulo
Betancourt and his successor President Leoni, in giving Venezuela one of the few progressive democratic governments in
Latin America. Yet the language in which my friend defined the
"position" of *Accion Democratica* seemed intransigently Marxist.
For a moment I thought that he must be expounding, in
Machiavellian fashion, the opposition's case in order the better
to refute it. But not at all. He was making the point that the
"position" of the AD was more genuinely Marxist than that of
the Castroite-Communist groups organising terrorism against
it. I was at a loss: why should a Social Democrat present his
case in these terms? A certain defensiveness towards the far
left, in view of the violent attacks the party has had to endure
from that quarter, might help to explain it. But it seemed, at
bottom, to resolve itself into a question of language. My friend
had spent many years in exile under the dictator Perez Jimenez
in Paris. The jargon of the Left Bank seemed to him the natural
language of progress and democracy.

This sheds a somewhat ironic light on the much-vaunted
présence française. President de Gaulle's expedition to South
America in the autumn of 1964, much boosted before the event,
turned out to be a nine-day wonder. Old Latin American
hands were not surprised. The French, who invented the term
Amérique Latine, had fallen into a trap; they had come to
believe their own propaganda. The Latin Americans played
hard to get. Like the rest of us, they do not care to be patronised.
And if one is to be patronised, why by *le grand Charles*, who has
little to offer, rather than by Uncle Sam, who at least has the
silver dollars? Certainly, Latin Americans are grateful for a
little attention. But they are also, and justifiably, on their
guard. They suspect French advances are less pure than the
rhetoric about "our Latin brothers' suggests. What, after all,
is Latinity? French Catholicism, it would seem, has little in

common with Spanish or Italian. Nor, say, does the status of women in French society correspond to their status in half-Moorish Spain. The intellectual instincts of the two peoples— the Frenchman analytic and system-loving, the Spaniard incurious and unreflective—could hardly be more different. Travelled Latin Americans know this quite well; they are not taken in. In Buenos Aires, Victoria Ocampo, the editor of *Sur*, pointed out to me that German existentialist philosophy was known in the Hispanic world, through Unamuno and Ortega, long before it was fashionable on the Left Bank. Many younger writers were as interested, say, in the novels of Günter Grass, or in the work of Saul Bellow, as in the *nouveau roman*. French cultural propaganda is intense; and Paris is still where a Latin American writer would choose to spend a self-imposed or involuntary exile (though not necessarily a painter: as many painters are attracted nowadays to New York as to Paris; as many stay at home). French cultural influence is still strong. But it is no more likely to go unchallenged than the political hegemony exercised by the "Colossus of the North". One advantage of being on the periphery is that you can be more cosmopolitan than the New Yorker or the Parisian. Young Latin Americans see no reason why they should not make the most of their opportunity.

Ironically, then, the *présence française* persists; but its main buttress is not M. André Malraux, but that fervent anti-Gaullist, M. Jean-Paul Sartre. Sartre is far and away the best-known foreign writer in Latin America. Yet, from a dozen conversations, I did not get the impression that Sartre was necessarily admired as a writer—or regarded, primarily, as a man of letters at all. Almost the entire Latin American intelligentsia is *marxisant*—Borges and Gilberto Freyre are among the very few exceptions. And it is the *bon socialiste* in Sartre, the anti-bourgeois, anti-fascist, anti-colonialist rebel who exerts so strong a hold on the imagination of Latin American intellectuals. What have most people actually read of Sartre? *La Nausée*, *L'Etre et le Néant*, *Les Mots*? Possibly. But for every intellectual who has read Sartre's literary or philosophical works, there are ten who have read his pronouncements on the Algerian question, the Jewish question, or the Cuban question. It is Sartre's *position* that matters and that is endlessly debated. A distinguished poet told me that Sartre's refusal of the Nobel Prize had caused him many pangs: how could any of us accept a literary prize now with a good conscience? In his Nobel Prize statement Sartre had referred to the "Venezuelan resistance" as a good cause he would like to see supported. On the day I arrived in Caracas an Open Letter from Sartre was published, protesting against the alleged torture of "resistance fighters" (the armed, Castroite FALN, who attempted to sabotage the 1963 elections through terrorism, only to be confounded by the overwhelming success of the moderate *Accion Democratica* and Christian Democratic parties. The terrorist campaign, however, continues). Sartre's Open Letter had set government circles in a tizzy. What would the Left think? A reply was hastily put out by a pro-government intellectual, Arturo Uslar Pietri, challenging M. Sartre to come and look at the facts. M. Sartre, so far as I know, did not come. He had made his "position" clear; let the facts take care of themselves.

Communism

Since Castro's coming to power—simultaneous with that of Betancourt—Venezuela has been the chief target of Communist and Castroite attack. Why should *Accion Democratica*, a party that had suffered under Perez Jimenez as much as, if not more than Castro's partisans under Batista, bear the brunt of this assault? The two régimes began as firm friends. But, once Cuba started to gravitate to the Soviet camp, polarisation was inevitable. Whether the US was wise to force this polarisation on Latin America is difficult to decide. It is often argued (usually by Liberals) that the US should have sought to retain Castro in the Western camp: on the assumption that this *could* have been done had wiser counsels prevailed. Yet the record shows that American policy, in the 1958–60 period, was remarkably indulgent towards Cuba. Once Castro was established in power, with tacit US support, the United States could do little to influence the course of events. My own view is that anti-Americanism, of a virulent kind, was a necessary ingredient in the radical, anti-imperialist, but not basically Communist revolution that Castro had in mind. The

Liberal argument is that the strategy of polarisation was wrong, because it led to a shift to the right in Latin America and to the subsequent military interventions. Indirectly, it did Castro's work for him. One's personal sympathies may be with those who see what happened in Cuba as a judgment on the US for her neglect of Latin America. Nevertheless, I doubt whether the Liberal conclusion is correct. That not all of Latin America was polarised to the right is shown by the example of Venezuela herself, where a social-democratic régime remained in power, supported by the United States, and became the chief target of Castro's invective. Nor, on a broader view, is the Liberal view easy to substantiate. In the long run, polarisation has probably hurt Castro, by isolating him and revealing his dependence on a "non-American" power, more than it has hurt the United States. That the US could or should have acted differently towards Castro in the early stages is arguable. But the policy the US muddled herself into has been, pragmatically speaking, more effective than most Liberals care to admit.

Will the Cuban experience be repeated? Articles and books continue to appear, exhorting Americans to "do more" for Latin America. The implied threat is that if more is not done a wave of Communist revolution will sweep over the continent. Considered now, ten years after Castro's rise to power, this must seem hysterical talk. Communism in Latin America has never been other than a sickly growth. It is perhaps because the indigenous Communist movements of Asia—in Vietnam, say, or in China—have dominated discussion that the analogy with Latin America is drawn. But it is not a valid analogy. In no Latin American country has Communism evolved into a nationally-based mass movement—not even in Cuba. And in Cuba the formation of a mass party, and the identification of Communism with nationalism, came about *after* the revolution had succeeded. Why was this? Communism has been active in Latin America for over forty years, longer than in Africa, and longer than in most of Asia. Why, then, has no Latin American Communist party developed a disciplined working-class membership on the French or Italian model, with the exception of Chile? Why has Latin American Communism thrown up no charismatic personality comparable to Tito, Togliatti or Ho Chi Minh?

The intellectual current, after all, has been flowing the Communists' way for a generation. Yet they have not secured the hold on the "new intelligentsia" that is theirs in much of Asia and the Arab world. The Communism of Latin America can boast famous names: Neruda in Chile, Siqueiros in Mexico. But because the jargon of many intellectuals—like my friend from *Accion Democratica*—has a *marxisant* ring, we should not mistake them for party-line intellectuals. It is even possible to take intellectuals too seriously. Except perhaps in the Liberal heyday of Sarmiento and Juarez, intellectuals have not enjoyed the political influence in Latin America that foreigners imagine. *Marxisant* talk is one thing; effective political action another. The most striking comment on the strength of Latin American Communism is that seldom, if ever, have Communist appeals to their own working class following to resist an anti-Communist coup met with success. This was demonstrated during the Brazilian "Revolution" of March–April 1964. Before the Army deposed President Goulart, many observers predicted this action of theirs would provoke violent opposition from the Labour Unions and the Communist-dominated student organisations. Yet, when the showdown came, nobody lifted a finger in his defence. Perhaps those who predicted trouble overlooked that gap between speech and action so characteristic of Latin America.

The fact is, Communism has remained profoundly alien to the Latin ambience. One reason for this we have noted: the Iberians, from the days of the Cid, have not been of an ideological cast of mind. Latin America, the cliché runs, is a "revolutionary continent". But this is too simple a picture. Most Latin American revolutions are no more than palace revolutions. In the European sense of the word—in which drastic social change is implied—there have been only two or three revolutions in all Latin American history: in Mexico, in Cuba and, perhaps, in Bolivia. Most "parties" are really traditionalist or personalist groups, owing loyalty to some strong man or *caudillo*. An ideological party on the Marxist-Leninist model makes little appeal. Even where Communist ideology agrees with popular sentiment—in anti-Americanism, opposition to the oligarchy, or to foreign capitalism—Communists have found themselves outbid by parties of the nationalist left. But there is a deeper reason for Communism's failure to make head-way in Latin America. It is that Latin America, whatever the headlines say, is not really a "revolutionary continent" at all.

Certainly, tremendous social changes have taken place over the past generation. But to assume that these changes are *politically* revolutionary is to beg the question. For example: since the war there has been a huge influx of migrant labour from the countryside into the major cities of Latin America. In consequence, these cities are now ringed with sprawling shanty-towns, whose squalor is rightly notorious. Here, surely, is the material for a revolutionary conflagration. Yet it has been shown that this *lumpenproletariat*—to employ Marxist termin-ology—is not in the least revolutionary. It is discontented, and would like to better its lot. But it is ready to follow any leader who promises better conditions. And it is not fastidious in its political preferences: in Lima it has voted for the ex-dictator Odria, in Brazil for Goulart, in Buenos Aires for Peron, in Chile for the Christian Democrat Frei. The reason is simple. However bad the conditions of slum life in the cities, these slum-dwellers are better off there than they would be in the country-side. (This was true, *pace* Engels, even of the industrial revolu-tion in Britain.) And there are other factors: these *campesinos* bring to the city the feudal outlook of the countryside. What they are looking for is a powerful *patron*, not a political party on the Leninist model. Slums breed discontent; but they also breed apathy. Revolutions are not made by men with empty bellies.

Nor are the other social groups on which Communists tradi-tionally rely—the organised working class, the student militants, the peasants—politically more dependable. Almost everywhere, the proletariat proper is very small. True, in some countries the skilled workers—the miners of Chile and Bolivia, the oil workers of Venezuela or Mexico—are in a powerful position. But this, from the Communist point of view, is part of the trouble. These groups form a "labour aristocracy". They are mainly concerned to preserve the differential between them-selves and the *lumpenproletariat* of the shanty-towns. They are militant; but in an economic, not a political, sense. So strong are they that there are few régimes in Latin America not ready to make concessions to them. The students are perhaps the most militant political force in Latin America today; they were instrumental in getting rid of Perez Jimenez, and thus paved the way for *Accion Democratica*. Many were disillusioned with Betancourt's moderation, and became an important source of recruitment to the far left. But students—*pace* Debray's arguments in "Revolution in the Revolution"—are not really a reliable political grouping. They have the common defect of the young: they grow up. A proportion may be recruited; but the majority, of middle and upper class origin, revert to the outlook of their class once they have left the University. Nor is the peasantry more reliable from a Communist point of view. What I have said of the *lumpenproletariat* is true, *a fortiori*, of the *campesinos* themselves. In many countries they are illiterate; and illiteracy disqualifies from the franchise. They have not yet awakened to political consciousness; and the active elements are drained off to the cities. Of the four groups, then, to which a Communist party might look for support—the proletariat, the slum *lumpenproletariat*, the students, the peasantry—none provides a dependable basis for a Marxist-Leninist party.

Perhaps, then, Latin America is not a "revolutionary continent" after all. Certainly, the pace of social change is accelerating, and demands for social reform grow louder. But these demands can be met as effectively by a military dictatorship *à la* Peron, a one-party régime like Mexico's PRI, a social-democratic régime like Venezuela's *Accion Democratica*, or by a Communist dictatorship on the Cuban model. On present evidence, it seems they are rather better satisfied by non-Communist régimes. But the point is that they are in general rather easily satisfied. And this suggests that those who prophesied red revolution in the wake of Castro's victory did not examine the evidence very closely. Indeed, they put the cart before the horse. They thought of Latin America as a revolutionary continent, with pockets of conservative resistance, whereas in fact it is a deeply conservative continent, with limited pockets of revolutionary activity. Take the urban middle class, which has grown enormously over the past generation. It cannot be compared with the European *bourgeoisie* of the nineteenth century. It is content to align itself with the ruling oligarchy, or with the military hierarchy, itself increasingly drawn from the middle class. The end-result of the Mexican Revolution, which destroyed the landed oligarchy, has been to create an urban, bureaucratic middle class, not unlike that "new class" of which Djilas wrote. (The end-result of the Cuban revolution may be not dissimilar.) An unromantic outcome; but then revolutions often end either unromantically, or in universal carnage.

Anglo-Saxons think of Hispanic society as caste-bound and inflexible. But what was true of the court etiquette of the Escorial was not necessarily true, as we have seen, of the lower reaches of Castilian society. Cortes and the Cid were not grandees; rather, each bore on his crest the bourgeois imperative: "*enrichissez-vous!*" That the spirit of free enterprise, and the social mobility that flows from it, was not lacking in later times, is evident from the fortunes made in Colonial Latin America out of silver and diamonds, sugar and cattle. The oligarchies retained control. But they retained control through their flexibility, by assimilating the nouveau-riche and the ambitious outsider. It is easy to forget that two of the most hierarchical organisations in Iberian-American life—the Church and the Army—are also ideal vehicles for the socially-ambitious individual. As in medieval Europe, the poor boy with intellectual ability can always hope for a career in the priesthood, and may rise to be Cardinal Archbishop of Lima or Mexico. More recently, the armies of Latin America have offered similar opportunities to those lacking advantages of birth. Nobody would claim that Latin America has inherited a just social order: few societies are more flagrantly self-seeking. But there is no contradiction between the continuing power of the oligarchs and a generous degree of social mobility. It is this degree of social mobility that helps to make Latin America so conservative a continent.

Indeed, a very curious thing has happened. The Communists themselves, against their will, have been assimilated into this conservative pattern. Until Castro's triumph, Latin American Communists had only once attempted to seize power by force of arms: under Luis Carlos Prestes, in Brazil, in 1935. Yet even this revolt was more of a barracks revolt by dissident army officers than a genuine popular rising: the working class failed to give it effective support. Castro's success brought guerrilla tactics back into fashion. Here, surely, was a more vigorous

alternative to the timid policies traditionally pursued by the
Latin American Communists? Yet the "traditional", Soviet-
line Communists have not been persuaded: only the Venezuelan party adopted this tactic, and even this party has now
reverted to orthodoxy. For the Communists of Latin America,
however ineffective they may be, are political professionals.
They know that Castro's success was freakish. Guerrilla movements do not succeed where the Army is not in sympathy or,
as in Cuba, seriously demoralised—as Che Guevara's débâcle
in Bolivia has conclusively shown. Castro owed his success
neither to his military tactics, nor to a peasant uprising (though
this is believed by the left all over Latin America). Castro won
because the greater part of the Cuban "establishment"—the
urban middle classes, the military, and the students—wanted to
be rid of Batista. Castro's initial success, then, was in the
conventional Hispanic tradition. There was no mass uprising,
no civil war. A *pronunciamiento* was issued and the incumbent
caudillo, finding he no longer had the support of the civil and
military establishment, retired from the scene. Old-style
Communists were not deceived. As they expected, the Castroite
wave then receded. Chinese attempts to infiltrate the Communist parties and alienate them from Moscow have largely failed.
It seems probable that they will revert to the pattern they
have followed since the 1920's—however passionately Castro
and his apologists, like Regis Debray, may dissent.

What were the elements of that pattern? They were, by any
standard, inglorious. Communists have more than once entered
into, and benefited from, political alliances with Latin America's more notorious dictators: with Trujillo, with Peron, with
Venezuela's Perez Jimenez—and, not least, with Batista. The
reasons for these tactics are interesting. The same factors that
deprive the Communists of a mass following—excessive rigidity
in ideology and discipline—give them remarkable stamina and
survival value. In a continent where political organisation is
feeble, their discipline has given the Communists an influence
out of proportion to their numbers. Politicians do not take their
local Communist parties seriously: they are too weak to constitute a threat. Yet they are strong enough, because of their hold
on key economic sectors, for it to be worthwhile appeasing them.
In Peru the oligarchy preferred to deal with the Communists

rather than with their more powerful rival, APRA. For APRA represented a threat to the oligarchy, whereas the Communists, who were bitterly anti-*Aprista*, could be relied on to bolster their power. The relationship needless to say is often mutually beneficial. The Communists continue to operate in conditions of legality; at the same time they secure better conditions for their working class following.

This is not, of course, what Marxist-Leninist theory prescribes. It is precisely that opportunist, "trade-unionist" mentality Lenin never tired of denouncing. Nevertheless, this is probably the only *modus vivendi* for a Leninist party in Latin America, unless it can infiltrate the government machine, as it has tried to do in Cuba. The pattern of Latin American Communism varies surprisingly little from country to country. It is only under "democratic" conditions that Communism attracts much popular support; even then it is outbid by the APRA-PRI-AD type of party. As soon as democratic conditions disappear, its mass support disappears, although a militant nucleus remains intact. It is then that Communist stamina pays off. Where other movements often vanish into thin air, the Communist party lies low, waiting for better days. Meanwhile, it has come to terms with the ruling dictator. Ironically, events in Cuba since 1959 seem to fit into this pattern. Castro was the *caudillo* who made the Revolution. The Communists provided the discipline and the political machine. The Communists of Latin America are nothing if not adaptable. They co-operate with Castro as they co-operated earlier with Batista.

Thus the Chinese, and the Castroites, are partly right when they ridicule the Communist parties for their conservatism and lack of enterprise. But they are not right in thinking that their brand of revolutionism would meet with greater success. The apparent failure of Castro-supported guerrilla movements in Venezuela, Colombia, Peru, Central America and Bolivia does not support this thesis. The Communists of Latin America have come to terms with their environment; they know their limits. It is easy to mock their timidity. But what else should they do? In their pre-war phase, they were pessimistic about the prospects for revolution for two main reasons. They were convinced that in a still largely agricultural continent the social basis for a Leninist revolution was lacking. They knew also that they could not hope for Soviet economic or military support in case of trouble. In the past thirty years the picture has changed. Yet, surprisingly, the Communists have profited very little. Industrialisation has gone ahead by leaps and bounds; the discontent of the peasantry has increased; students grow ever more radical in their attitudes. Yet the Communist party remains a sectarian political group, without mass support. In terms of geopolitics, the Communist position should be less unfavourable than in the twenties. Then, the Comintern's advice to its Latin American agents was to play a waiting game, to respect the fact that Latin America was the United States' back-garden. After the 1957 Sputnik triumph, and especially after Castro's victory in 1958, a bolder policy seemed to be on the cards. The US herself was within range of Soviet rockets; and the Bay of Pigs suggested that direct American intervention might be, partly for this reason, a thing of the past. The years 1958 to 1962 were consequently a period of euphoria for the Latin American Communists and their allies.

But the second Cuban crisis, in October 1962, dashed these hopes. It became clear not only that the Soviet Union could not bring its power to bear in the hemisphere, but that the attempt to rely on Soviet power must tend to polarize the situation in a way unfavourable to the Communists. The implications of the Cuban missile crisis were not lost on Latin American Communists. Thanks to the polarisation that had already taken place, it was not probable that another state machine would give in as tamely to a pro-Communist *caudillo* as had Cuba in 1958. Yet American support for moderate reformist movements, through the Alliance of Progress, was likely to take the wind out of the sails of those looking for more violent political solutions. October 1962, then, was the turning-point. The hopes raised during 1958–1962 that the Soviet Union might yet prove a *deus ex machina*—doing for Latin America what she had done for Eastern Europe after 1945—were seen to be illusory. The humiliation of the Soviet Union brought home to Latin American Communists how little the situation had really changed. A return to the *status quo ante* was indicated. That the US herself did not see the implications for her policy of Kennedy's triumph—as US policy in the Dominican republic was to show—is the more surprising. "Create two, three, four Vietnams!" cried Che Guevara. But Latin America is not Vietnam. When the smoke has cleared, the years 1958–1962 may well be seen to represent the high point of Communist advance in Latin America. No doubt, the coming years will harbour some unpleasant shocks for Western interests. But they are unlikely to bring much comfort to the Soviets either, let alone to their competitors in world revolution, the Chinese or the Castroites.

5

COLOMBIA:
or The Threshold of Violence

It is a land of violence. Thunder and avalanches in the mountains, huge floods and storms on the plains. Volcanoes exploding. The earth shaking and splitting. The woods full of savage beasts and poisonous insects and deadly snakes. Knives are whipped out at a word. Whole families are murdered without any reason. Riots are sudden and bloody and often meaningless. Cart and trucks are driven into each other or over cliffs with an indifference which is half suicidal. Such an energy in destruction. Such an apathy when something has to be mended or built. So much humour in despair. So much weary fatalism toward poverty and disease. The shrug of the shoulders, and the faint smile of cynicism. No good. Too late. It's gone. Finished. Broken. They're all dead. Ignore it. Use the other door. Sleep in another room. Throw it in the gutter. Tie the ends together with string. Put up a memorial cross.

What is cooking in there, with such ominous sounds, nobody now alive will ever know. A new race and a new culture, certainly. Perhaps an entirely different kind of sensibility, an original approach to life, expressed in other terms, another language. But whatever it may be, it is cooking. And it will go on doing so, mysteriously, noisily, furiously, through all the bad times that are coming.

The Condor and the Cows: Christopher Isherwood (1949)

E

Bogota

IF LATIN AMERICA is the forgotten continent, Bogota must be its most forgotten capital. It is partly a matter of association. We associate oil with Venezuela, tin with Bolivia, Aztecs with Mexico, beef with Argentina: what do we associate with Colombia? The Indian Chibchas, who lived in the highlands round Bogota, had a developed culture when the Spaniards overthrew them. But the intricately stylised gold-work they left behind, though appealing, cannot compete with the art of other, more famous Andean cultures to the south, or with the glories of the Valley of Anahuac. Again, the story of their overthrow lacks the high drama of Cortes and Montezuma, or of Pizarro and Atahualpa; and no Prescott has recorded it. Yet Colombia is no banana republic. In area, she is not much smaller than Western Europe; with her 18 millions, she is twice as populous as her better-known neighbour, Venezuela. The majority of her people are European-Hispanic (30 per cent), or *mestizo* (40 per cent); she has only 7 per cent pure Indian, and 5 per cent pure Negro. Like Venezuela, then, she is predominantly a White, European country. But whereas Venezuela has grown "whiter" since the war, thanks to a huge intake of European immigrants, Colombia's racial balance has changed little over the centuries. To all outward appearance she is a European country. Yet the appearance is deceptive. The outlook of the *criollo* is not necessarily that of the European stock he comes from. And the *criollo* pyramid rests on a *mestizo* foundation whose psychology is in many respects profoundly unEuropean.

Bogota, then, is the classic Latin American city. A Latin American tour ought to start here, one feels, rather than in Mexico or Rio, if the traveller is out for more than folk-art and flesh-pots and heroic landscape: the touristic *frissons*. Latin America, one sees, is not something invented by Buñuel and Eisenstein; by Renoir in *Orphée Nègre*, or Chris Marker in *Cuba Sí*. Latin Americans, according to that image, when not squatting picturesquely in the mud of their *barrios*, are dancing in the streets to dynamic neo-African rhythms. Buñuel's *Los Olvidados*, of course, is a different matter: like Oscar Lewis's *Children of Sanchez*, it is part of the truth about Latin America. But *Orphée Nègre* is too close, for my taste at least, to cultural tourism; it oversells the product. Much of Latin America is neither especially squalid, nor especially picturesque; it is disappointingly humdrum. It is almost like home. Consider Bogota. Alexander von Humboldt called her "the Athens of South America"; a phrase she has not forgotten and will not allow the visitor to forget. Certainly, her role in the liberation of South America was crucial. Bolivar's *quinta*, a modest eighteenth-century lodge on the slopes overlooking the city, may still be inspected; as may the house where, in 1794, Antonio Nariño translated the Declaration of the Rights of Man into Spanish. But Bogota's Periclean age was brief. Soon all was palace-intrigue, high-sounding, rhetoric, and sudden death. Athens had become Byzantium. Bogota still has the best bookshops in Latin America (Herr Buchholz's establishment, five storeys high, is a New World wonder: I found books on Herr Buchholz's shelves I never thought to see again outside the British Museum). Still, her Athenian aspirations invite gentle ridicule. A member of the British colony on his European leave, I am told, sent his fellow-exiles a postcard of the Parthenon. It bore, with an Athens postmark, the unkind greeting, "from the Bogota of Europe".

It is easy, then, to make fun of Bogota. And hard, perhaps, to make friends with her. For, unlike Mexico or Rio, she lacks surface charm. Her best friends would not claim that she was gay. James Morris described her as living "in a kind of perpetual damp October'. That was rude; but one knows what he felt. One stands in the street. One looks up apprehensively at that sombre, brutish whale-belly as it hovers around the Andean peak at the foot of which the city spreads out like a cloth. And one is seized with sudden depression. Colombia is the classical country, one recalls, of *la violencia*, strangest and most terrible of social diseases. Between 1947 and 1960, two hundred thousand people fell victim to this senseless fury. The Byzantine fever, once exclusively aristocratic, seemed to have gripped the masses; what had begun as politics ended in killing for killing's

sake. The huge rain cloud hovers, big with menace. It is always
about to rain; but it never actually rains. Tempers fray. The
bogotanos lean on their horns. The moustachio'd bandit who overtook you on the road to the airport would as gladly have cut
your throat. This is *homo hispanicus* on his mettle; cross him if
you dare. Or is it, perhaps, the altitude? At 8,000 feet, as an
unacclimatised *gringo*, you are not strong on your feet. A dozen
paces up one of Bogota's *calles*, and you gasp like a fish. Yet
born *bogotanos* are said to suffer too. Lack of oxygen is held to
shorten the temper. It is a much-heard argument, and a ready-
made excuse. One has heard something similar in Mexico,
and one will hear it again in Brazil. Either the mountains are
too high, and the plains too low; or the land is too wet, or too
dry. There is a geographical excuse for everything. Nature is
no friend to man: that is ancient Spanish wisdom. Spanish
America has a corollary: man would be perfectible—if only
the climate were in his favour.

   The sombreness of Bogota is not just a trick of the light.
People are, on the whole, drably dressed. Colombia's men of
God are numerous and combative. Sartorially, the male
population seems to approximate to them. Physically, as in
Spanish towns, two male types are dominant: there are the
young men, dark, willowy, fiercely handsome in the Manolete
style. There are the elderly and middle-aged: sallow, grave and
a little over-weight, who have taken on a certain distant
resemblance to General Franco. In a southern climate youth is
a brief fire. There is no middle ground. That Anglo-Saxon
type, the bronzed, middle-aged stripling, with his fruit juice,
chest-expanders and boisterous high spirits, is missing. You
will spot magnificent young men, if you study the street scene;
but for every Manolete you will spot three Francos. And the
women? The women of South America have a reputation.
They are supposed to be dark and sultry, passionate beneath
their tropical languor. As South Americans, they are the
children of a wild and uncorrupted nature. As Latins, they
inherit the sensuality, and the mother-worship, of the mediterranean peoples. They are born primadonnas. In a word:
Carmen Miranda. But if that is what you are looking for in
South America you are likely to be disappointed. Except,
possibly, on Copacabana beach, or at Acapulco, or at Punta

del Este; or in those Country Clubs where the *jeunesse dorée*
of Lima, Caracas and Bogota cavort. In the streets of Bogota
you see a handful of elegantly dressed, and rather more over-
dressed, women of wealth. But the norm, to be ungallant, is
dowdy and lacking in style. The Spaniards are not, like the
Italians, a visually imaginative people. The standard of public
and private taste, in Spain as in Spanish America, is uninspired.
Too often, in private homes as in public monuments, an arid
drabness prevails. Where it does not—as Fanny Calderon
noted—the tendency is to go to the other extreme. The women
of the *criollos* are like their churches. They cannot resist the
temptation to overdress.

This is not the Latin America of the steamship advertise-
ments. But the point about Latin America, as about Spain, is
that it is provincial. Certainly, provinciality has its charm;
much is preserved that is lost to the developed commercialism
of the North. But, praising it too much, we run into a dilemma.
To champion Spain, or Spanish America, is to champion the
past; and to champion the past is to fall under the suspicion
of being a reactionary. But to be a reactionary (it can be
argued) is to betray the interests of those you would befriend,
the people whose need of modern industry, hygiene and
education is so desperate. Perhaps that is why Mr Edmund
Wilson is wary of Hispanophiles. Certainly, this dilemma has
faced all Anglo-Saxon Hispanophiles, from Richard Ford and
W. H. Hudson to Gerald Brenan and Ernest Hemingway.
How to celebrate *hispanidad* without celebrating that *España
Invertebrada* of which Ortega complained? The visitor does well,
then, to tread lightly on this ground. Yet he should not seek,
for politeness' sake, to deny the provinciality. Whether it is
university standards that are in question, or the status of
women, he will run up against it. "Our women, you see"—he
will be told—"do not *want* to be 'emancipated', as you call it.
They demand respect as our wives, as the mothers of our
children. You *gringos* can keep your 'emancipated women',
and your psychiatrists, and your divorce rates!" That, of
course, is man's view: woman's view might be different, if
anyone thought to ask her opinion. Divorce may be low in
Latin America—in some countries it is very easy, in others it is
not permitted at all—but the soaring illegitimacy rates suggest

a different tale. There is not much divorce; but there is not much marriage either. There is no doubt that the woman of Latin America, by the standards of Europe and North America, is seriously underprivileged. Perhaps she prefers it that way; but she may not prefer it that way much longer.

It is not with disrespect that one insists on the provinciality of Latin America. That Latin America is provincial in regard to Europe no intelligent Latin American has ever denied. The intelligent young are even willing to admit their provinciality in regard to the United States. The relevant point is not whether Latin America is a province, but what she is a province of. And no one who walks the streets of Bogota or Santiago or São Paulo can be in doubt about that: Latin America is a lost province of Europe. You feel, in these cities, how profoundly European Latin America has remained. Say what you like about this strait-laced, Catholic, caste-bound society; but its principle of life is not North American. There was a time when North America, too, was provincial. She is not provincial now. Today she is a civilisation in her own right, a civilisation which the European may admire or despise, but in which he seldom feels at home. The European, in North America, falls victim to a curious kind of cultural weightlessness. In Latin America, for all her provinciality, her poverty, and her backwardness, the European feels at home. There is a riddle they set you in Bogota: "if you were kidnapped in the streets of London, New York or Paris, and catapulted to Bogota—where, when you woke up, would you think you were?" My answer, if I remember aright, was Cracow, Zagreb, or some other very Catholic, very industrious, very respectable-seeming city in Eastern Europe. The Monsignor lifts his hat to the Bank Director; the grocer speaks in low, respectful tones to the Notary's daughter; the flies buzz in the window pane among last year's unsold preserves; the trams creak painfully by. Bogota could be Bratislava, or Limerick, or some sleepy town on the Castilian *meseta*. She is European; yet somehow on the marches of Europe. Latin Americans bewail at times their undignified position as Europe's appendix, her forgotten, over-extended, phantom limb. What we want, they tell you, is to be *European*: see Paris and die! In all modesty, one is bound to contradict them. Latin America has many aspirations, noble and ignoble. But being

European need not be one of them. Why should it be an aspiration when it is a fact?

A Little History

Visiting a foreign country for the first time I, for one, appreciate a little history. It may be no more than a paragraph in a guidebook; but a little history helps. Without that extra dimension, the sights and sounds of a new city become a source of discomfort. That great, grim cathedral! Those charming, gabled houses behind the new, concrete apartment-blocks! That bulbous, outrageous, exotic Museum of Fine Art! The National Palace with its famous balcony and battle-scarred exterior! There they stand, higgledy-piggledy, baffling, enduring in an undifferentiated present, from which only Herr Baedeker's and Mr Murray's handbooks can release them. A morning's walk attenuates the discomfort. The grim cathedral is Romanesque, built as a fortress against heretics. The gabled houses are the old Jewish quarter, where a famous philosopher was born. The Museum of Fine Arts is *Art Nouveau*, a fitting monument to its epoch's vulgar wealth. And the National Palace; well, only last year they installed a Progressive President there. And only last week they chased him out with the traditional whiff of grapeshot. We have not learnt much; but we know enough to be going along with. That undifferentiated flatness is gone; the city has a third dimension. With a little further effort—a visit to the airless Historical Museum, some useful talk with an English-speaking Professor, a chat with a friendly barman—the scene comes into view. It is not pleasant; a sad tale of political violence, religious fanaticism and racial strife. But it makes a kind of sense; it falls into a pattern. We leave, on the tenth day, with a sensation of surprise. We have got a grip on the city now; we have won an intellectual skirmish. How pleasant to think that those brash people, with whom we shared a taxi from the airport, know nothing of this! They have spent their time between the hotel swimming pool and the local night-club. Such are the uses of history!

This game can be played as well with a Latin American as with a European city: here too are cathedrals, and museums, and places of historic interest. Perhaps it is a little more com-

plicated. But that is because it is unfamiliar. Of course, some
deny we can play the game at all in these latitudes. It is not
only that Latin America is something of a backwater. They go
further: Latin America, they consider, is without a significant
history to speak of. Who remembers the names of more than
half a dozen of her presidents? Who remembers during which
years Santa Anna was in power in Mexico—seeing that he
held power on no less than twenty-three occasions? No wonder
Latin American history has become a bad joke. But the
foreigner thinks of Latin America as being without significant
history in another sense. He sees no progress in it. And, seeing
no progress in it, he sees no sense in it. Latin American history
is a kind of Eternal Recurrence. Plots and counter-plots, coups
and counter-coups; but no clear-cut, dialectical progression.
Latin American history appears to be cyclical; and cyclical
history is not something the devout Westerner cares for. It
takes you nowhere; and the Westerner wants to arrive. Yet in
fact Latin American history is no more cyclical than European.
There is a pattern to it, which is not simply a pattern of
meaningless plots and counter-plots.

What is that pattern? Can it be demonstrated, not only for
individual countries, but for Latin America as a whole? The
visitor to Latin America is warned, rightly, to take note of
particularity and to scorn generality. Each country he visits is
unique: El Salvador is not Nicaragua; Peru is not Ecuador;
Uruguay is not Paraguay. Now this is wholesome advice, since
there is a natural tendency to confound and compound, if only
out of exasperation at the refractoriness of the subject-matter.
But, if we take it too literally, we miss the extent to which the
evolution of the twenty republics shows a common pattern.
Yet it is this pattern that gives shape and interest to Latin
American history. It demonstrates, not only that Latin
American history possesses inner consistency, but that it offers
striking parallels with other parts of the world—for example,
with the successor-states of the Turkish, British or Austro-
Hungarian Empires. In offering this sketch for a "typical"
pattern I assert no more than that certain broad similarities
are to be found between the histories of the twenty republics.
We shall examine certain of these parallels in more detail
later: at this point I wish only to establish that they exist.

With these reservations, then, the history of a "typical" Latin American republic might read as follows:

1765 Introduction of Bourbon reforms, *Intendente* system and freer trade has paradoxical effect. Meant to strengthen Empire, closer supervision through *Intendente* (always of "peninsular" birth) leads to greater Creole resentment at social and political discrimination. Freer trade welcome to Creole merchants, but disastrous to (formerly protected) local manufacturers. At the same time, trade for the Creole landowner not free enough, since he wishes to trade with non-Spanish merchants. Bourbon reforms, therefore, hasten dissolution of what they are meant to consolidate.

1795 Creole position stronger in army, and lower ranks of hierarchy; but increased status leads to increased resentment. Slow infiltration of ideas of French Enlightenment; first translation of Rights of Man. But conservative Creoles dismayed at course of French Revolution (and slave revolt in Haiti). Determination to prevent similar disturbances at home (suppression of Indian revolt of Tupac Amaru in Peru) prefigures concern that collapse of Royal authority will undermine Creole dominance. Both "conservative" and "liberal" elements therefore present in growing Creole resentment against *madre patria*.

1800 Foundation of clandestine Constitutional Society, group of lawyers and army officers influenced by French ideas. Arrest, trial and execution of dissidents by Spanish government. Street rioting. Remaining dissidents go into exile.

1810 Formation of autonomous *cabildo* in Capital, following Napoleon's occupation of Spain. Taste for self-government awakens among merchant class and leading landowners. Foundation of first newspaper. Ports thrown open to trade with Britain. Restrictions on import of foreign books removed.

1816 Temporary re-imposition of Imperial authority. Street rioting. Suppression of Free Press. Return of leading revolutionaries to exile. Preparations for military struggle

with Spain get under way, with British volunteers and
financial assistance.

1821 Final defeat of Spain. Declaration of Independence.
Establishment of Republican form of government, with
strong President on United States model. Commercial
treaty with Britain. Introduction of French educational
institutions. Constitutional Society (renamed Constitutional Club) rehoused in handsome neo-Colonial building on *Plaza de Armas*.

1836 Death of first President (*el Libertador*), former comrade-in-
arms of Bolivar, followed by period of anarchy. Beginning
of thirty-year struggle between Conservative or *Blanco*
party (representing land-owning interests) and Liberal or
Colorado party (representing mercantile and financial
interests). Conservatives favour Federal Constitution,
Liberals Centralism. Church support for Conservative
faction leads to rise of anti-clericalism in towns, demands
for church disestablishment.

1856 After twenty years of rule by military *caudillos*, final
triumph of *Colorado* party. *Colorado* victory owed to
increasing wealth of seaboard cities, control of commerce
with backlands, superior organisation and firepower of
European-type armies. Election of overwhelmingly
Colorado National Assembly. Church lands expropriated.
Civil marriage recognised. Chief orders of monks and
friars expelled. Slavery abolished.

1882 After new period of disorder, final settlement between
Blanco and *Colorado* interests. Policing and administration
of backlands left in hands of *Blancos*. Compromise in
Church affairs negotiated. Increasing prosperity, based
on export of coffee and beef to European markets,
reconciles antagonists. Beginning of long period of rule
by authoritarian, but moderate general, originally of
Colorado persuasion, who wins confidence of European
and North American investors. Railway system built
by British engineers and Italian labour.

1912 Stability of country once again threatened. New factors
on political scene: economic instability due to over-great
dependence on foreign markets and to inflationary boom
of past twenty years; rise of anarchist and socialist

influence among new proletariat. Border conflict with
neighbouring state leads to ignominious defeat, large
appropriations for new army and lack of confidence
among foreign investors. Situation resolved by coup, led
by *mestizo* general from backlands. United States replaces
Britain as chief supplier of capital.

1934 World economic crisis has political repercussions. Rise
of Revolutionary Action party, heir to older Liberal and
Radical parties, supported by literate Indians and
mestizos in countryside, lower middle class, and industrial
proletariat. Conservative oligarchy, allied with army,
decides on counter-blow. Radical government overthrown; oligarchy and military establish government of
"national concentration". Eminent writers exiled. Growing influence of Italian and German Fascism among
ruling groups. Communist influence replaces Anarchist
among élite working-class groups.

1944 Entry into War under Allied pressure. Boom in raw
materials leads to new prosperity. Decline of German and
Italian prestige accompanied by increased Russian
prestige. Growing strength of left-wing, but anti-
Communist Revolutionary Action party leads to coup in
its favour by young army officers, installation of its leader
as President with tacit American approval. Beginning of
New Era.

1949 On pretext of combating Communist influence in public
life, military coup by Navy and senior Army officers
(with tacit American approval) deposes Revolutionary
Action régime. Reform programme has antagonised
Church, landowning and industrial interests. Workers'
rising in support of régime does not materialise. Communist and Revolutionary Action parties banned.

1959 After ten years of military dictatorship, growing unrest
among miners, oil-workers, and students of National
University. Middle-class discontent at corruption and
galloping inflation. Overthrow of military dictatorship.
New junta of younger officers backs coalition of Revolutionary Action party (now moderate reformist movement) with Christian Democrats and rump of old Liberal
and Radical parties. Elections confirm new President by

large majority. Tacit American approval. Communist
party legalised, wins only 5 per cent of national vote.

1968 Reforming coalition still in power. Threatened on Left by
Castroite guerrilla groups in highlands and sporadic
terrorism in capital. On Right by rumours of new military
coup. Army divided between middle-class-democratic
and oligarchic-conservative factions; Navy strongly anti-
democratic. US support under President Kennedy
("one of the model states of our hemisphere") modified by
anti-Communist, stability-minded approach of subsequent
administrations. Economic prospects: good in long-term.
Foreign capital mandatory for development of oil and
metal extraction industries. But poor if commodity prices
cannot be stabilised and agricultural yields raised. Birth
rate 3·2 per cent. Outlook: political stability still jeopard-
ised by role of Army, but Revolutionary Action party and
new Christian Democrat party enjoy increasing support.
Communist poll, after peak of 15 per cent in 1946, mild
upturn (10 per cent) in 1961, amounts to less than 5 per
cent. Castroite groups dominant among students, but
guerrilla activity weakening. Verdict: military comeback
possible, but not certain; Communist take-over unlikely.

I make no dogmatic claims for this scheme. Of course much
is left out; and there are countries that deviate markedly from
the pattern. But the majority of individual items are true of at
least two-thirds of the twenty republics. That is a fair degree of
unity. And, in certain periods, the unity is still more marked.
Most countries experienced a long period of rule by *caudillo*
after Independence; a Liberal-Conservative struggle in the
mid-nineteenth century; and the rise of a labour-populist
movement over the past forty years. There are, of course, exceptions. There are countries where the Indian problem
does not exist. There are a few countries which escaped the
post-Independence period of *confusionismo* (Brazil). There are
countries where the Church has lost very little, or has now
regained its pre-Independence influence (Colombia and Peru).
There are countries where the older Liberal-Conservative,
Blanco-Colorado antagonism persists in a modified form (Colombia and Uruguay). And there is one country, as we have

seen, where the power of the military seems to have been broken: Mexico. Indeed, if our scheme shows anything, it shows that our previous contention was correct: Mexico stands apart from the rest of Latin America to an astonishing degree. Mexico is ruled, admittedly, by a party of the nationalist-populist type. But it is the only case in which a party of that type has swallowed the apparatus of the state itself. I am not holding up the dictatorship of the PRI as a model: that would be doing Latin America a doubtful service. But Mexico is the only one of the twenty republics where we can say with fair confidence that the cycle of instability has been broken.

The People of Aritama

I remarked earlier that these two northernmost countries of South America—for a time united in Bolivar's *Gran Colombia* —were "White" countries: that is, that they were basically European. I added the proviso that this Europeanness, though statistically greater than in Mexico, must be seen as an ice-berg reaching down into a different, alien, more ancient culture. In other words: that these "White" countries are a great deal more like Mexico than they appear on the surface. The statistics themselves point to this: 30 per cent of the population is classi-fied as "White", but at least 50 per cent has some degree of Indian blood. (It is a moot point, naturally, how far we can trust statistics of this kind: since "Whiteness" confers prestige, the proportion of "Whites", and even *mestizos*, tends to be exaggerated.) How far, then, can we speak of this huge *mestizo* base as also "European", in culture, if not in blood? Certainly, this huge proportion of *mestizos* would suggest that any "Europeanness" must be heavily diluted. Then there is another contradiction, one which we have noted already: is Latin America a "revolutionary" or a "conservative" continent? Or is it, paradoxically, both? It is too easy, as we have seen, to fall back on a cyclical reading of Latin American history. The revolutions of Latin America may seem to do no more than shuffle the faces on the Presidential balconies. Yet this never was an entirely true picture; and it has grown less true over the past generation. Social changes have taken place; new political forms have emerged. If we fail to recognise them, it is because they refuse to obey our Old World preconceptions.

Revolutionary or conservative? European or non-European? For us these are abstract formulations. But in Latin America they are the warp and woof of men's existence. *Mestizaje*, the sociology and psychology of racial intermixture, is now a fashionable topic among anthropologists. It is also of considerable political importance, as we have seen in the case of Mexico. Yet it is a topic peculiarly difficult of access. It can be approached, as Samuel Ramos and Octavio Paz approach it, through the literary-philosophical imagination. Both Ramos and Paz are perhaps guilty of intellectualising—and, at times, of romanticising—what is at bottom a practical problem. The "human biology" approach, on the other hand, may be no less misleading, for few of the variables are susceptible of exact measurement. A convincing account of *mestizaje* must take into account subjective factors as well. Since you cannot measure what is Indian you must measure what is thought to be Indian. This, with much else, is what Gerardo and Alicia Reichel-Dolmatoff have attempted in their fascinating book *The People of Aritama*, perhaps the most rigorous study of *mestizaje* yet undertaken. Conceived as an exercise in academic anthropology, their final conclusions—based on meticulous observation of the way of life of a north-Colombian *mestizo* village—shed light on many of the contradictions that we have noticed. Indeed, by attacking the problem at a deeper, and a more concrete level, they go some way towards resolving them.

The guiding assumption of *The People of Aritama* is that *mestizaje* is not a fixed condition, but a process. In the context studied by the Reichel-Dolmatoffs, the process turns on the gradual transformation of a "closed", highland, Indian village, rooted in the traditional culture, into an "open", *criollo*, Spanish-speaking community, similar to villages of the Colombian lowlands. The time-scale, in this case, is known with some accuracy: a century ago Aritama was practically untouched by *criollo* influence. To all intents and purposes it was an Indian village. Missionaries had made a temporary impact in the eighteenth century; but the new Catholic elements became absorbed into the local fabric of magic and ritual. At the end of the past century there occurred a migration of *criollo* peasants from the lowlands. These *campesinos* were racially of mixed provenance—Negro, Indian, and Hispanic. But culturally they formed part of the lowland, *criollo* way of life. They settled around the village *plaza*, and bought up the best land. By 1950, when the Reichel-Dolmatoffs began to study the village, they formed a distinct *barrio* of their own, separated by a fence from the Indian *barrio*, the "*loma*". Yet the two *barrios* did not live in total apartheid. Mutual interaction took subtle and, often, unadmitted forms. Many of the new techniques introduced into the village by the lowlanders were soon adopted by the *lomeros*. But the new ways were often adopted for what must seem strange reasons. The wearing of certain clothes had become general, not because they were suited to local conditions, but because they were held to confer "prestige"—the prestige of assimilation to a higher culture.

Indeed, prestige has come to rule the lives of the people of Aritama in every detail. Many of the *criollo* people of the *plaza* are desperately poor. Yet most would rather starve than plant potatoes, partly because agricultural work is degrading ("*trabajo por un indio*" is a common term of abuse in Colombia); but partly also because potatoes are considered "Indian food" and to eat them lowers one's prestige. But in matters of religion, magic, and medicine, the situation is often the other way about. Not much faith is put in Catholic observations. Grasp of Catholic doctrine is meagre: Corpus Christi is thought to be a festival of the Sun; the Trinity is considered to consist of Christ, the Virgin and the Devil; the saints are held to be the offspring of Christ and the Virgin. Christ himself is believed to be a local Indian shaman of former times who had won fame for his cures. There is no resident priest. In time of trouble, not surprisingly, it is to the shaman of the highland Indian tribes (who still speak no Spanish) that the people of Aritama, of both *barrios*, look for spiritual guidance.

Today, Aritama is a village between two worlds: an Indian world, whose metaphysical assumptions it partly shares; and a *criollo* world, commercial, aggressive, socially-mobile, but also prestige- and anxiety-ridden and unconfident of its assumptions. The picture the Reichel-Dolmatoffs draw is not flattering to either race. But then, it is an unspoken assumption of *The People of Aritama* that *mestizaje* is not a "racial" process at all. It is a process of acculturation, in which much that is valuable in the aboriginal condition is displaced, and much that is vulgar in the *criollo* tradition is imported. The Reichel-Dolmatoffs do not set out to assess profit and loss. In so far as they call these changes "progressive", they do so in a morally neutral sense. They merely record what is happening to Aritama. But it is evident that what has happened to the people of Aritama is happening to millions of their fellow-*mestizos* all over Latin America, and will be happening to millions of "pure" Indians tomorrow. In this larger sense, *mestizaje* is simply a name for that complex process of cultural adjustment in which half the population of Latin America is now caught.

The People of Aritama does not lend itself to easy quotation. The strength of the book is in its detail. But it is impossible not to see parallels with what other writers, in very different fields, have had to say on the subject: with Ramos and Paz, with Soustelle and Lévi-Strauss, with the Brazilian da Cunha and the Mexican Juan Rulfo. Nor is this surprising. For if the hidden history of Latin America in this century is really the history of *mestizaje*, and of its impact on the existing *criollo* structure, then the meditations of Paz, Ramos, and da Cunha, or even of Soustelle and Lévi-Strauss, are likely to coincide at many points. Take, for example, what is the earliest and most persistent stratum of all: the magical-religious world-picture of the people of Aritama:

> The general concept of the universe is that it is a complex magical system into which man is born and in which he exists without ever being able to achieve security and peace. The community of the living and the individuals that constitute it are nothing but passing shadows, unwelcome guests in a world controlled by unknown and unknowable powers which are essentially hostile to mankind. The structure and the function of the universe are thought to be far beyond human experience and understanding, and all speculations as to its meaning and all efforts to dominate even the most insignificant aspect of it, are deemed idle. . . . All attitudes towards life are eminently fatalistic.

If there is little grasp of the Catholic cosmogony, there is hardly more grasp of the pagan cosmogony that is Aritama's Indian inheritance. A mother-goddess, the source of fertility, is acknowledged. As is a Sun-god, to whom prayers are surreptitiously directed and sacrifices made—but who, if he were once the world's creator, appears to be now the enfeebled, Olympian spectator of its sorrows. More actual is the world of spirits. Yet here too much is vague and insubstantial:

> There is no love for the ancestors, no real worship. They are essentially evil and dangerous, and so they are feared: but they cannot be avoided. Their awful presence is felt at every step—in the tree that was planted by them, in the field they owned and cleared, in the trail they used to walk. They appear in dreams and nightmares. . . . They can be heard at night singing and talking in the dark, whistling in the air or moaning in the forest. They are a heavy burden each human being carries along on the road of life. . . . Belief in the ancestral spirits is in no way limited to the families of Indian origin. . . . It is easy to speak of stupid Indian superstitions and old wives' tales as long as there is a bottle of rum, while the hot noonday sun penetrates the darkest corners of the crooked streets . . . but once night has fallen and silence descends on the village and on the valley, these very same things begin to look different and there will not be a man, woman, or child who would not admit that the *sixguinyani* are lurking in the darkness, asking for food and threatening all and sundry with disease.

Tristes tropiques, indeed! Inevitably, too, Soustelle's characterisation of the world-view of the Aztecs comes to mind.

This, then, is the dim, twittering world out of which the Latin American *mestizo* is emerging. But what of the world he is likely to encounter? For, as the Reichel-Dolmatoffs point out —and as Soustelle insists with passion—not everything in that ancient pattern was unjust or ignoble. Soustelle admired the stoicism of the Aztec; and the Reichel-Dolmatoffs remark of the unspoilt Indian of Aritama:

> The conservative Indian peasant lives by a value system and demonstrates a personality type which are far more Western than the emerging *criollo* outlook on life. . . . The respect for due process of law, for family life, and village authority are in obvious opposition to the materialism of the average *criollo*, his hedonism, his disregard for law and authority, and his disrupted family life.

This is said in no sentimental spirit. It serves only to remind us that the transition is marked by loss as well as gain. But the transition is under way, is accelerating, and will ultimately prove irresistible. That many of the values these *mestizos* acquire are gimcrack is true, and no doubt deplorable. But we cannot alter it. It is the *fact* of evolution that is crucial. For it is this that has modified the social attitudes of Aritama. Here, the Reichel-Dolmatoffs' analysis closely resembles the Mexican autocriticism of Ramos and Paz. "Hispanic values", as they have come down to present-day Latin Americans, may justly be criticised—that is another matter. Less important than the content of these values, is the *fact* of their imposition, and the insecurity that results from it. Insecurity of some sort, no doubt, is incidental to all social change. But we should gloss over neither the pain involved nor the fact that this insecurity moulds the value-system of the people of Aritama today. How else can we interpret the goal of *ser respetado*?

> The ultimate goal of life is to be respected (*ser respetado*). . . . Leisure, capital, material progress, food, health . . . are really only means to the single aspiration in life: to be accepted by society; to be free of discrimination, persecution, and ridicule; to be respected. . . . Smiles, laughter, tears, rage, pain, or fear should never be shown and to maintain a "wooden face" (*cara de palo*) is a prerequisite for being considered a "serious person". On the street people, especially men, look straight ahead or downward and cast only furtive glances sidewards. . . . It is "formality" that is valued because only "the formal person" (*la persona formal*) can hope to be respected.

No wonder the Reichel-Dolmatoffs characterise Aritama, on the basis of these behaviour patterns, as a profoundly sick society. To them, as to Ramos and Paz, the neurotic element in these patterns of behaviour is obvious. But the political and sociological implications are no less interesting. I spoke earlier of the apparent contradiction between Latin America's conservatism and her revolutionism, between her European "feel" and those eruptions from the depths that seem so alien to the European observer. In the light of this analysis such contradictions become easier to understand. The "Europeanness" of much of Latin America is no illusion. The culture-pattern towards which *mestizo* society is moving is indeed the "European model"—as the *criollo* imperfectly understands it. To be respected is to adopt these characteristics, to blot out what is "Indian" in one's inheritance. Nor is there much doubt where this process will end: the Indian inheritance will be destroyed, the *criollo* pattern will triumph. But the tensions built up in this process will lead to outbursts of violence. And this is true not only between individuals; in Colombia's *violencia* it is impossible to distinguish political feuding from feuding between personal and social groups. To grasp the truth of this we have only to look at Mexico's revolution or at the strange episode of the Canudos revolt as described by da Cunha.

And the conservative-revolutionary paradox, too, becomes easier to understand in the light of this analysis. There are, as we have seen, many factors that make for political instability: Spanish *individualismo*, the tradition of the *patria chica*, poor communications, the general weakness of civil authority. But the insecurity inherent in the *mestizo*'s psychological make-up is itself a factor making for political instability. We must be careful not to press the argument too far: it is non-*mestizo* Argentina that has had the worst record of instability in recent years; and *mestizo* Mexico that has broken out of the cycle. Still, as the Reichel-Dolmatoffs point out, the rigid, neurotic formality of the *mestizo* is a different thing from the "conservatism" of the traditional Indian. Ridden by resentment and frustration, and a constant fear of "exposure", the *mestizo* is a disruptive and, in this sense, a "revolutionary" element in Latin America. Yet a deeper reading of the *mestizo* mentality does not offer the professional revolutionary much comfort. The social aspirations of Aritama are directed towards *criollo*, "European" norms. They are not quite sure what they are; but they are quite sure that they want them. *Mestizo* attitudes towards *criollo* culture are imitative and deferential: in a word —conservative. The *mestizo*, as a psychological type, cannot be other than a conformist. I have discussed why the Communist parties of Latin America have met with so little success. The Reichel-Dolmatoff analysis confirms the impression that Latin America, for all its endemic violence, is politically a conservative rather than a revolutionary continent. Not that we should rejoice unthinkingly at the discomfiture of the professional revolutionary. For the same factors that make revolution unlikely make change of any kind problematical. And it is this that makes Latin America the despair of her admirers.

6

PERU:
or The Place That Is No Place

"What country can this be?" said Candide. "It must be unknown to the world, because everything is so different from what we are used to. It is probably the country where all goes well, for there must obviously be some such place. And whatever Professor Pangloss might say, I often noticed that all went badly in Westphalia."

Candide: Voltaire (1759)

Lima

LIMA IS LATIN AMERICA at its most unregenerate. She is
Pizarro's city: the City of the Kings; capital, in her day, of all
Spanish South America. In the eighteenth century, by all
accounts, she was richer and more ostentatious than any city in
Europe. I have said that the women of the Creoles, like their
churches, could seldom resist the temptation to overdress.
Fanny Calderon, in her sharp Scots way, noted this with disapproval in the Mexico of the 1830's. But Mexico, of course,
had proved a disappointment to her *conquistadores*. On their first
visit Cortes's men discovered the treasure of Montezuma
sealed up in the palace wall; with impressive self-denial they
promptly concealed it again. On their second appearance the
treasure had been spirited away. Cuautemoc and his paladins
were put to the torture; but to no avail. The lost treasure of the
Aztecs, still hopefully dug for, has never been recovered.
Perhaps, in a sense, it was never really there. Perhaps, despite
that sealed treasure-chamber, it was always more in the minds
of the *conquistadores* than in the vaults of Tenochtitlan. For
Mexico and Central America, like Spain's first possessions in
the Antilles, were not rich in gold. Later, in the Mexican eighteenth century, picturesque, Baroque Taxco was to found her
fortunes on silver. But it was Spain's other Viceroyalty,
Pizarro's Peru, that for three centuries supplied Europe with
precious metals. The Eldorado of the Incas proved to be the
more rewarding. For Atahualpa's ransom Pizarro had a room
piled as high with gold as a man might reach. The ornaments and
vases were then melted down, and Atahualpa strangled. Pizarro
made sure of his plunder. His *criollo* heirs have never let go.
In Peru you are closer to the *conquista*, to the splendours and
miseries of the Colonial age, than in any country in Latin
America.

There is no statue of Cortes to be found anywhere in Mexico.
In Lima, proudly prancing in the *Plaza de Armas*, there is a
statue of the mounted Pizarro. In Lima's Cathedral there is a

chapel where the reputed skeleton of the Conqueror can be seen in its glass coffin. The walls of the chapel are covered with a mosaic. It shows Pizarro, sword in hand, drawing a line in the sand. Those who would follow him to Peru are bidden to step across it; the others, the faint-hearts, are promised a free trip back to Panama—and no share of the gold. This Renaissance gesture was the founding act of the second *conquista* and of Spain's authority over South America. It echoes—and perhaps it is a deliberate echo—the foolhardy, magnificent gesture of Cortes in burning the ships with which his men might have got back to Cuba. But then, at so many points the conquest of Peru, like the character of Pizarro, reads like an imitation. Who can doubt that Pizarro's bold seizure of Atahualpa was inspired by Cortes's seizure of Montezuma fifteen years before? Not, of course, that either could have played the role allotted to the other. Cortes was the originator; Pizarro the imitator. History, which is said not to repeat itself, offered each the role suited to his character.

Cortes, let modern Mexicans say what they will, was a great man. And we know that he was so regarded by the peoples he conquered. He was a purer-bred *hidalgo*, certainly, than his distant cousin Francisco Pizarro. But the qualities Cortes possessed had little to do with *limpieza de sangre*. Cortes was a man of his time; a Knight of Faith, but also a Renaissance *uomo universale*. He was noble, less by birth, than by nature. Proof of Cortes's nobility of spirit is that he grasped that quality in others, regardless of lineage or complexion of skin. Certainly, he could be as wily and unscrupulous as the next man. But Cortes was not a man of gratuitous violence: his violence was no greater than that of other great captains of his age and it was commensurate with the perils he faced. Few men ever found themselves in a more desperate situation. Cortes's situation was desperate in a physical sense, but also because he was ignorant of the nature of his opponent. Generals, in Wellington's axiom, like to know what is happening "on the other side of the hill". Wellington knew, or partly knew; he could study Bonaparte's battle-order over twenty years of campaigning. Pizarro had less to go by. But he could guess, by studying Cortes's campaigns, where the superiority of the European over the Inca would lie. Superiority lay in the fire-power and the

horsemanship of the Spaniard. But it lay also in an audacity of
spirit that owed something (it must seem to us) to the chivalry
of the Age of Faith, but something also to the European self-
awareness of the Renaissance. The Spaniard won because,
imaginatively, he could take the measure of his enemy; the
Indian lost because he could not. Pizarro knew also, through
Cortes's experience, where the weakness of the Indian would lie:
in his despotic, centralised system of government, and in his
necessary ignorance of any other social organisation than his
own. Pizarro, then, knew a little of what was happening on the
other side of the hill. But Cortes knew nothing. Yet Cortes
guessed right; and to guess right, at such odds, amounts to
genius. Cortes is the companion of Caesar and Alexander;
Pizarro a Renaissance *condottiere*.

We cannot, of course, put down the differences between
modern Mexico and Peru to the character of their conquerors.
Certainly, if there were any justice in history, there would not
be a statue of Pizarro in Lima's *Plaza de Armas* and none of
Cortes in the length and breadth of Mexico. In Cortes's time,
and indeed later, Mexico's rulers cared for the Indian as far as
they could: the Indian was Mexico's chief source of wealth. If
millions died, they died of diseases of which Europeans themselves did not know the cause or the cure. And there is no doubt
that many Indians welcomed the Spaniards as liberators from
cruel and arbitrary oppression. In Peru, it was the other way
around. If Peru's *conquistadores* were crueller and more rapa-
cious, it was because they were obsessed with her mineral wealth,
and careless of her agricultural potential. The Incas, as far as
we can judge, were better masters than the Aztecs—and
certainly better than the Spaniards, if the test be the well-being
of the people. The Aztec Empire was more crudely exploita-
tive, though it was less destructive of local freedoms. The
Incas imposed a *gleichschaltung* on their subjects that the Aztecs
never attempted. Still, this *gleichschaltung* had a beneficial
aspect. The Incas, at the price of unconditional obedience, saw
to it that their subjects were well cared for. Nobody was free;
but nobody starved. This welfare-state aspect of Incadom gave
rise to that notion of it as a South American Utopia which can
be traced from Garcilaso Inca de la Vega, through Voltaire's
Candide, to modern apologists like Mr Edward Hyams. There

are reservations to be made about that notion, as we shall presently see. But that the Andean Indian lost more heavily by his change of masters than the Indian of Mexico is not in doubt. Still, it is Pizarro who has a statue in his honour; and Cortes who goes unremembered. Not that this is the Indian's fault. It is his masters who decide the matter: in Mexico, the Spaniard-hating *mestizo* who has come into Cortes's heritage; in Peru, the hard, unregenerate progeny of Pizarro's swash-bucklers.

The stuff of which the Peruvian *criollo* is made is apparent from Peruvian history. As late as 1782, the leader of an Indian rising, the self-styled Tupac Amaru II, was torn limb from limb by wild horses in the Cuzco's *Plaza de Armas*, his wife and children having been tortured to death before his eyes. In the 1930's, Haya de la Torre's *Apristas* killed with savagery, and were punished still more savagely by the *criollo* military. Latin America has known violence in many forms; but only in Mexico and Peru has this violence taken on the horrors of "racial" warfare. In Peru, the *criollo* caste—a mere 12 per cent of the population—is fiercely loyal to *hispanidad*; a pure Castilian is spoken; all good Peruvians are *aficionados* of the bull ring; and the Church is narrower and more fanatical than in any other country in South America. Peru is very Spanish. Her violence is reminiscent of the dark side of Spain's history, of the Carlists and Franco. It is tempting to compare Peru's *criollos* with the White Settlers of British Africa. In Colombia, as we saw, the power of the *criollo* oligarchy and its hangers-on is great. But they are numerically stronger than in Peru, and no "racial" challenge to their supremacy is conceivable. It is only in Peru, Ecuador and Bolivia, and perhaps Central America, the countries where the "pure" Indian is in the overwhelming majority, and where Quechua or Aymara offers a potential unifying factor, that "racial" revolt is even conceivable. Not that it is in the least probable. A White Settler minority, as in South Africa, can usually keep power if it is sufficiently determined and has a monopoly of arms. The Peruvian *criollo*, then, combines Spanish ferocity with the rigid, anxiety-ridden stance of Africa's White Settlers. The Peruvians are the Afrikaners of South America. Beneath his Sevillian lightness of spirit, the *Limeño* suffers the nightmares of Prospero: terror may not yet stalk by day, but his dreams are of Caliban's destroying hordes.

This night-aspect of Peru may escape the visitor *en route* for the exotic delights of Cuzco and Machu Picchu. But it is the constant theme of her writers and *pensadores*. Two of the earliest and most interesting critics of the modern Latin American *misère*, the unorthodox Marxist Mariategui and the founder of APRA, Haya de la Torre, come from Peru. Their political and social ideas—they advocated, among other things, a return to the collective clan-unit of the Inca *ayllu*—influenced like-minded reformers all over South America (most notably the *Accion Democratica* in Venezuela). Not surprisingly, most of Peru's intellectuals incline to the extreme left. Cesar Vallejo, who fought in the Spanish Civil War, is the finest poet to have come out of Spanish America in modern times—Pablo Neruda and Ruben Dario, larger, if less perfect talents, excepted. Like Neruda, and like Mariategui, Vallejo was a Marxist. In those same years Ciro Alegria, in his epic *The World is Wide and Alien*, became the vocal champion of the downtrodden Indian of the Andes: Alegria was the South American Steinbeck. Younger writers remain faithful to this tradition. *Lima la horrible* is the title of a study by the late Sebastian Salazar Bondi: a title that requires neither translation nor elaboration. A novel by Mario Vargas Llosa, perhaps the most gifted young writer to have come out of Latin America in the past decade, *La Ciudad y los Perros* (*The Time of the Hero*), for all its borrowing from the *nouveau roman* is a passionately committed exposure of Peruvian society. Semi-autobiographical, *The City and the Dogs* describes the life of a military cadet college on the outskirts of Lima. The cadets, though brutalised by the system, imitate its brutalities in the secret society they form to protect themselves from its inhumanity. Symbolically, the endemic violence of Peruvian society erupts in the murder, by a sadistic cadet, of a comrade suspected of "sneaking" to the authorities. There exist horrific novels about life in English public schools; in his *Törless* Robert Musil gave, in a similar account of cadet school bestialities, an unflattering portrait of Habsburg Austria. In the writing of this newest, most exciting recruit to Latin American letters, the night-aspect of this most arrogant, yet most anxiety-ridden of Latin American cultures is not neglected. Today, Vargas Llosa lives abroad. His book has been publicly burned by the school authorities in his native city. An ironist, Vargas Llosa must savour this tribute to one of Spain's oldest traditions. Vargas Llosa will be accused, no doubt, of giving further sustenance to the Black Legend of Peru. But it is his opponents, not he, who see to that.

The Golden Legend, and the Black, are complementary; you cannot have the one without the other. Alas for Peru, the latter is more likely to catch the visitor's eye. Colonial Lima was the handsomest town in Spanish America. But so much has been destroyed, first by earthquakes, later by speculators in real estate, that you would not know it today. Lima has many fine churches; but the exuberant fantasy of Mexico's *churrigueresque* is missing. Picturesque shuttered balconies, known as *miradores*, behind which one imagines the ladies of Colonial Lima reclining, fanned by Negro pages, as they watch the world go by— of these many remain, though in a sad state of repair. But the low-slung eighteenth-century skyline, pierced by the new banks and the soaring luxury hotels, is irretrievably spoilt. The City of the Kings, which boasted more carriages than any city in Europe, has to be rebuilt in the imagination. An early nineteenth-century traveller conveys something of *criollo* opulence (Juan de Ulloa, *Voyage to South America*, 1807):

> The riches and pomp of this city, especially on solemn festivals, are astonishing. The altars are covered with massive silver wrought into various kinds of ornaments. . . . Divine service, in these churches, is performed with a magnificence scarce to be imagined, and the ornaments, even on common days, with regard to their quantity, and richness, exceed those which many cities of Europe pride themselves with displaying on the most solemn occasions.

The women of the *criollos* enjoyed a luxury only the wealthiest of peninsular grandees can have rivalled:

> They are fond of white silk stockings, made extremely thin, that the leg may appear the more shapely; the greatest part of which is exposed to view. These trifles often afford very sprightly sallies of wit in their animadversions on the dress of others . . . a lady covered with the most expensive lace instead of linen, and glittering from head to foot with jewels, is supposed to be dressed at the expense of not less than thirty or forty thousand crowns: a splendour still more astonishing, as it is so very common.

Visually, little of that Lima remains. No painter recorded that feckless, profoundly materialistic society in the days of its glory. The *criollo*'s notion of art did not extend beyond the decorative. True, in the sketches of Johann Georg Rugendas, done in the eighteen-thirties, we catch something of the sunset-glow of that gold-gorged society. Rugendas was a German of the Romantic generation, a protégé of von Humboldt, who spent many years in Brazil and Spanish America, recording their exotic landscapes and scarcely less exotic manners. Rugendas is a minor figure in the history of painting. But without Rugendas we should know little of how Latin America looked to the foreigner's eye on the morrow of Independence. Or rather, we should be dependent on the written word: on Fanny Calderon, on Charles Waterton, on Maria Williams, on Darwin's *Voyage of the Beagle*. What took Rugendas' fancy in particular was the unique head-gear of the ladies of Lima, the *tapada*. The *tapada* was a black silk shawl, draped over the face, neck and shoulder, a single dark, lustrous eye remaining visible to the beholder. A provocative garment; and Rugendas, the northerner, became infatuated with it. He painted *tapadas* on the street, behind *miradores*, at Viceregal balls; mysteriously veiled, his *Limeñas* are caught up in a perpetual round of flirtatious intrigue. His painting of a bevy of *tapada*-clad ladies kneeling in languorous devotion in the cathedral—a minor Romantic masterpiece, surely—suggests the correct adjective for Lima: she is Andalusian. The hot blood, the love of display, the provocative combination of seclusion and flirtatiousness: all these are Andalusian, indeed Moorish characteristics. The splendid palace of the Marquises of Torre Tagle, best-preserved of Lima's Colonial mansions, is unmistakably Andalusian. Lima, then, is the Seville of Spanish America. For the origins of the *tapada* we need not look far: the *tapada* is what Catholic Peru has made of the *yashmak* of the Moors.

Cuzco

Nature divides Peru into three parts. Lima, though the most powerful of these parts, is the least in extent and, to most foreigners, in interest. At the turn of the century, Lima was one of the minor cities of Latin America, her glory diminished since

Colonial days. (Peru was the only real loser, apart from Spain herself, in the Independence struggle.) But this has changed over the past generation: today's Lima, with a population of two million, ranks with the half-dozen major cities of Latin America. In another generation, she will be what Mexico City and São Paulo are today: a huge, sprawling, squalid, yet potentially immensely dynamic concentration of human energy. There are other important cities in coastal Peru: Trujillo in the north, and Arequipa in the south. But Lima is, and will remain, what Pizarro meant her to be: the Queen of the Pacific. Still, coastal Peru, though it dominates political and economic life, is only one tenth of the country by area and has hardly more than a quarter of the population. It owes its economic power to the presence of guano and petroleum; and to the circumstance that this coastal plain, otherwise a rainless desert, can be made fertile by irrigation. Beyond the dry coastal strip rise the massive walls of the Andean *sierra* which, towards the south, merge into the high, infertile plateau of the Bolivian *puna*. The Andean valleys are fertile and, towards the east, well-watered. It is here that the mass of Peru's population is to be found. But here a "racial" difference becomes marked. Apart from a tiny, landlord class of *criollo* descent, and a *mestizo* middle class in the towns, the *serranos* are pure Indian. They are the direct descendants of the Incas, and of the tribes subjugated by the Incas; and they speak Quechua in preference to Spanish. Indeed, many still speak no Spanish at all.

Beyond the *sierra* lies a third Peru, one scarcely better known to the Peruvian than to the foreigner. This huge area of tropical forest and jungle, the *montaña*, forms 60 per cent of the land area, though it has no more than 12 per cent of the population. It is said to be potentially rich in oil and tropical products; and Peruvian politicians like to picture it an economic Eldorado, able to solve Peru's economic problems (economists are more sceptical as to its potentialities). This vast hinterland the conquerors, like the Incas, scarcely penetrated. Geographically, it forms part of the rim of that huge steaming saucer, more than two thousand miles wide, that is the "green heart" of South America. Only a few miles to the east of the *sierra*, therefore, we enter a world that is more familiar from North America: the world of the Plains Indians, from which the Aztecs emerged.

On the *sierra*, and along the coastal strip, civilisations have
risen and fallen over the ages. Across the Amazonian saucer,
even within historical times, vast nomadic migrations and
völkerwanderungen have occurred: these survive in legend, but no
historical record of them is likely to be recovered. This is a
different world: that "savage" world, primitive but complex,
Lévi-Strauss depicts in *Tristes Tropiques*. Peru is the place for
those who like their history romantic. An hour in the plane
from Lima, and you are back in the Middle Ages: two hours
and a half, and the Faucett Company's time-machine lands
you safely in the neolithic.

   To visit Cuzco, even in the air age, is something of an expedition. Cuzco and Machu Picchu, of course, are *yanqui* tourist
attractions. Not that they are to be left out on that account;
they are among the most extraordinary places in the world.
Still, it is well to be forewarned. There is trouble with the
altitude: Cuzco lies at 11,000 feet. The mountain-dwelling
Incas may not have flinched at this. Indeed, it may have given
them a decisive advantage over the softer-living coastal peoples,
the head-waters of whose valleys they were able to control.
But it is a height the most robust of modern globe-trotters will
find trying. The Mountain Indian is adapted to this environment; his broad body, low stature, and swinging gait are
nature's answer to the thin air of the *sierra*. When the *serrano*
comes down to work on the coast, it is he who is maladapted.
As the Spaniards found—it was one reason why they imported
Negro slaves—he falls an easy victim to disease in this environment. The European, too, can adapt to life in these altitudes;
his haemoglobin increases; he learns not to over-exert himself.
But it takes time, and an hour's flight from Lima is not time
enough. The scene in the airplane, as you cross the crumpled
cardboard of the Andes at 18,000 feet, is both painful and comic:
something between a maternity hospital and an Arabian orgy.
You lie back obediently, and suck in the life-giving oxygen
from long, hookah-like rubber tubes dangling from the roof
of the fuselage. Maternally, hostesses warn of the dire effects of
withdrawal: *soroche*, the mountain-sickness, nausea, loss of
consciousness. Looking around—a lady has just fainted—you
note the penalties of disobedience: you suck dutifully, and
survive. Still, the ordeal is not over. The flight is bad enough;

but return to *terra firma* brings no relief. Life at 11,000 feet is like learning to walk all over again. Don't lift your feet! Don't exert yourself unduly! You do not need the warning. Your feet have turned to lead. It is all you can do to drag yourself up to your hotel bedroom to take the mandatory two-hour rest before exploring the wonders of Cuzco.

Cuzco does not disappoint. Despite the earthquake of 1950, most of its churches and palaces, built by Pizarro's men on the ruins of the Inca Cuzco, are still in good condition. *La Compañia*, the Jesuit church, the Cathedral, and the monastery of *La Merced*, are as fine ecclesiastical architecture as is to be found in the Americas. At a first glance, Cuzco seems as Spanish as a small cathedral town in Castile or Extremadura. Here in Cuzco, as in Santillana del Mar or Trujillo, are those modest, rectangular town houses of the local *hidalgos*, their escutcheons carved in grey stone over the doors. Pizarro and his brothers, illegitimate sons of a Trujillo swineherd, built themselves houses such as these; first in Cuzco, then—as if to make doubly sure of their hard-won nobility—in their native Trujillo. Interestingly, nobility was never thought to be a property of Spaniards alone. On the contrary, the Spaniards were anxious to confirm their title to the land by marrying the best blood they could find. Thus, near *La Merced* stands the stone house where the father of Garcilaso de la Vega, author of the *Royal Commentaries*, lived in great state with his concubine, an Inca princess and niece of the Huayna Capac. The notion that Inca society came to an end with Pizarro's killing of Atahualpa is too simple. The Spaniards—anticipating the British formula of "indirect rule" —had Manco II crowned Inca in 1535. Withdrawing to Vilcapampas, Manco II set up a neo-Inca state, which survived until his successor, Tupac Amaru, was captured and barbarously put to death in Cuzco in 1572. Two hundred years later his supposed descendant, Tupac Amaru II, led an Indian revolt against the Spaniards—Francisco de Miranda, first of the liberators of Spanish America, brought it to Pitt's attention in London—and was executed in the city. Some paintings in the church of Santa Ana, dusty and neglected, but uniquely fascinating, show church processions of the late seventeenth century in which the drum-majors (as Mr Sacheverell Sitwell calls them in his *Golden Wall and Mirador*) are to be seen wearing

Inca costume. The populace looks on at the spectacle, as it looks on now, with the same cool, deferential indifference we noted in the descendants of the Aztecs and the Mayas.

Once again, then, the Spanish veneer is no more than skin-deep. There is no way of calculating the volume of Spanish blood flowing in *cuzqueño* veins; but it cannot be very great. The clerks and shopkeepers of Cuzco belong to the *cholo* (*mestizo*) caste. Their women wear the curious grey-felt bowler hat, the status symbol of the *cholo* from Ecuador to Bolivia. That "caste" is the right term nobody who visits the "colourful Indian market" of Pisac, near Cuzco, can doubt. The tourist attraction of Pisac is Sunday mass, to which the Indians and *cholos* of the surrounding countryside come, and during which —at the moment of elevation—a weird cacophony of conch-sounds is let loose upon the ether. It is a strange scene, more like something in Ethiopia or Tibet than anything in Catholic Christendom. Yet nobody who has witnessed it can doubt that, had it not been for the friars and Jesuits who followed in the wake of the *conquistadores*, Spain would have left little impression on the Indian mind. (In Cuzco, I was lucky enough to witness the performance, in the open air, of a Nativity play in Quechua; a lineal descendant, no doubt, of those Didactic Plays in Quechua the Jesuits introduced in the seventeenth century.) In the market of Pisac something different may be observed. The distinction between *cholo* and Indian is apparent to the eye. The *cholos*, the mixed-blood market women, wear their felt hats and their more-or-less European-style clothes. The Indian women wear their "native" skirts and *ponchos*; and it is their colourful costume that attracts the tourists to Pisac. How "native" these costumes really are may be questioned. The fine weaving and dyeing may well be an Inca or even pre-Inca inheritance; but the designs point to borrowings from European costume of the sixteenth or seventeenth centuries. Like most European *volkskunst*, Peru's art of the people is really an imitation of the art of their masters.

Criollo; cholo; indio: there are further subdivisions, imperceptible to the foreign eye, but it is this threefold caste system that dominates *serrano* society. We discussed the appropriateness of the term "caste" in the Mexican context. We concluded that, if allowance is made for a degree of upward mobility between "castes"—the Indian who adopts European dress and speaks Spanish acquiring *mestizo* status—the term is apposite. This mobility, as in the case of Aritama, is as much collective as individual. The individual Indian can shed his skin as the individual Black American or South African cannot. Whether he can hope for complete acceptance by the "White" ruling group will vary from country to country. In Peru and Ecuador he probably cannot; in Bolivia or Venezuela his chances are better. Collectively, it is evident that just as a low Hindu caste can hope to improve its stature and achieve greater "respect" within the caste-structure, so an Indian village can acquire *mestizo* or *cholo* characteristics and merge into the general life of the nation. This is the grain of truth in Latin America's much-boosted claim to have "solved the race problem".

We noted that this mobility had interesting political implications. It worked against the formation of a separate "Indian" consciousness, and indeed against "revolutionary" consciousness in general. The populist parties of Latin America have two characteristics which are closely related. All are *mestizo* parties; and all have moved away from their revolutionary origins towards a moderate social-democratic view. It is true that Western European socialism has evolved in a similar direction. But it would be a mistake to read European influence into this shift of position. (There are few political ties between these Latin American parties and their European counterparts.) These parties are an indigenous American phenomenon. Their shift to the centre, at a time when anti-Americanism and Castroism are powerful, must be explained in indigenous terms. APRA itself, it is true, only achieved power for a brief, disastrous period after 1945. It has long since ceased to be true to its founding title of "American Popular Revolutionary Alliance". But it has called into being other parties—ex-President Belaunde's failing *Accion Popular* and the Christian Democrats—which appeal to the same electorate in the same language. The Communists, as elsewhere in Latin America, have little more than nuisance value. They are strong, as it happens, in the Cuzco area; but their power is not great in the advanced coastal strip of Peru. We have looked at the reasons for the failure of Communism in Latin America. The same reasons help to explain the opposite phenomenon, the success of these left-

wing, but only vaguely ideological parties. It is at bottom the
mestizo basis of these parties—with all that it implies of a desire
to assimilate to the *criollo* norm—that causes them to gravitate
to the political centre. If we choose to listen, what we hear in
those movements is the voice of the *mestizo* caste demanding its
place in the sun.

Despite appearances, then, Peru fits into the Latin American
pattern. For all her reactionary traditions—long spells of rule
by military *caudillo*, a narrow and selfish oligarchy, an ecclesiastical hierarchy as hidebound as any in the Latin world—
today's Peru is a progressive country by Latin American
standards. It is true of Peru, as it is of Brazil or Argentina,
that the military hold the ultimate sanction: all political
advance takes place in the shadow of the man on horseback.
But it would be wrong to identify the military with the *criollo*
oligarchy. There are political divisions among the military
themselves. There are extreme, right-wing *"gorilas"*; and
youngish, "Nasserist" colonels, whose sympathies lie with the
reformist politicians and the new technocrats. If the reformers
should seem to go too fast, like Peru's APRA and Venezuela's
Accion Democratica between 1945 and 1948, the Army withdraws
its support. But that is not the end of the matter. Once rid of the
politicians the Army must run the show on its own. This
proves more arduous in practice than it seemed on the sand-
table. Allies must be sought, compromises entered into. Soon
enough, the Army finds itself playing the same game as the
politicians it has bundled out of office. It is then that disillusionment sets in. Two courses are open; continuance of military
dictatorship, with all the risks of growing unpopularity and
growing unrest, or strategic withdrawal, followed by new
elections. Thus the past relatively progressive constellation
of forces in Peru—APRA, *Accion Popular* and Christian Democracy—was less fragile than it seemed. Experience shows that
military intervention can postpone demands for social reform.
But it can seldom eliminate them altogether. The military—
or at least some elements among the military—are by now
aware of this. They fear most, of course, the abolition of their
privileged position. But as long as that position could be preserved, they seemed willing to tolerate the new political forces.
There was nothing sentimental about this tolerance: it was dictated

by political opportunism. Now, intervention has taken place:
we shall examine its logic in greater detail in Argentina's case.

Machu Picchu

Modern Peru, then, resembles her neighbours more closely
than one might think. Still, a startling difference remains: of
Peru's thirteen millions half are Quechua-speaking *serrano*
Indians, and these are excluded for all practical purposes from
the life of the nation. Only in Ecuador and Central America do
we find anything like this: but these are small fry, while Peru
ranks fifth among the nations of Latin America. And Peru, lest
we forget, was the seat not only of the Spanish Viceroys, but
also of the greatest empire of pre-Columbian America. Here
then, in the *sierra*, is Indian country *par excellence*. The dwelling-
unit is the ancient, pre-Inca *ayllu*; and the still-spoken Quechua
tongue is thought to have changed little since Inca times. To
all intents and purposes, then, these Indians of the *sierra* are the
same people Atahualpa ruled four and a half centuries ago.
Yet what does that tell us? Are they the inheritors of that
culture in any meaningful sense? It is the same problem we met
in Mexico and Guatemala: granted the Mayan and the Aztec
enjoyed an advanced civilisation, how much of it can be said to
survive in his lineal descendant? And how much of what survives
can be carried over into the modern culture of the nation?

The answer, in the case of Mexico, was inclined to be negative. Despite the official propaganda, *pace* the Indigenous
Institute and the Anthropological Museum, it seemed inevitable that progress—in education, in hygiene, in technology—
must mean Hispanisation. True, the collective agricultural unit
favoured by the Mexican Revolution—the *ejido*—is claimed to
have pre-Hispanic roots. As we have seen, similar claims are
made for the pre-Hispanic *ayllu*; and other parties have adopted
this part of the traditional APRA programme. But how
seriously can we take this? To the foreigner the Mexican *ejido*
looks like the Israeli *kibbutz*: more ideological shibboleth
than economic cure-all. It is tempting, again, to draw parallels
between the agrarian revolutionism of Mariategui and Haya
de la Torre and the theories evolved by Mao Tse-tung at the
same period. According to Chinese doctrine, Latin America,

and particularly her indigenous Indian population, form part
of that peripheral, agrarian zone whose revolt against the cities
is the distinguishing feature of our time. The parallel is tempting; but almost certainly misleading. We have seen the fallacy
of this view in the case of Cuba. Castro and Guevara were
fond of citing Mao's theories; but they based their practice on
Hispanic tradition of guerrilla fighting. And, whatever the Latin
American left may think, they did not come to power by these
means. Their victory was altogether conventional within the
Latin American context.

It may be said that the *campesino* or the *gaucho*, under a powerful *caudillo*, has been a revolutionary factor in the past. Up to
a point this is true. The post-Independence anti-Centralist
caudillos often drew on this potential; and the tradition persisted in such figures as Gomez of Venezuela, Vargas of Brazil,
and even Argentina's Peron. But the end-result was always the
same. A "federalist" *caudillo*—Rosas or Gomez or Obregon—
had only to win power at the centre to become the very model
of a "centralist" dictator. And naturally so. For a centralised,
bureaucratic government machine is one of the chief legacies of
Spanish rule. The quarrel is over who should control this
machine, the legitimacy of which, unlike that of its masters, is
never in question. Such a government machine, situated in the
capital, cannot be anything but an agent of Hispanisation. This
is evident in the case of Mexico; we can follow the stages by
which the agrarian radicalism of a Pancho Villa or a Zapata
yielded to the centralism of Calles and Obregon—themselves,
of course, provincial *caudillos* by origin. And this is the universal
pattern. Whatever its validity in Asia, with its ancient village-
centred cultures, in Latin America agrarian revolution is a
myth. Power is always centred in the city. The Communists,
as we have seen, are aware of this. They make it their business
to keep in with those who wield power at the centre; with
Trujillo, with Batista, with Peron, with Fidel Castro. Nor is it
accidental that Latin America's first Communist government
should be the most centralised of them all.

Must we conclude that the "Indian" heritage, or what
survives of it, is doomed? And doomed the more certainly, the
quicker the forces of progress do their work? It would certainly
appear so. And I am not alone, I suspect, in finding the prospect

distressing. Sceptical as one may be of the *indigenistas*, it is natural to shed a tear at the passing of these remnants of ancient America. We have touched on that cruel irony underlying Latin America's "racial tolerance": that the racially-tolerant Iberians may prove to have been more deadly enemies to the aboriginal cultures with whom they came in contact than the Anglo-Saxons. There are, of course, good reasons why this should be so. The Anglo-Saxon impact was neither so intense nor so long-lasting; and the resilience of the aboriginal cultures was generally greater. Indeed, so great was their resilience that in many cases European hegemony merely provided the shock needed for internal renewal (India and China are the obvious examples). But nowhere in America, Latin or Anglo-Saxon, has that proved the case. We can be fairly certain that the traditional values of India, China and Japan will be carried over into modern society. But the traditional values of pre-Columbian America, where they are not already lost, seem certain to receive their *coup de grâce* at the hands of a mongrel Europeanism. The steel mill and the oil derrick will finish the job Cortes and Pizarro began.

Machu Picchu is the spot for such melancholy reflections. This lost Inca town among the Andes has become one of the high places of pan-American romanticism—and a major tourist attraction. That it does not, historically, deserve its reputation disturbs nobody any more. Hiram Bingham, who discovered the city in 1911, was an American Schliemann (appropriately, Machu Picchu looks remarkably like Mycenae). Bingham maintained the Virgins of the Sun had fled here after the sacking of Cuzco, and that the city remained a secret centre of resistance to the conqueror. In fact, there is no reason to think that "Machu Picchu" (we do not know its Inca name) was more than one of a chain of forts built by the Incas to keep the tribes of the *montaña* at bay. Its interest is that it was never discovered by the Spaniards, and has remained relatively unspoilt. Its terraced gardens and exquisitely finished masonry can be found elsewhere, though rarely in such good condition. They are striking evidence of Inca competence in the arts of practical civilisation. Competence, perhaps, is the word: for I admit, personally, to a lack of enthusiasm for things Inca. The Incas may have been good administrators and good

engineers. But as artists they were as inferior to the cultures
that preceded them (Nazca, Paracas, Tiahuanaco) as were the
Romans to the Greeks. Though possibly less bloody-minded
than the Aztecs, they seem to have lacked their syncretistic
genius. With the Aztecs one feels that the elements of a great
civilisation were present, and were brutally cut short. With the
Incas one is less sure. The uniformity the Incas imposed on
their Empire is impressive—the Aztec Empire was no more
than an agglomeration of tributary cities—but also depressing.
The Inca's passion for administration and engineering suggests
that the developed Inca civilisation might have been not unlike
Imperial Rome. It would have been a body without a soul;
materially imposing, at heart hollow and weary of life.

These are heretical thoughts. And they matter little: for the
significance of Machu Picchu is symbolic. Here, the setting
helps. It is as if Mycenae were set, not among the chiselled,
weathered ranges of the Peloponnese, but in a landscape altogether harsher and more savage. To Claude Lévi-Strauss
this virginal quality, this innocence of humanity, is the defining
characteristic of American landscape—an *Urlandschaft*, if ever
there was one. Yet we should be on our guard. In one of his
greatest poems, "The Heights of Machu Picchu", Pablo Neruda
has invoked Machu Picchu in this spirit, as a "place of beginnings", with a certain poetic licence, for the Andes are young
as mountains go, and retain the awkward angularity of
youth:

> Here is permanence of stone and the word:
> The city is raised up, like a bowl, in the hands
> Of mankind, the living, the dead, the unsleeping; sustained
> By this death; a bastion; their lives like a blow
> Of stone petals falling: rose of permanence; place
> Of fixed abode in a glacial sea; reef of the Andes.
>
> Now when the hand, hand the colour of clay,
> Turns back to clay, and the tiny eyelids shut
> Full of rough walls, peopled with castles;
> When our human thread's tangled and torn—
> There remains, hoisted high, a truth of precision;
> This is the high place of humanity's dawn
> A lofty vessel replete with silence;
> A life of stone outlasting so many lives.

Neruda being the controversial figure he is, malicious tongues assert that, having hauled his great bulk up the mountain side, he stayed no more than ten minutes in the place. But why so pedantic? Machu Picchu has long since ceased to belong to the archaeologists. It fulfils a need, a need not easily satisfied in the Americas. "*America, du hast es besser, du hast keine verfallenen Schlösser*". But Goethe was wrong: America, expecially Latin America, does have her monuments, her palaces, her places of pilgrimage. It is this that gives her that "European" aspect seldom found in the United States outside New England and the South. Still, it is not enough. Latin America is an ambitious culture. And she lacks those shrines of national identity which Europeans take for granted: the Parthenon, St Peter's, the Escorial, Versailles, the Palace of Westminster. It is not that Latin America is too young to be the proud possessor of such shrines. She is not in fact so young; and her Mayan ruins, and even Antigua and Ouro Preto, can hold their own with Europe's *verfallene Schlosser*.

The problem is this: the traveller cannot avoid a sense—Latin Americans evidently have it too—that the centre of this civilisation lies, as it were, beyond its own circumference. The Escorial, for traditionalists, may be such a centre. But most Spanish Americans have put aside Spain and her Black Legend. For a few sophisticates, and for many intellectuals, Paris is such a centre. But France, *positiviste* or *marxisant*, is too tidy, too rationalist a culture to suit most Latin Americans. For the good Catholic, no doubt, Rome is such a centre. But at home? There are the monuments, secular and religious, of the Colonial Age. But these are, precisely, *colonial*. They have decorative charm; but there is little original or creative about them. There are, of course, the great monuments of pre-Columbian civilisation. These cannot be denied originality. But what meaning do they bear for the Latin America of today: *criollo*, *mestizo* or pure-blooded Indian? The need for a Latin American Parthenon, a high place the nations can feel to be the cradle of their race, the source and focus of their energies, is therefore acute. In his *Canto General*, the great epic about America from which "The Heights of Machu Picchu" is taken, Neruda was in search of such a place. That he chose Machu Picchu, beloved of the *yanqui* tourist, has a certain irony. A lesser man would

have been glad to borrow Machu Picchu's latterday fame. It is
a measure of Neruda's stature that he has added to the fame of
Latin America's most famous ancient monument.

Realistically, then, Machu Picchu is neither the world's
navel, nor the place of humanity's beginnings. It is a pictures-
quely-situated Inca hill-fortress, of rather slight artistic interest,
probably predating the Conquest by not more than a century.
Culturally, it should be classified rather with Hadrian's Wall
than with the Parthenon. Not that it matters. Neruda is a great
poet, and deserves a poet's licence. Still, Neruda's is a traditional quest—more traditional, perhaps, than he realised.
According to the Black Legend, the *conquistadores* were a band
of gold-grabbing roughnecks, clothing squalid ambition in the
rhetoric of the *Siglo de Oro*. But the *conquistadores'* motives cannot,
as we have seen, be reduced to a formula. They were Spaniards,
and Spaniards of the Renaissance; but in the Spain of the
Renaissance, of a sudden Europe's leading power, lingered
more of the crusading spirit of the Middle Ages than in the
rest of Europe. The Spaniards of Cortes's time still read their St
Thomas and their St Augustine. But they also read St Thomas
à Kempis, Petrarch, and Erasmus—especially Erasmus—and
Amadis of Gaula: all the new literature flooding from the
printing presses of Europe. It was as if Flanders had undertaken
the education of Castile. The *Conquistadores* were the last of the
Crusaders. But they were also practical men who saw no
reason why Christian men, fighting the *paynim*, should not look
to their fortunes. They had, then, much of Sancho Panza in
their make-up. Yet, like Don Quixote, they were great readers
of the novels of chivalry. That it should be Romantic writers
—Keats and Southey and Washington Irving—and Romantic
historians—Prescott and Ticknor and Parkman—who first
broke the anti-Hispanic mould of their society and responded
to the romance of the *conquista* is appropriate. For the *conquistadores*, too, were Romantics. If we wish, we may see the
Conquest of the New World as the first of the gold-rushes.
But we miss the point if we do not see it at the same time as the
most sustained of Europe's mythopoetic enterprises.

If we wish to understand Latin America, then, we must be
careful to distinguish the myth from the reality. But we must not
despise the myth. We have seen how elusive is the search for

"the Indian": he is a being mysteriously present and yet not present. Yet of the importance of "the Indian" in the collective psychology of Latin America there is no doubt. For the *mestizo* he is a potential threat: he represents the magical past from which he is trying to escape. For the *criollo*, the Indian is also a threat, but in a different way. He is not a threat to the integrity of his personality. But he is the original owner of the land, refusing even now to accept the conqueror and his ways. He is a watchful, unsleeping eye, never wholly to be exorcised. Here then, the myth invades the reality. Of the actual life of the Indian in the Guatemalan highlands, or in the Peruvian *sierra*, the *criollo* knows little. But it makes itself felt. The *criollo*'s myth of the Indian, of course, is as unflattering, and as inaccurate, as the White Settler's myth of the African. But the "bad" Indian myth of the *criollo* has this in common with the "good" Indian myth of Rousseauvian Europe: it is not the actual, but the imputed qualities of the Indian that count. If we wish to explain the myth of the Noble Savage we must psychoanalyse the European, not the Indian; Prospero, not Caliban.

Brave New World

Perhaps, then, we cannot distinguish the myth from the reality after all. Even the earliest explorers—it is from them we derive our myth of the Noble Savage—cast the spell of their subjectivity over the world they had discovered. The tragedy of the New World is that she never had a chance to be new. No sooner discovered, she became the field of projection of her conquerors' fantasies, fantasies that had their origin in the turbulent, questing spirit of late-medieval Europe. Yet the paradox is that this New World, whose tragedy is that she was never new, becomes a new world again for each European enquirer who sets foot on her soil. Of his first trip to the New World Lévi-Strauss wrote in *Tristes Tropiques*:

> The charcoal skies and lowering atmosphere of the doldrums summarise the state of mind in which the Old World first came on the New. This lugubrious frontier area, this lull before the storm in which the forces of evil alone seem to flourish, is the last barrier between what were once—quite recently—two planets so

different from one another that our first explorers could not believe they were inhabited by members of the same race. The one, hardly touched by mankind, lay open to men whose greed could no longer be satisfied in the other. A second Fall was about to bring everything into question: God, morality and the law. The Garden of Eden was found to be true, for instance; likewise the ancient Golden Age, the Fountain of Youth, Atlantis, the Gardens of the Hesperides, the pastoral poems, and the Fortunate Islands.

A definitive history of this strangest of human adventures has not been written. Nor would it be easy to write: for the discovery of the New World, coming when it did, exercised the imagination not only of historians, but of theologians and philosophers, poets and statesmen and merchant-adventurers. A history of that encounter would be a history of the aspirations and illusions of Europe in the Age of the Renaissance and the Reformation. Lévi-Strauss remarks of that encounter:

> Never has the human race been faced with such a terrible ordeal; nor will such a one ever recur, unless there should one day be revealed to us another earth with thinking beings on it.

It may be that such a history is impossible to write. The field is too vast and ill-defined; the theme, of its nature, lacks coherence. For the discovery of the New World meant all things to all men. To the Puritan, the New World was a citadel for the Saints of God. To the Kings of Spain it was a sign of God's favour to the hard-pressed champions of the Counter-Reformation. The New World became a projection of the aspirations of the Old. And these aspirations were as contradictory as the age that bore them.

Can that be all? Is there nothing these aspirations have in common apart from their newness? Is the fascination of "newness" mere seeking for novelty? If we turn the question round we see that there may be, after all, a common element. To call it "optimism" would be putting it too low; to call it "millenarianism", perhaps, too high. But why is it—to put the question in its naïvest form—that the Europeans of the sixteenth century should have thought a new world likely to be a *better* world? Europeans had long been aware of the existence of civilisations unlike their own. The Spaniards, with their experience of the *reconquista*, more than most. They had accepted for centuries that Islamic civilisation—and possibly Indian and Chinese—were in certain respects superior to their own. Yet they never felt about these cultures as they felt about America. The American discoveries, it may be said, came as a shock; the European mind was unprepared for them, and the degree of strangeness was out of all comparison. But how far is this so? Nothing is stranger in Bernal Diaz's account of the *conquista* than that the *conquistadores*, for all their sense of wonder, found Aztec ways so little strange. Practical men, they applied what they had learnt in Flanders, or in Italy under *el Gran Capitan*, to this new field of action. The Aztecs were pagans and idolaters: we would expect the Spaniards to take this in their stride; many of them must have fought against the Moorish infidel in Africa. True, we do not expect conquerors to indulge in sentimental fantasies about a ferocious and hardly-vanquished enemy. This is for the camp-followers, moralising priests like Las Casas, self-appointed champion of the Red Man, in the safety of the Court of Castile or the University of Salamanca. How, then, do we account for that uprush of Utopian sentiment about the Red Man, both in his savage state and as an Imperial master? Within fifty years of the Conquest Montaigne could write:

> Our world of late has discovered another, no less large, fully peopled, yielding in all things and mighty in strength than ours; nevertheless so new and infantile that it has yet to learn its ABC. . . . If we rightly conclude about our end, the late world shall only come to light when ours shall fall into darkness. . . . It was an unpolluted, harmless, infant world. . . . They were nothing thanking us, nor beholding to us for any excellence of natural wit. . . . The magnificence of the never-like seen cities of Cuzco and Mexico . . . show that they yielded as little to us in cunning and industry. But concerning unfeigned devotion, awful observance of laws, unspotted integrity, bounteous liberality, due loyalty and free liberty, it has greatly aided us that we had not as much as they, for by that advantage they have lost, cast away, sold, undone and betrayed themselves.

We know something of what lay behind such sentiments, in which we hear Rousseau's thought anticipated. There are parallels in every European country: in the England of Thomas

More and of Shakespeare (Prospero's island is based on an
account of Bermuda); in the Germany of Dürer, or the Florence
of Benvenuto Cellini (who saw and admired the treasures the
conquistadores sent to the Emperor Charles V; the unwilling
tribute, as it were, of the New World to the Old). Anti-Spanish
feeling among Protestants played a part. Las Casas' indictment
of the violence of the Spaniards in the New World—the
origin of the Black Legend—bred a counter-legend. In the end,
the Spanish Court adopted Las Casas' view that the Indians had
souls: they could not justly be enslaved. They must be treated
as subjects of the Crown and brought into the Catholic fold.
But many champions of the Indian went further. Indians might
not be subjected to the attentions of the Inquisition; it could be
said of them, as it could not of Jews or Moors, that they knew
not what they did. This theological argument protected the
Indians from many of the horrors to which other non-Europeans
—black-skinned slaves from Africa, for example—were later subjected. (Why it was contrary to Aristotle's doctrines to enslave
Red Men, but not to enslave Black Men, remains a mystery.)

Can we not detect in this argument the seed of Rousseau's
Pelagianism: the heretical thought that for the people of the
New World the Fall might not have occurred? Certainly, the
danger is plain. For to assert that human societies exist, of
equal antiquity to our own, that have remained free of the
curse of original sin, is close to asserting that there are some men
who do not need Christ, being innocent by nature and capable
of self-redemption. Perhaps, then, it is society that is at fault?
Perhaps, if that evil mould were broken, the salvation of Man
might be assured—assured, that is, by Man? Such thoughts, no
doubt, were far from the minds of Las Casas and his friends.
But the implication is there. There is a road from the benevolent exaggerations of Las Casas to the Pelagianism of
Montaigne and Rousseau and the ideologists of the modern
age.

Let us, at this point, draw the threads together. I have
identified the Utopianism of the modern age with Pelagianism;
that is, with Christian heresy, implying neither assent nor disapproval. But it is a fact that, in traditional Christianity, these
notions represent a deviation from the norm of orthodoxy. If a
man can see to his own redemption, then he does not need

Christ. And if he does not need Christ, then he does not need the Church and its teachings. Further, if man is able to see to his own redemption, it becomes meaningful for him to direct his efforts to that end. The age of faith is past; let the age of good works commence! If America had been the home of a perfectible society in the past, why should man not build Jerusalem on her soil in the future? That these heretical notions should have arisen in the Age of Discovery may be coincidental. It is likely that they would have arisen in any case. Their appearance at this moment, however, gave the discovery of America a significance it would not otherwise have had. Tenochtitlan was conquered while Luther, in the shelter of the Wartburg, was translating the Bible into vernacular German. Luther, least of all men, would have given his blessing to the Utopian notions the discovery of America was to set in train. How ironical, then, that it should be the originally Augustinian, anti-Pelagian Reformation that contributed the most powerful element to the Pelagianism of the modern world: the civilisation of North America. If America—and by America I mean Latin and Indian, as well as Anglo-Saxon America—often seems a tragic continent to the European, the reason is plain. It is because America is a region of his own mind. For the American, America may be God's own country. But for the European she is something disturbingly familiar; she embodies Europe's greatest heresy.

American Utopianism has taken many bizarre forms. According to taste, we may find the practical or the theoretical implications of greater moment. Certainly, the intellectual repercussions of Columbus's landfall are of unique fascination. The train of thought it set in motion is not exhausted even now. Yet it is, perhaps, the practical implications that should concern us: the painful contrast, for example, between the triumphant North American conquest of the wilderness and the sense of failure that dogs the America of the Latins. We shall see this theme worked out in two of the greatest works of Latin American literature: Sarmiento's *Facundo* and da Cunha's *Rebellion in the Backlands*. Certainly, even in the world of practical men, there are no limits to the extravagances American Utopianism can inspire. Sir Walter Raleigh ruined himself on the Orinoco expedition; three centuries later men were ruining themselves in the gold-rushes of Yukon and California. In literature, the theme recurs in each generation. It inspired W. H. Hudson's *Green Mansions* at the turn of the century, as it inspires the work of a contemporary Cuban, Alejo Carpentier's *The Lost Steps*. In both novels, the sophisticated "European" protagonist is lured into the "green mansions" of the Orinoco jungle, travelling up-river in pursuit of the lost secrets of a natural, primeval humanity. Both heroes are granted something of what they seek. Hudson's Rima, an elusive woodsprite, sweetly, teasingly sexless in the late-Victorian manner, has her counterpart in Carpentier's hero's love-affair with an Indian woman, Rosario. (Characteristically, Hudson's paradise is asexual. For the modernist Carpentier, on the other hand, sexual fulfilment is the symbol and sacrament of Paradise.) Yet both heroes are to be disappointed. Rima is murdered by the natives, who fear her magic; her lover, his paradise lost, must flee for his life. The hero of *The Lost Steps*, a North American composer, comes to see that his idyll in the jungle cannot last. To finish the musical composition he is working on he finds that he requires, after all, the resources of civilisation. The theme of Hudson's *Purple Land* is not dissimilar. It is the theme of all American Utopias: the desire to seek a new life, untrammelled by civilisation, to become one with primitive nature or with primitive people. Primitive virtue is here imputed, not to the Red Man, but to the patriarchal, ceremonious, honour-loving way of life of the people of the Uruguayan backlands. Once again, euphoria is followed by disillusion. And so it must be. For it is the vision itself that is flawed. No earthly paradise exists; if it did, an angel with a fiery sword would forbid man entry to it.

The most celebrated, if not the most serious, evocation of a South American Garden of Eden is Voltaire's *Candide*. Voltaire's sources must have been similar to those of Montaigne and his own contemporary Rousseau—at whom, with Leibniz, the mockery of Candide is directed. Historically, the legend of the Noble Savage derives from the accounts of French explorers of the Brazilian coast in the mid-sixteenth century. But there is one source, probably not available to Montaigne, whose influence is even more evident: Garcilaso Inca de la Vega's *Royal Commentaries*. 'The New World, you see, is no better than

the Old . . . let's return to Europe as quickly as we can,"
Cacambo persuades Candide, after their unhappy experience
in the Jesuit Missions of Paraguay (that strange echo of the
benevolent despotism of the Incas). Disappointed, Candide and
Cacambo decide to make for Cayenne. At an inn on the way,
they hear of a country called Eldorado: "The country", as
Candide says, "where all goes well; for there must obviously
be some such place." At the inn, to their surprise, Candide and
Cacambo find their offers of gold coin refused, though with
exquisite politeness:

> Gentlemen, it is obvious that you are strangers here; and we are
> not used to foreigners. So please excuse our laughter at your
> offering to pay us with stones off the road. . . . All inns run for the
> convenience of tradespeople are paid for by the government.

Voltaire's source here must be Garcilaso. The "inns" are the
tambos at which Inca government runners were put up; and
the Indians' contempt for the Europeans' love of gold is a theme
that, though it is found in Garcilaso, occurs even earlier. Many
of the details of life in Eldorado—it is the same Eldorado,
Voltaire tells us, Raleigh had tried to reach—are borrowed
from Garcilaso, if sometimes in comically modified form. We
hear of "two large red sheep, saddled and bridled for riding"
—the "sheep", presumably, being Peruvian *llamas*. Nor is the
Temple of the Sun in Cuzco forgotten:

> They walked over to a modest little house, and went in. The door
> was mere silver, and the rooms were panelled with nothing better
> than gold; but the workmanship was in such good taste as to vie
> with the richest panelling. It is true that the hall was incrusted
> only with rubies and emeralds, but everything was so well
> designed as to compensate for this extreme simplicity.

The religious beliefs of the inhabitants of Eldorado are satisfactory. They are, more or less, eighteenth-century deists; they
believe in God, but will have no priests in their kingdom. The
inhabitants of Eldorado are not Incas, we are told; the kingdom
once belonged to the Incas, but "they imprudently left it to
subdue another part of the world, and were finally exterminated
by the Spaniards'. Voltaire's Eldorado, then, is the earthly
paradise of the *philosophes*. It is a state founded on pure reason.
Yet Voltaire is plainly bored by this earthly paradise he has

invented. It appears, certainly, to have no particular flaw in it
—unless boredom itself be the flaw. Voltaire is eager for Candide
to move on to fresh pastures; which he soon does, being anxious
to find out what has become of his lady Cunégonde. The conclusion? "It goes to show", as Candide puts it, "that people
ought to travel". It must be admitted that Voltaire's use of the
legend is a bit of a let-down. Unlike Hudson or Carpentier,
he does not make the tragic-ironic point that since the paradise
his hero seeks is a projection of his own desires, ecstasy must be
followed by disillusion. There is really no good reason why
Candide should leave his paradise—the King begs him not to
go—except that Voltaire does not want to spoil a good story.
Admittedly, Voltaire is anxious not to let the optimists get
away with it. But *Candide* does not altogether make it clear why
they should not. *Green Mansions* and *The Lost Steps*, obviously,
are less brilliant books; but they extract a deeper irony from
their theme.

Garcilaso was the child of a Royal Inca mother and a
Spanish father. Brought up in Inca Cuzco, he went to Spain as a
young man, fought in her armies, and lived the life of a Spanish
hidalgo. When in old age he composed his *Commentarios Reales*,
writing for a Spanish audience as a distinguished *mestizo*, he
was inclined to paint the Inca past in rosy colours. But that is
not all: Garcilaso was writing in that narrative convention so
popular in the Europe of his time—the convention of pastoral.
The *Royal Commentaries* cannot, then, be compared with Diaz's
True History. It is not simply that scholarship has shown them to
be unreliable (Bernal Diaz is unreliable too); Garcilaso's book
was intended from the beginning as an apology. He is, then, to
be read with a pinch of salt. That he is not always so read is
evident from the flood of pro-Inca apologetics his work has
provoked in the past and still, apparently, provokes today. One
recent example is Mr Edward Hyams's *The Last of the Incas*,
another Mr Peter Shaffer's *Royal Hunt of the Sun*. Mr Hyams's
thesis is that the Incas deserve to interest us because they were
the first socialist society, a society rudely shattered by "White
imperialism":

> The *tahuantinsuyu* was, economically, a socialist state. All the means
> of production, distribution, and exchange were in the state's
> hands. The country was extremely flourishing, and the worst

evils of our own world, a grinding and degrading poverty, were completely absent. Our freedom, in Western Europe and North America, was a product of inexhaustible and readily accessible natural resources; we could afford therefore to limit co-operation and specialisation well short of social conscription. But the Andean peoples could not, their communities could grow, their wealth accumulate, only if they built and operated vast irrigation systems . . . and the only way to accomplish such works was to combine under a discipline which accepted all the restraints on freedom which in our own times have been imposed on the Communist half of the world's population and are being slowly and grudgingly accepted by ourselves. . . .

The reader will catch Mr Hyams's drift. Mr Hyams does not believe in Communism for himself (or only in prophylactic doses); but he believes in Communism for other people—underdeveloped people. It is part of his thesis, admittedly, that Inca despotism was not "imposed", being based on a voluntary social contract:

Where can we find an equivalent social organisation? Obviously, in the Communist states of our time. In them, the state is despotic. But it is a projection of the people's own will. If a great public work has to be undertaken, Soviet citizens may, and in fact often do, sacrifice their personal interests and even sink their identity altogether, in order to accomplish it. It seems to have been exactly so in Peru.

It is instructive to compare Mr Hyams's tone (Mr Hyams has written a laudatory history of the *New Statesman*) with that of his distant original. One thing plain from the comparison is that Garcilaso had a modern talent for apologetics. The following, one feels, could have been written of Stalin's deportations:

The Incas transplanted Indians from one province to another for special reasons, some for the good of their vassals, and others for their own purposes and to secure their dominions from insurrections. In the course of their conquests the Incas found some provinces to be naturally fertile, but thinly populated. To these districts they sent Indians who were natives of other provinces with a similar climate. This precaution was taken so that no injury might befall the settlers. They also removed Indians from barren and sterile tracts to such as were fertile and prolific, with a view to the benefit both of those that remained and of those that went; because, being relatives, they would help each other with their harvests.

So much, then, for the idyll. What of the reality? If the Incas have enjoyed a better press than the Aztecs, it is because they have enjoyed better public relations. Aztec "cruelty" is all too easily set against Inca "benevolence". Aztec art has always been admired; but no one had written about the Aztecs (until M. Soustelle) as Garcilaso and Mr Hyams write about the Incas. What is the truth of the matter? The central point we have already noted. The Incas were the only American people who developed a true Empire. Artistically, they were far inferior to earlier civilisations; but of their political genius there can be no doubt. They had mastered the subtle arts of power diplomacy. They had learnt that if war is the continuation of diplomacy by other means, the contrary is also true, and often more effective. Naked *machtpolitik*—we have seen it in our own time—calls countervailing forces into being which finally prove its own destruction. Lasting power is built, not by military force, but by political skill. And political skill implies tolerance, vision and flexibility: virtues which the Incas possessed in considerable measure.

But it can hardly be empire-building skills that Mr Hyams admires. Or, if he does so admire them, it is only by the sleight-of-hand of calling them "socialist". The truth is that if the Inca system had merits, they are precisely those to be found in the benevolent-despotic "hydraulic societies" for which Wittfogel has found the name "Oriental Despotism". The founding principle of this type of social organisation, according to Wittfogel, is the need to combine human energies for purposes of flood-control and irrigation: China, Egypt, and Mesopotamia are standard examples. It is a corollary of Wittfogel's argument that the totalitarian societies of Russia and China have become what they are because they are built on these proto-totalitarian foundations. It is characteristic of these societies, as of Inca Peru, that no merchant or feudal class ever developed. Wittfogel's thesis therefore confirms one part of Mr Hyams's contention: a society of this type could be said, theoretically, to rest on a social contract, in which large-scale economic planning is an essential element. But Wittfogel is not an ally

Mr Hyams can be anxious to embrace. For it is a corollary of
his argument that the values of Western civilisation would
probably not have arisen, and can flourish only with difficulty,
in such a soil. And Mr Hyams, despite a sneaking admiration
for Communist methods, is clearly of the opinion that these
values are worthwhile—otherwise he would not regret our
having to give them up.

The truth is, Mr Hyams and the Incas' other modern
admirers are too ready to blink the fact of Empire. Empires are
historically the product of the will to power of a specific human
group; and we all know that power, once attained, becomes its
own justification. The power-drive implied in this process is an
ugly thing, as Mr Hyams should be the first to admit. Such
power is pursued for its own sake, and has no natural limits.
Thus it is significant that the Incas, having devoured "the
known world", were on the point of devouring one another
when the Spaniards came on the scene. There may be good
reasons for admiring the Incas; but they are not those given by
Mr Hyams. The fact is, the reasons for admiring the Incas are
as good, and as bad, as the reasons for admiring any of history's
"Oriental Despotisms". Let me quote what an authority on
ancient Peruvian history, Mr Alden Mason, a more pragmatic
writer than Wittfogel, and a more sober one than Mr Hyams,
has to say about the way in which Empires—the Inca Empire
among them—came into being:

> It is coming to be realised that, with only minor deviations,
> practically all of the great civilisations of the world developed
> along more or less the same lines. A fortunately situated people,
> on a hunting and gathering plane of economy, developed or
> adopted agriculture . . . the pressure of population and the
> resultant competition for the means of food production resulted in
> violent conflicts between adjacent groups, and mastery by a few
> of them. Finally one of the latter, compelled by its lust for power
> rather than by a real need for economic security—although
> generally offering the latter as an excuse—achieved power control
> over all others within its sphere, establishing an Empire.

Alas for Utopians! There is little in this account to support the
fine structures of millenarian fantasy Europe has built on
Garcilaso's narrative.

"*Tristes Tropiques*"

It is tempting, perhaps, to dismiss these fantasies as an adolescent aberration of the European mind. Machu Picchu is not the world's navel; it is a common-or-garden hill-fort. The high Andes conceal no Eldorado of noble-minded savages—only the wretched, coca-chewing descendants of a defeated culture. The reality of the *Green Mansions* of W. H. Hudson is the *Green Hell* of Colonel Fawcett and Colonel Fleming. If in the jungles of the Amazon and the Orinoco are preserved nature's most intimate secrets, then modern man cannot share them. As Voltaire put it, mocking Rousseau: we cannot be expected to go on all fours again. It is easy, then, to mock. The etymology of Utopia, after all, is not "good-place", but "no-place". But it is perhaps not enough to mock. European man, at the dawn of the modern age, delighted to dream dreams. These dreams, it is true, tell us more about the dreamer's mind than about the object of the dream: the life of the Red Man, the green mansions of the jungle, the Incas' earthly paradise. But it does not matter. The mind was that of nascent Europe; and in it were prefigured the contours of our own.

Perhaps, then, these fantasies may deserve our attention after all. For they proceed from something that is of the essence of the Western mind; and which is, possibly, unique to it. In its simplest terms, that something may be called self-awareness. Few cultures have been so acutely self-aware and yet so able to stand apart from themselves, seeing themselves from the vantage-point of another society, real or imaginary, that lives by values different from its own. Why, Lévi-Strauss asks, should anthropology be so quintessentially a product of the Western mind? What other cultures have interested themselves so passionately, and so meticulously, in the behaviour of other human groups? Granted, if we look more closely, this *penchant* may not be quite as flattering as its uniqueness suggests:

> It has sometimes been said that only in Western society have anthropologists been produced. Therein, it was said, lay its greatness. . . . But the contrary argument could also be sustained: that if the West has produced anthropologists it is because it was so tormented by remorse that it had to compare its own image

with that of other societies, in the hope that they would either display the same shortcomings or help the West to explain how these defects could have come into being. . . . If anthropology cannot take a detached view of our civilisation or declare itself not responsible for that civilisation's evils, it is because its very existence is unintelligible unless we regard it as an attempt to redeem it.

The anthropologist as Redeemer! An absurd notion? Not altogether: for anthropology, more than historiography, is the putting into practice of that urge to see oneself by others' lights characteristic of the Western spirit. It is doubly a legacy of its Christian past; springing, on the one hand, from radical self-doubt and self-distrust and, on the other, from a conviction that the evil in man is not of his essence, but is capable of redemption. Anthropology is not interested in truths of the calendar; in dates, in decisive battles, in great men. It is concerned with how human beings live in societies different from our own, and with the values by which they live. It is the most intimate of the sciences, not only in subject-matter, but also in inspiration. In this light, Lévi-Strauss argues, Rousseau does not seem so ridiculous after all:

> Turning over these problems in my mind, I become convinced that Rousseau's is the only answer to them. Rousseau is much decried these days; never has his work been so little known; and he has to face, above all, the absurd acusation that he glorified the "state of nature" for its own sake. . . . What Rousseau said was the exact contrary. . . . Rousseau, of all the *philosophes*, came nearest to being an anthropologist . . . for there is only one way in which we can escape the contradiction inherent in the anthropologist's position, and that is by reformulating, on our own account, the intellectual procedures which allowed Rousseau to move forward, from the ruins left by the *Discours sur l'Origine de L'Inégalité* to the ample design of the *Contrat Social*, of which *Emile* reveals the secret. He it is who showed us how, after we have destroyed every existing order, we can still discover the principles which allow us to erect a new order in their stead.

What are the principles of this "new order"? We do Rousseau an injustice if we take his distaste for mechanical civilisation to mean that he wished men to go on all fours. Rousseau's point was that humanity "should aspire to the middle ground between the indolence of his primitive state and the questing activity to which he is prompted by his *amour-propre*". This "middle ground", Lévi-Strauss points out, is not necessarily a "primitive" condition; it is to be found in all ages, at all levels of material culture. In *Tristes Tropiques* Lévi-Strauss evokes the life of the "savages" of the huge basin that stretches away from Machu Picchu, on the hot, wet Amazonian watershed, across the vast expanse of Amazonia to the Atlantic:

> The study of these savages does not reveal a Utopian state of Nature, nor does it make us aware of a perfect society hidden deep in the forests. It helps us to construct a theoretical model of a society which corresponds to none that can be observed in reality, but will help us to disentangle "what in the past nature of Man is original, and what is artificial". It also helps us "to know closely a state which no longer exists, which may never have existed, which will probably never exist, and of which we must, nevertheless, have an exact notion if we are to judge our present situation correctly".

This, then, is the new Utopia. Utopia is no-place. Yet we are bound to seek it, as we are bound to find it, in every place. For there is one task that is common to all human societies: the task of so ordering man's life that his potentialities may be realised, and not perverted into instruments of self-destruction:

> As he moves forward with his own environment, Man takes with him all the positions that he has occupied in the past, and all those that he will occupy in the future. He is everywhere at the same time, a crowd which, in the act of moving forward, yet recapitulates at every instant every step that it has ever taken in the past.

This Utopia has no specific content; for it embraces every content, every experiment in living on which man has embarked. Yet it is not for that reason hollow or vague. The grace we seek is to be found in the opportunity such studies offer us of escaping from the prisons we build ourselves:

> This is the grace for which every society longs, irrespective of its beliefs, its political régime, its level of civilisation. It stands, in every case, for leisure and recreation, and freedom, and peace of body and mind.

Objections are easy to anticipate: if traditional Utopias were impractical, what of this new Utopia, whose motto is *nihil humanum mihi alienum*, where everything exists in potentiality, and nothing in actuality? But Lévi-Strauss insists that the anthropologist is not interested in merely abstract possibilities. He deals, professionally, in practicalities. That is why his discoveries may be of direct application to our own society:

> Other societies may not be better than our own. . . . But knowing them better does none the less help us to detach ourselves from our own society. It is not that our society is absolutely evil, or that others are not evil also; but merely that ours is the only society from which we *have* to disentangle ourselves. In doing so, while not clinging to elements from any one particular society, we make use of one and all of them to discover those principles of social life which may be applied to the reform of our own customs. . . . In relation to our own society, that is to say, we stand in a position of privilege. . . . For our own society is the only one which we can transform and yet not destroy, since the changes we would introduce would come from within.

No wonder then, that the euphoria the New World inspired in the Europeans of the Renaissance, with their demonic curiosity, unassuageable *amour-propre*, their amalgam of self-confidence and self-doubt, still has such fascination for us:

> For those of us who are earth-bound Europeans, our adventurings into the heart of the New World have a lesson to teach us: that the New World was not ours to destroy, and yet we destroyed it; and no other will be vouchsafed to us.

Our wilful destruction of the New World takes on, indeed, a new significance. For if in discovering this new world we awoke to potentialities concealed in our nature, by destroying it we were brought face to face with the fact that no earthly paradise exists. Did such a paradise exist, we would forfeit our right to inhabit it by our violence and our folly. The true pain of the Discovery was that it brought Western man face to face with himself. So, apparently helplesss—an "infant world", Montaigne calls it—the New World took its unwitting revenge on the old. Yet all is not tragedy. For, if Lévi-Strauss is right, the perspectives then opened up are not less available to the present age than to the age of the Discoverers. Utopia is not mocked: it is a necessary function, both of the self-awareness of the West, and of the aspirations of humanity. Retrospectively, the Utopian adventure, from Thomas More to Campanella, from Bacon to Rousseau, receives the blessing of the modern anthropologist:

> If our race has concentrated on one task, and one alone—that of building a society in which Man can live—then the sources of strength on which our remote ancestors drew are also present in ourselves. All the stakes are still on the board, and we can take them up at any time we please. Whatever was done, and done badly, can be begun all over again: "The golden age, which blind superstition situated behind or ahead of us, is in ourselves."

7

CHILE:
or The Making of a Small Earthquake

It is amazing to observe the ingenuity with which the Birmingham artists have accommodated themselves to the coarse transatlantic tastes. The framed saints, the tinsel snuff-boxes, the gaudy furniture, make one smile when contrasted with the decent and elegant simplicity of these things in Europe. The Germans furnish most of the glass in common use: it is of bad quality to be sure; but it, as well as the little German mirrors, which are chiefly bought to hang up as votive offerings in the chapels, answers all the purposes of *Chileno* consumption. . . . Some few German artificers are also established here, and particularly a most ingenious blacksmith and farrier, one Frey, whose beautifully neat house and workshop, and his garden, render him an excellent model for the rising *Chilenos*.

Journal of a Residence in Chile: Maria Graham (1824)

Leftward Ho!

WE HAVE GROWN TOO ABSTRACT. Like those others, we have been seduced by Utopia, the-place-that-never-was. We need to remind ourselves that America is not a region of the mind, but a landscape with figures, a place of complex humanity and squalid, agonised reality. Let us add, though, that it may be as facile to agonise as to enthuse. How many tears have been shed by television commentators over the *favelas* of Rio, and the *barrios* of Mexico City? And how much good has it done their wretched inhabitants? True, the spectacle of such squalor, allied to such abundance, is not without effect on the Northern conscience. Ashamed at his new-found affluence, Uncle Sam accustoms himself to the role of Joseph the Provider. It is not a role that will bring him tangible reward, or even common gratitude. Seven fat years, and the people will thank God; seven lean years, and they will blame the United States. If Uncle Sam is eager to do good, let him do it by stealth: good works, over-advertised, are counter-productive. We have looked at some of the implications of the Latin-*yanqui* antagonism; an antagonism which has grown worse over the past generation and may grow worse yet. The fault, we said, lay on both sides. But there was something sado-masochistic about the relationship. If the Latin were not so apt to be dominated, all the power and wealth of the *yanqui* could not dominate him. That is why the wholesale acceptance of development theory *à la* Rostow is disastrous: it gives the underdeveloped world the perfect, self-confirming proof of its inferiority. But it distorts no less the perspective of the nations that are "economically mature". Seen through Rostovian spectacles, the hundred-odd nations of the Third World look much alike. Distinctions become blurred; the variety of the world vanishes in a fog of generalisation. The people of under-developed countries become underdeveloped people. As objects of our pity, our generosity, our good intentions, they cease to be quite human. It is we, as much as they, who are impoverished if we look at the world through such spectacles.

What, then, is the answer? To affirm that Latin Americans are not mathematical digits, but people—people, as they say, "like you and me"? That does not seem quite satisfactory. For one thing, it is a trifle patronising. For another, it is not true. Latin Americans are not like you and me; they are very much themselves. They are not Spaniards or Portuguese or *yanquis* or Afro-Asians; they are Latin Americans, a species to themselves. Chileans are very different from Argentines; Peruvians do not greatly care for Ecuadoreans; Colombians consider Venezuelans brash and materialistic. The traveller will fall in with one or the other of these prejudices. For myself, I confess I found Chileans among the most agreeable of Latin Americans. When Chileans tell one that Argentines are arrogant and ill-mannered, and Peruvians either hidebound or frivolous, I know what they mean. Still, to the foreigner, all are recognisably Latin American: people who share certain characteristics, not to be found elsewhere in precisely this conjunction. This may seem too bold, and too bald, a statement. Is there really a distinguishable Latin American type? There is no *one* type, certainly. But there is a gallery of types that go to make up the spectrum of Latin American life today. To judge, say, from Maria Graham's *Journal* it does not seem that the spectrum has changed much over the past century and a half.

Let us return to the concrete: to Señor Pedro de Osman, say, of the city of Lima. Where else could one hope to meet such a character but in Peru, brooding over his unique collection of Colonial treasures, preening himself like a *conquistador* on the loot of the Incas? Is Señor de Osman typical? For all his seigneurial charm one hopes fervently that he is not. He remarked to me, as he showed off his treasures, that the Christian Democrats in Peru were as bad as the Communists. Not, of course, that he cared for *yanquis* any better. "Surprise! surprise!", he would cry, opening the silver doors of a Cuzco reliquary to reveal the exquisite ivory statuette within. "Surprise! surprise!" That was the reaction you would expect from a *yanqui*—for which, I suppose, he must have taken me (until it dawned on him that I was an *ingles*, whereupon I was taken to admire a photograph of "the Prince of Wales and party", prized relic of their trip to Peru in the twenties). Don Pedro, then, is a snob. He is an unabashed reactionary. His views are not nice. He

looks, and probably thinks, like General Franco. It is quite
impossible to approve of him. Even his "love of art" may not be
what it seems. Much of his collection is really expensive *kitsch*.
There is little in Don Pedro's private museum (no visitor should
miss it) to compare with the pre-Columbian Nazca pottery or
the Paracas textiles to be seen in Lima. Don Pedro, then, is
everything the Anglo-Saxon ought to disapprove of in Latin
America. And yet? And yet it would have been a loss not to
have made his acquaintance. An hour at Don Pedro's tells you
more about Latin America than a dozen ministerial interviews.

Don Pedro, then, is a rare specimen: rarer and more interesting than the objects in his collection. But naturally, whom the
traveller meets, and what impressions he forms, will depend on
the circles he moves in. If his introductions are to artists, writers
and intellectuals, he will meet few Don Pedros. And that will be
a pity. For only a handful of Latin American intellectuals are
men of the Right. Indeed, after half a dozen interviews—with a
Mexican painter, let us say, a Guatemalan writer, a Venezuelan
economist, a Colombian philosopher—the traveller must take
care: if he believes all he is told he will go away thinking Latin
America is indeed on the brink of red revolution. Like the bull
in the ring, he will respond to the red flag draped before his
misting eyes with bursts of rage and frustration. He will have
the mortification, too, of knowing that the *aficionados* are enjoy-
ing it all hugely: the bull, so strong and yet so clumsy! The
matador, so frail and yet so self-assured! But there the analogy
ends. For in this game—the national sport of the Latin intelligentsia—it is really the bull, teased and provoked beyond
endurance, that has the last word. It ought of course to be the
other way round. Handsome, agile Ariel, with his brave red
flag, ought to triumph over Caliban's brute force. Alas, it is not
so. Left-wing politics in Latin America is a sport for Don Juans,
for doomed, elegant masochists desirous to cut a figure. When
the athlete enters the arena, he does not expect to leave it to
shouts of triumph. He is murmuring under his breath, "We,
who are about to die, salute thee, Caesar!"

The motto, then, of the Latin American intellectual is the
French: "*personne à ma gauche!*" It is not hard to see why. To the
Left are to be found—as he sees it—internationalism and ration-
ality and freedom from social restraint. To the Right there is, at

best, small-town stupidity and narrow-mindedness; at worst, the whole paraphernalia of the Black Legend—from the Holy Inquisition to Don Pedro de Osman. To be on the Left is to proclaim one's solidarity with a wider world, one's independence of the paltry provincialism of the *patria chica*. To be on the Right is to accept the limited horizon of the *patria chica*, and of the Hispanic-Catholic tradition; and few intellectuals, laboriously acquiring a cosmopolitan outlook, are likely to find this appealing. (That Borges, most cosmopolitan of writers, should declare himself an old-fashioned *conservador*, is something of a joke; only the spectacle of Peron's demagogy explains such a pose.) The traveller, then, must be on his guard. He will meet few intellectuals who do not think of themselves as "left-wing". And of these very many will call themselves Communists.

How "Communist" are they in fact? Certainly, there are grades of commitment. Pablo Neruda is a Communist, in the sense that Mayakovsky and Brecht were Communists: though it is true that some of his worst poetry is "committed", and most of his best poetry is non-political. The young Mexican novelist, Carlos Fuentes, and the young Peruvian novelist, Vargas Llosa, are often called Communists by their enemies; and they would certainly consider themselves "left-wing". Having met and liked both, I cannot see that either deserves the description of "Communist". They are certainly rebels and non-conformists; and one can see how, in the context of modern Mexico or Peru, they would think it dishonourable to be anything else. But neither they nor most other "left-wing" intellectuals are Communists in any conventional sense. Question them, and you find they abhor the oppressive aspects of Communism (of which, after numerous free trips to Communist countries, they are quite aware) as much as any Anglo-Saxon liberal. But they do not wish—and this is understandable—to be labelled as militant anti-Communists. There is, at bottom, something of a time-lag in all this. Like French, German or Anglo-Saxon intellectuals in the nineteen-thirties, they feel that the Communists, though strayed sheep, are yet of the left-wing fold. The grim experiences of the Nazi-Soviet pact, the Hungarian Revolution and the rape of Czechoslovakia, have largely passed them by.

Pablo Neruda

Needless to say, none of these generalisations fits Pablo Neruda. What generalisation could? I have compared Neruda with Brecht and Mayakovsky, as his genius deserves. Here, at least, is no parlour-pink, no self-deluding fellow-traveller. This man is acknowledged to be the world's leading Communist poet, and probably the greatest poet to have come out of Latin America. Neruda knows all this, and acts the part. There is neither conceit nor false modesty in the man. I made the pilgrimage to his seaside house at *Isla Negra*—an experience not quickly forgotten. *Isla Negra* is the house of a retired sea-captain or eccentric colonial governor (Conrad and Lord Cochrane on the bookshelves). There is a flagstaff in the garden; and an ancient Birmingham steam-roller, lovingly cared for. The house is the poetry and the poetry is the man. It is full of objects: sea-shells and butterflies, logbooks and rock specimens; and these, too, are the props of Neruda's poetry (one thinks of the *Elemental Odes*). Here Neruda holds court; and one is reminded of Goethe in Weimar, also holding court, also surrounded by a magpie-hoard of precious objects.

But there comparison breaks down. Both men, certainly, may be classified as egotists—though to carp at egotism on such a scale merely reveals the critic's own pettiness. Yet the difference is not uninstructive. Goethe's egotism is very personal: the objects the visitor is shown at Weimar are personal trophies, tokens of love or friendship, or proofs of the great man's cosmopolitan *Bildung*. Neruda's egotism is utterly impersonal. Neruda's objects are chosen not for what they mean to Neruda, but for what they have meant to others. They are tokens of that natural world which Neruda does not need laboriously to collect and classify, since it belongs to him by right. Neruda's egotism, then, is both greater and less than that of Goethe. Greater in that it knows no natural limits, no renunciation, no *entsagung*. Less in that Neruda appears to claim nothing for himself, is himself an object among objects—though to be sure, a not inconspicuous one. And the character of the men is the character of their poetry. Goethe was something of a culture-vulture; Neruda, the noble savage, has no use for the stuff.

It is here that Neruda, though he lacks Brecht's intellectuality and his dramatic sense, comes closest to the poetry of his contemporary. Indeed, Neruda might almost be a character out of Brecht. He is Baal, the roistering, innocent, gluttonous child of nature; the little pagan *Glücksgott*, beyond good and evil. Brecht, too, was a lover of well-used objects. And Neruda's *On Impure Poetry* reads at times like an echo of Brecht's *Messingkauf*:

> It is very appropriate, at certain times of the day or night, to look deeply into objects at rest: wheels which have traversed vast dusty spaces, bearing great cargoes of vegetables or minerals, sacks from the coal-yards, barrels, baskets, the handles and grips of the carpenter's tools. They exude the touch of man and the earth as a lesson to the tormented poet . . . the flawed confusion of human beings shows in them, the proliferation, material used and discarded, the prints of feet and fingers, the permanent noises of humanity on the inside and the outside of all objects.

I have said that Neruda is no parlour-pink, but a self-confessed Communist whose political orthodoxy, both in public and private (from all one hears), is a good deal more unquestioning than that of either Brecht or Mayakovsky. In Chile, and in Latin America in general, Neruda is an important figure: his personal influence and patronage are enormous, and the Communists know it. Yet one cannot help being sceptical. What is, after all, a good Communist poet? Is he a poet who toes the party line and was never detected in a deviation? Very well: Louis Aragon is a great Communist poet. But Louis Aragon, however sure in his orthodoxy (until recently), is not a great poet. Brecht and Mayakovsky are very great poets; yet their orthodoxy is seriously in doubt. In what sense, then, is Neruda a great Communist poet? There is, as I have said, no doubt of his practical orthodoxy. But then Neruda's is not a doubting, or even an inquiring mind. Neruda is that rare thing among modern artists: a non-intellectual. He has written some "good" —that is to say, deeply-felt—Communist poems, like those he wrote about the Spanish Civil War. But he has written some very bad Communist poems, on subjects varying from Stalin to the United Fruit Company. What cannot be said of him, as it can of Brecht, is that Communism—in the sense of the just ordering of man's social relations—is the committed centre of his art. For Neruda is not all that interested in human relations.

He is concerned with Man, certainly. But it is Man in deadly combat with Nature, with a cruel, tempestuous environment (in which, nevertheless, solace may be found) that is the true subject of his poetry. And he is writing here out of his own experience. Neruda grew up in Southern Chile, where nature's action is not unlike that attributed to her in his poetry. It is this apprehension of nature, found in his earliest as in his latest writings, that makes Neruda so uniquely *American* a writer.

Indeed, one can go further. I have cited Mr Philip Rahv's distinction between American writers of the Redskin and the Paleface tribe. Clearly, to find a parallel to Neruda in North American literature, we must look to Walt Whitman or William Carlos Williams, not to Hawthorne or Henry James. Certainly, Neruda is a more considerable poet than either Whitman or Williams, though a strangely old-fashioned one. Neruda is only superficially a modernist. He is a poet of objectivity, and little given to abstract rhetoric. Compared with him Carlos Williams, though they share certain poetic ideals, seems thin-blooded. It makes good sense, then, to see Neruda as a Redskin. But to do so is perhaps to cast doubt, not on Neruda's strengths, which are considerable, but on the conception of Neruda as a Communist writer. Brecht was a Communist writer (if an unorthodox one) in that he put man's injustice to man at the heart of his dramatic enterprise. The Peruvian Vallejo and Mayakovsky were good Communist writers, because they gave lyrical expression to the faith that suffering man may redeem his personal pain by merging it with the pain of the generality of men. Of all this there is little trace in Neruda. Neruda's vision of Man and Nature has a grandeur, an affirmativeness, a naïvety, for which there are no parallels in modern poetry. It is a unique vision; and one that is perhaps no longer possible in those regions where man, in overcoming nature, has suburbanised, homogenised and trivialised her out of existence. But is it a Marxist vision? I doubt it. Marxism is about men, not about Man. Marxism is about men in conflict with each other, with themselves, with the alien social structures they have created. Only when these conflicts have been resolved can the Marxist poet (or so Brecht thought) write of Man and Nature with an easy conscience. The artefacts of this struggle are to be found in Neruda's poetry, but not the substance. Neruda is a good Communist, and a good poet; he is also very likely a great man. But it would be doctrinaire, or worse, to hold that these three are one.

The New Demonology

Neruda is too big a fish to be caught in any ideological net. Yet his influence is immense; and in his political stance, of course, he is far more typical than Borges. The traveller is all too likely to get the impression that the Left has an intellectual monopoly. Yet "left-wing" is a remarkably elastic term. The traveller must be prepared for some bizarre effects. I have cited my Venezuelan friend, the spokesman for *Accion Democratica*, who appeared (to naïve European ears) to be defending his party's anti-Communist position with the arguments used by its opponents. There are stranger things than this. It was at a lunch at one of Mexico City's smarter restaurants that I heard the story of how British oil interests, expropriated by Cardenas in the 30's, had revenged themselves by hiring two British authors to do dirt on Mexico's Revolution. Present were Carlos Fuentes—the "angry young man" of the Mexican intelligentsia—the Chilean novelist, Jose Donoso, and Victor Urquidi, the Mexican economist. Which authors, I was eager to know? Who were these shameless lackeys of imperialism, these intellectual prostitutes? They were, it seems, Graham Greene and Evelyn Waugh! Carlos Fuentes, playing (as he put it) the "wild Mexican" to Urquidi's urbane, statistician's bedside manner, assured me that it was true: "everybody knows it" (a statement I was able to confirm). Fuentes had been initiating me into the art of drinking Mexican *tequila* (with salt and lemon): drinking it boldly, Russian-fashion, I gasped for air, "Are you telling me . . .?" But one got no further. Politeness ruled out direct rebuttal; and it would have been useless. Throughout, Urquidi remained silent and sceptical. Even moderate, bearded Donoso, a Chilean neutral, failed to rise. I was left to make what I would of this extraordinary statement; nobody threw me a lifebelt. I realised that it was not a statement it was useful to challenge. This was simply something that "everybody knew". Latin America, for all its love of the new, is not a rigorously inquisitive place: it is rarely rigorously anything. So, out of polite cowardice, I did not challenge it. The point, after all, turned on a probability rather than a fact. If it could be believed, in Mexican left-wing circles, that the talents of Mr Waugh and Mr Greene are for auction on the capitalist market—well, then anything could be believed. (I have since wondered what Mr Greene, an admirer of Castro's Cuba, would have made of it all.) But then, it is not what people believe that is interesting; what is interesting is what makes them believe it.

The demonology of the Left would require a book to itself. It is worth noting, though, that it overlaps with the demonology of the Right. As in France, so in Latin America, the anti-Americanism of the Right is often indistinguishable from the anti-Americanism of the Left. Nor is this anti-Americanism simply the product of malignant fantasy. America's power is indeed a threat to the integrity of smaller states. Not because America is especially irresponsible or interfering—she is less so than those whose mantle she has inherited—but because her strength is such that she cannot but interfere in their affairs. The United States is an elephant. The elephant is by nature a peaceable, vegetarian beast. But even an elephant imbued with the ideals of Albert Schweitzer cannot lie down in the jungle without crushing a number of lesser beasts. The trouble with America is not that she is very strong; but she does not yet know her strength, and what to do with it. Her dilemma, I believe, is something new in world history. And it is the very novelty of her situation, as much as her "immaturity" as a world power, that accounts for her confusion. Her arrival at world power has coincided with the destruction of the old Empires, and with the setting up of a hundred dwarf-powers, any one of which (other factors being equal) she might crush with a swing of her trunk.

The idea, popular on the Latin American Left, that the *yanqui* goes about like a roaring lion, seeking whom he may devour, is a long way from the truth. By the standards of the past (and not just the recent past), it would have been natural enough for America to have taken up the White Man's Burden as Kipling demanded, and built a political empire. The "advanced" nations have grown economically and militarily stronger, relative to their ex-colonies, over the past two decades. Indeed, the nuclear powers enjoy an absolute superiority over the non-nuclear (though they may be inhibited from using it) which has no parallel in previous ages. The New States owe their independence less to their own strength than to the quarrels among their one-time masters—and to the simple fact that old-fashioned colonialism is not a paying proposition. What is extraordinary about America's post-war policy, I believe, is her *restraint* in the use of power (Vietnam excepted). What is extraordinary about her political thinking is not its occasional immaturities, but the remarkable patience she has shown in the face of a new historical situation. This, I realise, is anathema to America-haters of all colours. Unless one is careful, one will find oneself in the company of Messrs Greene and Waugh. But it is a truer picture, I believe, than the demonology of Right or Left. It does not imply an uncritical attitude to the United States; it asks that America's situation be seen for what it is. The real charge against America is not that she is sometimes insolent or maladroit, but that she is muddled in her basic aspirations. To intervene or not to intervene? Who can tell? If the US intervene, as in Guatemala, she will be accused of taking up Teddy Roosevelt's Big Stick. If she does not intervene—as with Batista, Trujillo, and Perez Jimenez—she will be accused of conniving at dictatorship. In the circumstances, it is hardly surprising that American policy is sometimes inconsistent. The wonder is that it is not more so.

The demonologists would do well to recognise, then, that America is a fallible giant. I have suggested that the real harm done by theories of development-economics is that they undermine the self-confidence of the people they are meant to help. Much the same may be said of this anti-American demonology. It harms North America not at all; but the damage done to Latin American self-confidence is incalculable. And the same is true of much of Afro-Asia. Most Latin American intellectuals suffer, in any case, from a feeling of impotence. Chile, for example, is one of the more "advanced" countries of Latin America, and has enjoyed stable civilian government for most of her history. Yet despite industrial advances since 1930, the gap between rich and poor has grown. Since the war there has been an actual decline in income per head; the population explosion, and an inequitable distribution of income, combining to produce this sorry result. In addition, inflation has continued unabated; and Chile's extractive industries are as much at the mercy of international market forces as ever. Much of this is not within Chile's power to alter. Only an international agreement on commodities—such as exists for Latin American coffee—can secure a dependable price, say, for Chilean copper or Venezuelan oil. Such agreements are difficult to achieve; they are certainly impossible without the co-operation of the United States. And this not simply because she controls (despite Frei's 'Chileanisation') the Chilean coppermining concerns. If they were expropriated outright it would be impossible to find a substitute for the US market. Anti-Americanism is understandable; but it is simply not practical politics in countries so dependent on one market.

Yet there is much that Chile could do to strengthen her position. It is absurd that Chile should import foodstuffs and raw materials she could produce at home. The problem can be simply stated: Chile possesses much fertile land, but that land is inefficiently used. What is the answer? Predictably, the cry goes up that Chile needs "land reform". This is at once a truism and cliché. It is of course true that Chile needs land reform. It is also true that it is political pressures that prevent this. But the problem is not so simple. Take the case of agriculture: the problem is not to take from the rich and give to the poor, like some latter-day Robin Hood. The problem is to ensure that the right crops are grown on the right soil, and that the right tools and expertise are available to the right people. Chile has some of the best agricultural land in Latin America, and her people are above the average in skill and intelligence. Yet at present only 17 per cent of this land is used; and of this much is wrongly used. Thus "intensive" crops are grown on the huge central *fundos*—estates dating back to the time of the *conquistadores*—whereas "extensive" crops, like wheat and rye, are grown on the small farms of the Chilean south. This is the exact reverse of what economic rationality would require. Yet this pattern cannot be altered without active state intervention, which powerful vested interests conspire to resist. "State Intervention" need not mean expropriation and collectivisation, which might prove still less economic. The state must devise fiscal and other means to ensure the profitable use of national resources. If Chile is short of food, the fault does not lie with Chile's natural endowments. Chile has 1·01 hectares of agricultural land per head, a figure which compares favourably with Mexico's 0·79, India's 0·29, or Japan's 0·07. It is also more than twice the average in Europe. The fault lies with the social structure Chile, like the rest of Latin America, inherits from the age of the *conquistadores*.

It is this, together with Chile's exposed position in international trade, that gives rise to the profound feeling of impotence among her intellectuals. What results is a kind of paranoid nightmare, in which the local Oligarchy and Army, the CIA, the Pentagon, and the World Bank become fused into a single monster, ever ready to swoop and smother the helpless dreamer. It is the equivalent, in modern terms, of the haunted dream-life of Soustelle's Aztecs or of the people of Aritama. Here is the root of that demonology which fascinates, while it paralyses, the intellectuals of the Left. The blame for the obstacles to reform that are built into Latin American society is imputed—this is psychologically understandable—to an outside force, the United States of America. Yet this can only compound the feeling of impotence. There are some men—Mexico's Victor Urquidi, and the excellent economists of the Economic Commission for Latin America in Santiago among them—who see the perils of this demonology. They are in a position to offer more rational explanations and solutions. But they are dependent on politicians to carry them into effect. Their number is growing; and in them lies the chief hope that Latin America will cope with the problems that face her during the coming decades. Chilean agriculture is merely one example. But it is sufficient to show that rational solutions can be achieved, if the will is there. Still, one should not be too optimistic. These new technocrats are a small minority; much they would like to see done runs contrary to powerful vested interests. Nor can the doctrines they preach compete with the emotionally satisfying if paranoid demonology of the *marxisant* Left. Among the intelligentsia that demonology has a long life-span in front of it.

It is tempting to mock the world-view of this left-wing intelligentsia. But we must be cautious: in their ranks, if anywhere, shall we find the ten just men on whose account the city is spared. As I have said, it is not easy to respect those who reject out of hand the "commitment" demanded by the Left: a commitment that implies a radical critique of the existing structure of Latin American society. To be on the Left, in this sense, is to be patriotic—Latin America being a place where nationalism is universal, and patriotism very rare. It is because the demonology of the left seems to me a recipe for despair that I am opposed to it. That Latin Americans should feel impotent to alter the conditions under which they live is understandable. But it is tragic that the ideology this sense of impotence causes them to adopt should be one which, far from freeing them from their fears, freezes them in a deeper intellectual pessimism. It is, to be sure, an ironic outcome. Marxism is generally reckoned a philosophy of optimism. Marx complained that, whereas the philosophers had *explained* the world, the point was to *change* it. But it seems that Marxism can also be a recipe for doing nothing. If Marxism teaches that the forces of *imperialismo* have a grip on the country from the outside, it teaches equally that given the existing internal constellation of forces—lack of a class-conscious proletariat or even a class-conscious bourgeoisie —no true social change can be expected. True social change, on Marxist premisses, is only possible through revolutionary action; and in Latin America the prerequisites are lacking.

What society needs is a Big Earthquake; small earthquakes do no good at all. Indeed, small earthquakes do harm, because they falsely persuade the peoples of underdeveloped countries that a reformist alternative to revolution is feasible. Logically, then, Marxists must sit back and wait until conditions are propitious. Political action will be limited to tactical support of "progressive" movements, and the building up of class-consciousness among the masses: more is not possible. This, as we have seen, is pretty much the position taken up by the orthodox Communist parties. Not surprisingly, it is for this habitual passivism that the Castroites mock them. But few left-wing intellectuals, of course, are Communists in any organisational sense. Nor are they personally prepared to take a rifle and disappear into the local *Sierra Maestra*. For them the appeal of this demonology is that, in explaining their world, it explains why it is not possible to do anything about it. It is arguable that a consistent Marxism, lacking the élitist activism Lenin infused into it, must always lead to a despairing fatalism of this kind. But then it must be admitted that Marxism is a profoundly reactionary force in Latin America. In adopting it, her intellectuals are exchanging Hispanic-Catholic fatalism for a fatalism in no way less damaging.

We may take the argument a stage further. What I have said of the *marxisant* tendencies of the Latin American Left is three parts of the truth: it is not perhaps the whole truth. It is possible to take the Marxism of the Latin American Left too seriously— more seriously than they take it themselves. Beneath the Marxist trappings one detects an emotional syndrome of a different order. The fact is, Latin American attitudes to *imperialismo*, American or British or French, appear to be profoundly ambivalent. One should hesitate before using psychological categories to explain political phenomena. But one cannot look at the phenomenology of Latin American leftism without a psychological analogy coming to mind. Oscar Mannoni has taught us that the colonial relationship has many points of similarity with the relationship between Father and Son. It is an illuminating comparison. In nothing does Latin America, and the Third World generally, show the persistence of a colonial psychology more strongly than in her wish to be simultaneously independent of the Father and protected by his strong right arm. I recall a conversation with a Chilean Marxist. Beginning with a standard denunciation of American *imperialismo* it moved, imperceptibly, towards a complaint that the United States had *neglected* Latin America. The inconsistency seemed glaring; yet my friend seemed not to be aware of it.

The conjunction was revealing. Yet what had happened? Merely, the sign outside the bracket had been changed. By this Manichean algebra, the omnipotent demon of *imperialismo* had suddenly acquired the potentialities of an infinitely tender and caring force for good. At first, I was astonished at the reversal. Yet the psychological mechanism was clear. The angry vengeful father alternates with the all-loving father in whose infinite power one's own impotence is subsumed. Common to both images, of course, is a numbing sense of impotence. But the fact that, by changing the sign, the anti-imperialist demonology can be transformed into its opposite is significant. It is something that Americans should bear in mind when they read of the "anti-Americanism" of their southern neighbours. Beneath the Latins' often justified resentment of American tactlessness and arrogance, there is a profound need to be loved and provided for. It would be healthier, perhaps, if this were not so; if the nations of the Third World were able to achieve psychological as well as economic independence. But these are not emotions that Americans, of all people, should find it difficult to understand. No people, after all, shows as powerful a need to be loved as the people of the United States.

Christians and Democrats

"Small Earthquake in Chile": this headline—it bore the subheading "Not Many Killed"—was an easy winner in a pre-war competition Mr Claud Cockburn and his *Times* colleagues set up for the "most boring headline of the year". Of course, the joke is a little grim. Earthquakes are nature's curse on Chile's green and pleasant land: small as they seem to the staff of *The Times*, they have cost thousands of Chileans their lives and homes over the generations. Still, we must not spoil a good joke. And the small earthquake I have in mind is political, not geographical: the coming to power of President Frei and his Christian Democrats in September 1964. By world standards—Khruchshev was about to fall, Wilson about to be elected, Goldwater about to be demolished—this was a very small earthquake indeed. Yet many people thought at the time, and subsequent events support them, that Frei's victory was an event of more than ordinary interest. A new political force, Christian Democracy, had come to power for the first time in Latin America. Now Chile is one of few countries in Latin America with a well-organised, mass-based Communist party. A succession of popular front governments had ruled Chile, not unsuccessfully, from 1938 to 1950. A similar left-wing alliance, the FRAP, had run the Radical President Alessandri a close second in 1958, and was tipped by many to win the Presidential election of 1964. If the FRAP won, Chile would become the first Latin American country to elect a Castro-sympathising, quasi-Communist government by a free vote. The State Department was shaking in its shoes. If the Reds could win power by democratic means in traditionally stable Chile, what might not happen in more unstable countries all over South America?

In fact, the scare was unjustified. On the spot, few people thought it likely that FRAP could win a plurality. Nevertheless, within Chile itself, the scare was remarkably effective. For fear of letting in Allende's Socialist-Communist alliance, the parties of the centre and the right began to rally to the centre-left Christian Democrats. The Chilean "Socialists" are not social-democrats in the European sense; they are a loose coalition of Castroite, Trotskyite, anarcho-syndicalist and more moderate opinion. They are rather more "revolutionary", and certainly more unstable, than the solidly Soviet-oriented Communist party. Who, then, are the Christian Democrats? They are relatively new to the Latin American scene. The name is derived from the highly successful Christian Democratic parties of post-war Europe: the German CDU, the Italian *Democrazia Christiana*, the French MRP. So far, the Christian Democrats of Latin America have achieved only limited success. Apart from Chile, they have won a strong electoral base, or governmental responsibility, only in Venezuela, Peru, Ecuador, and El Salvador. However, it is as misleading to identify the Christian Democrats of Latin America with their European namesakes as it is to identify *peronismo* with Mussolini-type Fascism, or APRA with European-style social-democracy.

It is true, as its opponents point out, that Frei's party started life as a splinter group of the old Conservative party, and that it was known for a time as the Falange (the same is true of the COPEI in Venezuela). But the notions of a "corporate state", and of "vertical syndicalism", with which young radical Catholics played in the 1930's have long since given way to the semi-socialist teachings of the great Encyclicals. Much of the financial backing for Catholic activity in Latin America is West German (there is a committee in Essen to which projects have to be submitted for approval). But this support has not, it seems, influenced policy-making. The trend of the German CDU under Adenauer and Erhard was from the centre-left to the centre-right. The Latin American Christian Democrats, like their Italian comrades, have moved ever further to the left. In this, of course, they are responding to the general trend in Latin American politics. In most countries, the political sentiments of these parties as well to the left of the clerical establishments whose creatures they are accused of being. How could it be otherwise? If they are to appeal to the new electorate, they will have to compete still more vigorously with the parties of the conventional Left. It happens that in Chile the Church hierarchy is not reactionary in the Hispanic-Catholic tradition.

But in many countries this new Catholic involvement in politics will lead either to a leftward re-alignment of the Catholic establishment, or to a radical split between the Catholic parties and their sponsors.

This is heady stuff for the average Latin American Catholic. Don Pedro, you may remember, thought the Christian Democrats of Peru little better than Communists. There were Conservative Chileans who looked on Father Vekemans, the intellectual mentor of the Christian Democrats, in much the same light. Father Vekemans, a Belgian Jesuit, is one of the more remarkable characters on the Latin American scene. A tall Fleming, still youngish, hugely energetic, he is no sufferer of fools gladly. Vekemans may not be universally beloved; but he is universally respected. And he has done something which, in Latin American terms, is indeed a small earthquake. He has challenged the left-wing monopoly of intellectual prestige. If it is true that it takes a Jesuit to outwit a Marxist, Vekemans's order has every reason to be proud of him. At debates in the students' societies, it is now the Jesuits' men who have the facts at their fingertips and the mastery of dialectic. Marx is in danger of becoming old hat; Maritain is the man to read.

But Vekemans beat the Communists at their own game in more unexpected ways. He organised Catholic youth groups, and sent canvassers into the shanty-towns of Santiago to persuade the slum-dwellers to vote Christian Democrat. Curiously, but perhaps significantly, it had not occurred to the Communists to use electioneering techniques of this kind; and the Christian Democrats won heavily in these areas. Women too, as in Europe, voted for the Christian Democrats in large numbers, even where their husbands voted Socialist or Communist. This shows, of course, what modern-minded political techniques can do when applied to a semi-developed country like Chile, polarised between a conservative-minded Oligarchy and a scarcely less conservative-minded Communist Party. Vekemans himself, despite this triumph, is modest about the prospects of Christian Democracy in Latin America. He looks forward to Catholic parties holding power in Venezuela, El Salvador and perhaps Peru: but he is not over-sanguine. Himself a Jesuit technocrat—one is reminded of those energetic Jesuits, mocked by Voltaire, who organised the Indian "reductions" of

Paraguay—he is doubtful whether the technocrats are Latin America's best friends. They may feel they can work as well, if not better, with the kind of "Nasserist" régime that *Peronismo* foreshadowed. As for Chile, Vekemans was confident that Frei, given some outside help, could tackle her social and economic problems. Roger Vekemans, like Victor Urquidi, is a moderate of the left, a man of rational analysis and limited solutions. Still, if his formula can be made to work, the tremors of this small earthquake will be felt all over Latin America.

"Latin America is Catholic, as we all know. Half the world's Catholic population lives on this continent, and we're supposed to be the bastion of the Church. But how many of our Catholics actually go to church, or live Catholic lives? A tiny percentage! We're 'Catholic' in the bad sense of the word: easy-living, indulgent, casuistical, corrupt. Oh, we're very good at forgiving: we forgive ourselves everything. Catholic without being Christian, you see. Catholic, very Catholic! I would say: *hopelessly* Catholic!" Thus Father Vekemans: he has, as you see, a line in Pauline shock-tactics. After three centuries of bromide, he is eager for Christ to be once again a stumbling-block to the faithful. I do not know how much of the Christian Democrats' success can be attributed to Father Vekemans, but my guess is: a great deal. No less important, of course, has been the failure of the old centre-right parties to adapt to the newly industrialised Chile of the past generation. The bourgeois parties of Germany and Italy disintegrated under the impact of Fascism, leaving a gap which Christian Democracy was to fill. In a similar way, the Conservative, Liberal and Radical parties in Chile had begun to seem increasingly anachronistic. The history of one family illustrates this. In the twenties, the Radical Alessandri led a middle-class revolt against the Conservative oligarchy. Thirty years later his son became President with the support of a Radical-Liberal-Conservative alliance. But, by the fifties, such an alliance was no longer politically viable. If the strong "popular-front" FRAP was to be successfully opposed, a regrouping of the forces of the centre was required, as in Germany and Italy. Christian Democracy has filled this gap. It looks as if the Christian Democrats will come to occupy a reformist centre-left position, with a weakened Liberal-Conservative block to the Right, and a numerically powerful, but disunited

Socialist-Communist block to their Left. Such a constellation of forces is like that to be found in Venezuela and elsewhere. Which suggests that Latin America's political salvation lies with those parties of the centre-left which can depend on the support, or the acquiescence, not only of the traditional establishment, but of those "middle sectors" of society whose aspirations are reformist rather than revolutionary. As we shall see, it is the failure of Chile's powerful neighbour, the Argentine—where the "middle sectors" are still more strongly entrenched—to develop such a constellation of forces that has led to the *confusionismo* of the past generation.

Creole and Cosmopolitan

Strictly speaking, Roger Vekemans is no Chilean at all: he is a foreigner, a *gringo*. But it is characteristic of Latin America, as of North America, that the foreigner is assimilated remarkably quickly—more quickly than is possible in Europe. This, indeed, is one of Latin America's most "American" characteristics. It strikes the foreigner how many of Latin America's outstanding men are in fact sons of recent immigrants. Among political leaders there have been President Leoni of Venezuela, ex-President Frondizi of Argentina, ex-President Alessandri of Chile: all of immigrant Italian stock. Chile's Frei is of German-Swiss, Brazil's Kubitschek of Czech stock. The great hero of Chilean Independence was Bernardo O'Higgins, son of an Irish Viceroy of Peru; and the Edwards family has long been famous in Chilean commercial and public life. The great fortunes made since the war have been made as often as not by newcomers to Latin America: Hans Neumann, for example, the Venezuelan industrialist and patron of the arts, arrived in the country as a penniless post-war refugee from Hitler's Europe. But the Italians have played a unique role. The plutocracies of Buenos Aires and São Paulo—the Matarazzo dynasty, for example—are to a great extent Italian in origin. What is interesting, sociologically, is how much more successful Italian immigrants to Latin America have been than their cousins in the United States. It is tempting to argue that in a Catholic, Latin country difficulties of assimilation are not so great. This is certainly true; but it is not the whole explanation. Whereas the Italian immigrants to the United States had to face the competition of people technically more sophisticated than themselves, the Italians who flooded into the Argentine, Uruguay, Brazil and, to a lesser extent, Chile in the late nineteenth century were superior technically to their Latin American hosts. Also, the immigrants to South America were largely North Italian, whereas the immigrants to the United States were often from the economically less advanced *Mezzogiorno*.

The immigrant's role, then, has been different in Latin America and in the North. What has taken the Jews, the Italians and the Irish of New York generations to accomplish, their Latin American counterparts accomplish in one generation. "Racial" explanations for this will not do. Slavs and Germans and Anglo-Saxons, though much less numerous, appear to assimilate no less easily than do Portuguese, Spaniards, or Italians. The explanation, I think, lies in a factor we have already mentioned: the differential—in economic skill, in adaptability, in intelligence, and in sheer application—between the native-born *criollo* and the immigrant from Europe. In the United States this differentiation is not absent. Until quite recently, the highly-trained European professional (the German-Jewish immigrant of the 1930's, for example) had a similar advantage over the native-born. But in the United States this differential is becoming a thing of the past. Not so in Latin America. There, the superiority of the immigrant is still apparent, and very significant. For it points to a real weakness in Latin America, a weakness none the less real for being taboo to some of her self-appointed champions: I mean the inferior quality of her spiritual and intellectual life.

A colonial society prides itself on its pioneer qualities. But that is not the whole story. As striking to the outsider is the lack of competitiveness, the narrowness, the conservatism of a colonial society. A colonial society, inevitably, is a low-pressure society. It is a society where a few men—a Pablo Neruda, a Borges, a Roger Vekemans—stand out in a way that would not be possible in Europe. They owe their stature in part to the flatness of the surrounding landscape. It follows that the immigrant from a more high-pressured society has an advantage. But this was no less true in Colonial times. Indeed, it forms part of the psychological background to the Independence movement. Here, for example, is what the Chilean historian, Francisco Encina, had to say about the conflict between *criollos* and *peninsulares*:

> The Spaniard was irritated by the indolence, the frivolity, and the superficiality of the *criollo*, and especially of the tropical *criollo*. At heart he felt him to be an inferior, a bastard off-shoot of his race, an empty-headed chatter-box, incapable of any serious task. For his part, the *criollo* hated the *peninsulares* with all his soul; he regarded the mental deliberation of the Galician as stupidity; he saw the Catalan as a miser and the Basque as a bird of prey, and he felt of all of them as parvenus and climbers, who wanted to monopolise wealth, and marry the richest heiresses. . . . Viewing this antipathy from another point of view we can see that the social ideals and values of *peninsulares* and *criollos* were quite different. The *criollos* delighted in an extreme generosity, in bold adventure and reckless courage, in skill at *criollo* sports and exercises and in an intense enjoyment of the present without thought of tomorrow. But for the Spaniards who came to America in the eighteenth century, regularity of conduct, economy and foresight were everything.

That these "peninsular" attitudes should be precisely those of first- and second-generation immigrants to Latin America over the past century is an eloquent comment on the quality of *criollo* civilisation.

A Catholic Culture?

This is, perhaps, what Roger Vekemans meant when he said that Latin America, though not especially Christian, was "hopelessly Catholic". In both Americas the passionate, otherworldly faith of the founders has lost its vigour, and has become secularised. But whereas no one can doubt that the "Protestant spirit", of which Paul Tillich wrote, lives on in present-day North America, in Latin America the rot has gone deep. It is arguable, of course, that freemasonry, the *positivisme* of Comte (there are still Comtiste chapels in Brazil), and even Marxism, are to some degree products of Catholic secularisation. The Jacobin is first cousin to the Jesuit; and Mexico's Juarez reminds us of the fanaticism anti-clericalism was once able to arouse. But the balance of the comparison is unfavourable to Catholicism. Whereas Protestantism has plainly moulded North America in its image, this cannot be said with confidence of the Catholicism of Latin America. The reasons for this are various; but the facts are not in doubt. It is only necessary to compare the highly-organised, socially and politically powerful Catholicism of the United States (whose Catholics are some forty million strong) with the permanently under-staffed, impoverished, and miserably-educated priesthood of Latin America (with a nominal total of some two hundred million Catholics).

Thus even today a good many priests are *"peninsulares"*—or Frenchmen, Germans, and Belgians. According to figures published by official Catholic sources, the situation among the laity is no less catastrophic. One survey, in 1959, estimated that whereas 93 per cent of the population of Latin America was nominally Catholic, *not more than 10 per cent* could be claimed as practising Catholics. Another source puts the figure as low as 3·5 per cent of church-attenders for the male population, and 9·5 for the female (Stephen Neill, *A History of Christian Missions*). It might be thought that Chile, with its Christian Democrat government, would be a Catholic stronghold. But this is not so. Only 11 per cent of the population are officially claimed as practising Catholics, which is about the same number of Chilians who are active members of evangelical churches. Yet Chile is classified by the above-quoted Catholic source, along with Guatemala, Cuba, and Venezuela, as a country where Catholicism is "holding its own". Only in Mexico (paradoxically), and in Costa Rica, Colombia and Argentina, is the Church classified as "strong". In Bolivia and Paraguay, in much of rural Brazil, in Panama, the Dominican Republic and Honduras, the Church is actually said to be "dying".

Considering the monopoly the Church has enjoyed in Latin America for over four centuries these figures are striking. The militant Catholicism of Latin America turns out to be a paper tiger. If we can speak of a pervasive Catholic influence in Latin America, it is only in the negative sense implied in Roger Vekemans's comment: Latin America is "hopelessly Catholic". It is Catholicism's mediterranean, pagan elements, apparently, that Latin America has taken to heart. Soft, indulgent, and permissive, it shies away from the inexorable, Semitic imperatives of traditional Protestantism. Are these the reasons for

Catholicism's relative failure in Latin America? Not entirely:
the reasons for the failure are various. But that list of countries
in which Catholicism is said to be "dying" gives us a hint.
These, after all, are the most backward areas of Latin America;
they are, to a large extent, Indian or Negro, or *mestizo* or
mulatto, in racial complexion. The countries, on the other hand,
where the Church is said to be "strong", are predominantly the
"white" countries of Latin America—with the exception of
Mexico.

The position of Mexico seems anomalous. But it may also
yield the key to the mystery. It was in Mexico that the great
work of the religious *conquista* began, and it was there that it
penetrated most deeply. The anti-clericalism of *Reforma* and
Revolution may have reflected the anti-clericalism among the
peasantry, but it did not reflect anti-Catholicism. Even in the
era of Porfirio Diaz's *positivisme*, and Obregon's and Calles's
socialist secularism, the Church never lost its hold on the masses.
The unofficial *rapprochement* that has now taken place with the
PRI régime is, as in Communist Poland, the result of irresistible
popular pressure. But in the other Indian countries of Latin
America missionary penetration did not go so deep. It is clear
from *The People of Aritama* that Aritama's Catholicism is no
more than a veneer beneath which pagan beliefs linger on. The
same is notoriously true of countries like Guatemala and Honduras, where complex syncretistic cultures have grown up. Or
of Haiti and Cuba, or the Brazilian North-East, where Voodoo
or *makumba* cults flourish. In the "White" countries, on the
other hand, the strength of the Church seems to be a reflection
of these countries' Europeanism. If this is correct, it would seem
that Catholicism has remained—except in Mexico—inextric-
ably bound up with *criollo* culture. Where that culture is not
predominant, the aboriginal peoples have either rejected
Catholicism or turned it to uses of their own.

The historical reasons for this failure are plain. The early
missionaries, the Franciscans and the Dominicans, and later
the Jesuits, performed acts of staggering courage and endurance. They learned and transcribed the native languages, protected and instructed the Indians, and were often martyred for
their pains. But they also made certain mistakes which—speaking
with historical hindsight—explain the weakness of Catholicism

in Latin America today. Thus the earliest conversions were rather too easily effected. Peter of Ghent, a Belgian friar, wrote from Mexico in 1529:

> I and the brother who was with me baptised in the province of Mexico upwards of 200,000 persons—so many in fact that I cannot give an accurate estimate of the number. Often we baptised in a single day 14,000 people, sometimes 10,000, sometimes 8,000.

No wonder the early missionaries were impressed with the docility, the Christ-like humility, of these uninstructed natives! But effective Christianisation of these mass-converts depended on intensive education and instruction: and this was beyond the resources of Spain and Portugal. Even so, it seems that more could have been done, had the Church been willing to treat her converts as adult human beings. But this was seldom the case. The Indian churches were almost always "non-communicating". The sacraments of Baptism, Matrimony and Penance might be administered; but seldom the sacrament of Confirmation. Only under bishop's licence might the sacrament of the Eucharist be administered. No attempt was made to build up an indigenous Ministry. In 1535, the first Council of Mexico forbade the admission to orders of anyone of "Moorish race"— which was taken to include Indian, *mestizo* and *mulatto*. Such rules were not always observed. But it is significant that in the most ambitious missionary experiment of all—the Jesuit "reductions" in Paraguay—no Indian candidate was ever prepared for the priesthood. The Indians, in fact, were treated as children. Once the Jesuits were expelled, the "reductions" fell into decay and their inhabitants reverted to paganism. Paraguay is classified today as a country in which the Church is dying.

Failure to develop either an indigenous priesthood or an educated laity seemed to have been the fundamental mistake of the Catholic missions—a mistake which the Catholic Church, which claims to be freer of colour prejudice than the Protestant Churches, might well take to heart. Nor has the situation changed much today. In Brazil, according to one Catholic source, only 2·3 per cent of priests are *mulattos*, only 0·4 per cent pure-blooded Negroes; yet *mulattos* and Negroes make up 36 per cent of the population of Brazil. That the growth of semi-pagan, syncretistic *makumba* cults among Negroes and *mulattos* is related to this can hardly be doubted. But the weakness of Latin American Catholicism, not simply as a system of dogma, but also as a system of morality is equally evident. By nature, Latin Americans may be no more immoral in their financial or sexual habits than other people. But in any given society much will depend on the threshold of tolerance. And there is no doubt that in Latin America the standard is often set staggeringly low. In financial matters this is well-known; as in Latin Europe, the tax-collector is considered fair game. Equally, it is accepted that a politician or a government servant may line his pockets at the expense of the state. When a dictator is overthrown, it is noticeable that this is seldom one of the charges brought against him: his successors are too busy doing it themselves.

But there are other matters with which Catholic morality is traditionally concerned. For example, the stability of the mono-gamous family. We have only to look at the figures for illegiti-macy in Latin America to realise how far the Church has failed to mould society in its image. At present, the illegitimacy rate in Chile is 20 per cent; this compares well with 23 per cent in 1949, and with 39 per cent in 1917. But it is very high by North American or European standards. Yet there are countries far worse off than Chile. Indeed, Chile occupies a middle position between the relative familial stability of Uruguay or Argentina and the staggering instability found in the Caribbean countries, or in Colombia or Venezuela. It is only when outside standards are applied that the extent of the trouble becomes apparent. Thus in Chile about 50 per cent of all males of eligible age are married. This compares well with the figures for Peru (26 per cent), and for Venezuela (20 per cent). (These figures show, incidentally, that poverty is not the only reason for familial instability; Venezuela has the highest income per head of any Latin American country.) Yet even Chile's 50 per cent com-pares unfavourably with the figures for non-Latin countries: Sweden (60 per cent); the United States (70 per cent); New Zealand and South Africa (75 per cent). The factors influencing familial stability are complex. But the differential between New Zealand's 75 per cent and Venezuela's 20 per cent can hardly pass without comment. The Protestant churches appear to have impressed their basic morality on society far more effectively than the Church of Rome.

These failures are freely admitted by Catholic writers. More money and effort is being put into missionary activities than at any time since the eighteenth century. In Bogota, the Church has her own radio station; by distributing transistor radios to the *campesinos* of the backlands, she has ensured herself a captive audience. We have looked at the remarkable socio-political work done by Father Vekemans. But Father Vekemans is only one of the growing army of Jesuits and Dominicans who have taken the pessimistic results of these surveys to heart, and look on Latin America as a virgin field for Catholic proselytising. (For the Jesuits the Latin American field is a special challenge. It was there that their greatest conquests were made, and it was largely as a result of their expulsion that the level of Catholic intellectual activity sank to its present state.) Nevertheless, it is going to be an uphill struggle. It has been estimated that, for pastoral work alone, at least fifty thousand more priests are required than are at present available. Clearly, unless Catholic education is drastically improved, the majority of these men will have to be drafted in from abroad.

Will Latin America, in a generation's time, still deserve the title "Catholic"? Indeed, how far does it deserve it now? The truth is, for more than a century the Church has fought a war on two fronts. It has been up against the perfunctory Catholicism of the semi-converted Indian, *mestizo*, and *mulatto* masses. But, among the educated élite, it has also been up against the ideals of the Enlightenment and the *positivisme* of nineteenth-century France. Whether the cancer of scepticism had struck deeper with the educated Latin American than with the educated European is impossible to say. But that it had gone very deep, even in Colonial times, is evident from Maria Graham's account of a meeting with the Liberator of Chile, San Martin:

> He quoted authors whom he evidently knew but by half, and of the half he knew he appeared to me to mistake the spirit. When we spoke of religion . . . he talked much of philosophy and he . . . seemed to think that Philosophy consisted in leaving religion to the priests and the vulgar, as a state-machine, while the wise man would laugh alike at the monk, the Protestant, and the deist . . . His natural shrewd sense must have led him to perceive the

absurdity of the Roman Catholic superstitions which here are naked in their ugliness, not glossed over with the pomp and elegance of Italy . . . it has been observed that the Roman Catholic system is shaken off with much greater difficulty than those which are taught in the Reformed churches, but when it loses its hold on the mind, it much more frequently prepares the way for unlimited scepticism. And this appears to me to be exactly the state of San Martin's mind. From religion . . . the transition was easy to political revolution. The reading of most South American reformers is mostly in a French channel. The age of Louis XIV was talked of as the direct and only cause of the French Revolution and, consequently, of those of South America. . . .

A century later, according to Lord Bryce's account in *South America, Observations and Impressions* (1912), the attitudes of the *criollo* upper class had changed relatively little:

> Men of the upper or educated classes appear wholly indifferent to theology and Christian worship. It has no interest for them. They are seldom actively hostile to Christianity, much less are they offensive when they speak of it; but they think it does not concern them, and may be left to women and peasants. In the more advanced parts of South America it seems to be regarded merely as a harmless Old World affair which belongs to the old order of things just as much as does the rule of Spain, but which may, so long as it does not interfere with politics, be treated with the respect its antiquity commands.

"So long as it does not interfere with politics": that is not the spirit of Father Vekemans and his fellow-partisans. And it may turn out to be the opposite of the truth. One thing, at least, is clear. When all allowances have been made for the courage and humility of those who defended the Indians against the excesses of the Conqueror, the fundamental reason for the Church's failure to hold the territory it won in the sixteenth century remains her identification with the Colonial system. It was this that caused her to fight a losing battle throughout the nineteenth century against the growing power of the urban middle classes, and against the discontent of the peasant masses on the *estancias* of her Conservative allies.

What is the likely pattern of the future? The spirit bloweth where it listeth: for all we know, Latin America may be on the brink of a second religious *conquista*. Who can tell? For what it is worth, my guess is that Catholicism will indeed undergo a revival in the course of the next generation. If we may judge by European experience, it is likely that a part of the rapidly growing middle class will return to the fold—especially if threatened by militantly atheistic left-wing movements. The political commitment towards which the Church is moving—is, indeed, being dragged—will be different from anything it has experienced in the past. Most educated Catholics realise that the Church's past identification with the Conservatives was mistaken, and would prove disastrous if repeated. This means that the Church must look to the political centre or centre-left. This in turn may enable the Church to evangelise the new urban masses of the *barriadas* and the *callampas* more effectively than it evangelised the rural masses four centuries ago. The success of Christian Democracy is not essential to this goal; but it may well play a part in it. The one factor that would inhibit any renewal of Catholic activity would be a return to the doctrinal and political rigidities of the past. But this is not likely. The liberalisation of Vatican policy, and the obvious need to adapt to the trends of Latin American politics, suggest that the chances of a Catholic revival may be better today than at any time since the age of Las Casas.

8

ARGENTINA:
or Civilisation and Barbarism

The first colonists who made their homes in this vast vacant space called the *pampas* came from a land where the people are accustomed to sit in the shade of trees, where corn and wine and oil are supposed to be necessaries, and where there is salad in the gardens. Naturally, they made gardens and planted trees, both for shade and fruit. . . . No doubt for two or three generations they tried to live as people live in Spain. . . . But now the main business of their lives is cattle-raising, and as their cattle roamed at will over the vast plains and were more like wild than domestic animals, it was a life on horseback. . . . They gave up their oil and wine and bread and lived on flesh alone. They sat in the shade and ate the fruit of trees planted by their fathers and their grandfathers until the trees died of old age, or were blown down or killed by the cattle, and there was no more shade and fruit.

Far Away and Long Ago: W. H. Hudson (1918)

Buenos Aires

IN THAT CHILDHOOD GEOGRAPHY, sad vestige of hours spent poring over the schoolroom atlas, Argentina is a fat turnip-root tapering gently polewards, Chile an unnaturally elongated tuber struggling down the Pacific seaboard. We do not know much about either; but at least we know where they are. And that is more than we can say for Paraguay, Uruguay, Guatemala or Nicaragua. Actually, the childhood image is not so misleading. Chile is impoverished and constricted; Argentina is open and ample. The soil of central Chile is as rich as any in Latin America. But its wealth cannot be compared with that of the *pampas* of Argentina. Around the turn of the century, as Chile grew rich on copper and nitrate, Santiago cast its modest colonial skin and became an Edwardian metropolis. Argentina, belying her name, had no such resources—she had no silver, no copper, and little enough iron and coal. Still, during that age Argentina's beef and cereals had made her rich too—indeed, much richer. Santiago was to Buenos Aires as Winnipeg was to Chicago. Today, both Santiago and Buenos Aires have a down-at-heel air. They have the look of cities that have known better days.

Thanks to past trade connections these three countries of the Southern Cone—Chile, Argentina, Uruguay—are the Latin American countries the British know best. Two smart Buenos Aires' suburbs rejoice in the names of Ranelagh and Hurlingham. "Harrods" is the biggest department-store in Buenos Aires. The British introduced horse-racing and polo and five o'clock tea. And, of course, the *pampas* railway system, which Peron nationalised out of the sterling balances accumulated during the war, and on which the Argentine—*Schadenfreude!*—has lost money ever since. Argentina still exports more to Britain than to any other country. But she imports less from Britain nowadays than from either Germany or the United States. It is the *norteamericanos*, here as elsewhere, who inherit the ambiguous sceptre of economic hegemony. I was told I would find anti-American feeling decreasing as I travelled south: "the Cubans and the Mexicans may hate us *yanquis*; but in Buenos Aires and in Santiago they've got more sense". Not so, not so at all. If anything, anti-Americanism in the Argentine is more reckless than in Mexico, whose people, over the years, have come to terms with it. Britain, on the other hand, is once more quite popular. Salutary to reflect—*Schadenfreude* again!—that a generation ago the brickbats were aimed at us.

The countries of the Southern Cone show a different mood, a different attitude to the past, from anything we have yet come across. They knew better days, not in far-off Colonial times, but only the day before yesterday. It is easy for Colombians and Ecuadorians and Bolivians to claim that they never had a chance. It is also, because of this, easy to claim that things can only get better. But the peoples of the Southern Cone have seen prosperity come and go; and both rise and fall seem equally mysterious. Was our prosperity always built on sand, or were we cheated of our inheritance? (It is fair to say that to many economists the cycle of wealth and decay is no less mysterious.) The pessimism of these countries is therefore different from the Catholic-Hispanic or Indian-*mestizo* pessimism of Mexico or Peru. It is a specifically modern pessimism and thus, for the visitor, profoundly disturbing. We have become so development-conscious, so compulsively optimistic, that the spectacle of economic failure, of an actual decline in production or in wealth per head, is acutely shocking. It is something we would rather not know about. Things ought to go up and up; the entelechy of history is progress and, in particular, economic progress. If things should go wrong, if the curve should falter, we are at once plunged in despair. Argentina has the largest middle class in Latin America. Ought she not to be stable, affluent, and democratic like ourselves? The commercial and industrial skills of the seven million inhabitants of Buenos Aires have no equal in Latin America. Yet 97 per cent of Argentina's exports are still of livestock and agricultural products. She is as dependent on foreign markets for these as she was fifty years ago. A certain defeatism, then, lies behind the at first so startling malaise of this solidly-based, comfortable bourgeois society. It is as if the Depression of the nineteen-thirties, ancient history to millions of Americans and Europeans, had somehow

persisted into the present decade. And not only the stark economic facts of the Depression, but the gamut of rage, frustration,
and political hysteria that accompanied it.

For all that, Buenos Aires is no mean city. Compared with its
shabby-genteel Edwardian air, modern Caracas, Mexico City
or Lima seem brash and raw; not cities, but sprawling, un-
disciplined human agglomerations. Why this difference?
Buenos Aires was not founded until fifty years after Lima and
Mexico City. Until the mid-eighteenth century she was not
allowed to trade with Europe; goods, imported through Panama, had to be carried on donkey-back across the Andes and
the Bolivian *puna*. In 1780, when Lima and Mexico City were
at the height of their glory, Buenos Aires was still a provincial
outpost, with a population of 25,000. Like Caracas, she was
something of a *parvenu* (it is no coincidence that Bolivar and San
Martin, twin liberators of South America, came from these
neglected poles of Spain's South American Empire). Nor did
her early years hold great promise for the future. Under Rosas,
most notorious of South American *caudillos*, Argentina enjoyed
a terror-spree that lasted seventeen years. At the fall of Rosas in
1852 (thanks to Brazilian and Uruguayan intervention), the
population of Argentina was hardly more than a million; that
of Buenos Aires only 90,000. Only in the sixties and seventies
did the surge of immigration from Europe get under way that
made Argentina, by 1910, the richest and most powerful of all
Spanish-speaking countries in the Americas. Between 1857 and
1930 six million Europeans, mostly Spanish and Italian, came to
settle in the Argentine (another 650,000 arrived between 1947
and 1951). Over half Argentina's population is therefore of
first- or second-generation immigrant stock: a much higher
proportion than in the United States, and a contributing cause
to the instability of Argentine political institutions.

By 1900, Buenos Aires was the largest and wealthiest Spanish-
speaking city in the world. She could hold her own with
Barcelona and Madrid; her only rivals in Latin America were
Brazil's Rio and São Paulo. Visitors to Latin America in those
pre-war years (Lord Bryce, for one) did not hesitate to predict
that the twentieth century, in Latin America, would be the
century of Argentina. In Buenos Aires, the visitor found
splendid boulevards, operas and theatres, elaborate parks and

weighty municipal statues. He was impressed by the restless vitality and ingenuity of her people, to whom the great Sarmiento, writer-president of Argentina in the 1880's, had thrown down the challenge of doing for South America what the energetic *yanqui* had done for the North. The visitor saw in Buenos Aires, for all her *parvenu* qualities, a true daughter of the cities of the West: Rome, Paris, Vienna, London. In 1910 Argentina celebrated her hundredth anniversary in a blaze of ostentation. There seemed no clouds on the horizon.

Why did Argentina, most promising of Latin American states, flounder in this way? That Argentina, and to some extent Chile and Uruguay, should have betrayed their promise of fifty years ago, is obviously profoundly disturbing. These countries, after all, appear to have all the presuppositions of social and economic development. Or is it, perhaps, that our presuppositions are more open to question than we realise? There is no simple answer. But pointers are not lacking to certain of the reasons for this malaise. One is self-evident and not unique to Argentina: the Colonial structure, whether pastoral or agricultural, or based on coffee or oil or mineral extraction, of most of the economies of Latin America. In the years before 1930, Argentina was the chief beneficiary of this profitable, but fundamentally lop-sided state of affairs. It is logical, then, that she should also have been the hardest-hit, first by the failure of North American and European industrialism in the 1930's (one reason, certainly, for the Fascist sympathies of the military revolutionaries of 1943), and then by the shift in the. terms of trade against the producing countries that took place after 1950.

We have already touched on one other possible reason: the social atomisation resulting from the immigration of the pre-1930 period, and from the internal migration (from the countryside to the city) that set in after 1930. But does mass-immigration necessarily make for political instability? The United States weathered a similar storm with her institutions intact. So, in a smaller way, did Australia and Canada. But in the Argentine there were significant differences. First, the immigrant alluvium was deposited, in the Argentine, on ground itself shifting and unsteady. This was not the case in the United States. There, the Constitution and the conventions of representative government were firmly rooted before mass-immigration began. Then, in the second place, the scale and the distribution of this immigrant flood were different. By the mid-nineteenth century the battle between Federalists and Central-ists was decided: Buenos Aires *was* the Argentine. Today, one-third of the population lives in Greater Buenos Aires; and it is here that the proportion of immigrants is highest. Thus, com-paring Buenos Aires with New York—the other great immigrant terminal of the Americas—we are bound to note that New York is not the United States. For the analogy to fit, we would have to imagine a United States in which the ethnically-mixed immigrant population of Chicago, Boston and New York, having achieved economic dominance over a traditionalist, WASP countryside, were yet unable to find any focus for their aspirations in the traditional pattern. This is what happened to Argentina when she opened her doors to the immigrant flood. In Argentina, the barriers were swept away. In the United States the barriers stood, and her immigrants adopted the norms of the traditional society.

Comparison with New York is inevitable. But the differences are at least as interesting. Buenos Aires, like New York, is a cosmopolitan city; she makes most Spanish American capitals look provincial. The busy bookstalls on her boulevards offer a varied menu: *Der Stern, La Prensa, Paris Match, The Times, Life en Español, Corriere della Sera.* These are devoured, not by would-be cosmopolitans, but by people whose first language is Italian, French, English or German. The women of Buenos Aires are notably more elegant—this must be the Italian strain—than elsewhere in South America. One test of a city's cosmopolitan-ism is the telephone book. In Lima, Bogota or Mexico City, if you glance down the names of subscribers, you seldom come on a non-Spanish surname. In Bogota you find pages devoted to the Jaramillos, the Gonzalezes, the Echevarrias. These are the names, much-multiplied, of the earliest Spanish settlers. These are the descendants, legitimate or otherwise, of the *conquistadores*; or the descendants of *mestizos* or Indians who have adopted (as in Europe) the name of their feudal *patron*. In Buenos Aires, Montevideo or Santiago, such names are found too. But they are no longer dominant. Equally common are names of second- or third-generation Italian immigrants:

Germani, Manzi, Pezzoni. Less common, but still numerous, are those familiar-unfamiliar combinations that point to ethnic intermixture. There are the Joneses and the Browns and the O'Haras (but Señor Jose Brown Gonzalez speaks, very likely, no English at all). There are the Schultzes, the Schmitts and the Pickelbergers (but Señor Juan Rodriguez Pickelberger, unless his mother sent him to the *Deutsche Schule*, probably speaks little German). Argentina, again, is the only Latin American country to have a sizeable Jewish population: close on five hundred thousand, mostly in Buenos Aires itself. If Eichmann found kindred spirits among the exiled Nazis of Buenos Aires, he also chose (perhaps fatally) the most Jewish city in Latin America to set up house in.

This city of seven millions then, the largest in the Americas after New York, and by far the largest in the Spanish-speaking world, may not even have a majority of people with Spanish blood in their veins. It is not quite so humiliating an outcome, perhaps, as the overwhelming of the old WASP population of New York by successive waves of Irish, Italians, Jews, Negroes and Puerto Ricans. But it is a situation without parallel in Latin America, except in São Paulo and, more recently, in Caracas. Yet in one respect the contrast is striking: assimilation is much further advanced in Buenos Aires than in New York. In Buenos Aires, unlike in New York, the "melting-pot" has melted. The colour problem, admittedly, does not exist: like Australia, Argentina prohibits coloured immigration altogether. (Buenos Aires' formerly numerous Negroes—a quarter of the population at Independence—appear to have been completely absorbed.) Buenos Aires has assimilated both her Latin and her non-Latin immigrants far more effectively than is the case in New York —there is no equivalent to the ingrained communalism of New York social and political life. That is a remarkable achievement. But the paradox of Argentina is that though she has assimilated her immigrants with success, she has not drawn the political dividends to which this achievement would seem to entitle her.

The Argentine Malaise

If Argentina is the most exasperating, she is also in many ways the most interesting country in Latin America. There is a sense, of course, in which she is not "typical". She has few Indians and almost no Negroes. Her population, far from starving, enjoys a higher calorie-intake than that of the United States. Her oligarchy scarcely counts today as a political force, having been displaced by a middle class and a working class, recognisable as such by European criteria. Nor is Argentina, in the strict sense, "underdeveloped". Areas of the back-country are still very primitive. But the great industrial complexes of Buenos Aires, Rosario, and Cordoba belong not to the underdeveloped Third World, but to the most advanced regions of the northern hemisphere. And yet Argentina is not the country that these data, according to the best theories, ought to have made her. She is troubled not at all by the perverse psychology of *mestizaje*. She is highly literate; and she has the best institutions of higher education in Latin America. Her problems are not those of the "Indian" countries of Latin America. Her difficulties cannot be put down to the climate, which is temperate; nor to the soil, which is fertile. All the components of a progressive, stable polity are present: only the trick of combining them is absent.

Since 1930 almost everything has gone wrong. In that year the middle-class Radical régime of President Irigoyen, unable to cope with the effects of the Depression, was bundled out of office by the Army under the semi-Fascist General Uriburu. Uriburu's attempts at a conservative-élitist reaction were a failure. The power of the oligarchy, broken by the Radical triumph of 1916, could not be restored. Yet any return to constitutional democracy meant a return to the *status quo ante*, which was as unacceptable to the Army as to the oligarchy. The upshot was the period of "indirect" military rule, in alliance with the Conservatives and the right-wing of the Radical party, that lasted until the Army took over again in the coup of 1943: the prelude to the emergence of Peron as the Argentine's strong man. Peron, as we shall see, hit upon a formula for political and social stabilisation which must seem, in retrospect, of great historical interest. We might say that Peron invented "Nasserism" a decade before Nasser. Unwittingly, he became the spiritual progenitor of that brand of authoritarian populism that has spread throughout the Third World over the past decade and a half.

H

Still, Peron's formula did not work in the long run either. Peron was thrown out by the Army which put him in power; a new period of oscillation between direct military intervention and precarious civilian control began. In 1958 the left-wing Radical Frondizi was elected by a large majority, which included the *Peronista* working-class vote. By 1962, Frondizi had few friends left, and the Army stepped in again, dismayed at Frondizi's failure either to stem the *Peronista* tide or to provide a stable government of the centre. In the following year, the moderate ("Blue") faction in the Army insisted on a return to civilian rule and Arturo Illia, ex-country doctor and moderate Radical, was made President. In 1966, the army took over again, under General Ongania. About Argentina's present mood, over two years later, it would be wrong to be dogmatic. A certain disillusion, a weariness with the ins and outs of the military and civilian factions, has descended on the country. Nevertheless, there is no serious resistance to the régime. There is, perhaps, a sense of shame. Argentina, Argentines ruefully protest, is no banana-republic.

These are the dry bones of politics: and they make melancholy reading. It is clear, I think, that a full explanation must be sought at a deeper level: in the sociology of urbanisation; in the spiritual and intellectual formation of the Argentine élite; in the conflict of inherited values with the needs of modern society; and in the many foreign influences, ideological and economic, that have touched the Argentine over the past two generations. One explanation, the economic, we have looked at already: it explains a good deal; but it does not explain everything. If it explains the malaise of the 30's, we must admit that the Argentine economy made a creditable revival in the late 30's, and that it was thanks to the credits piled up during the war that Peron financed the bonanza of his first years in office. Not until 1950 did the Argentine run into serious difficulties. Since then, admittedly, the economy has been almost stagnant; production per head has even declined. We may note that these facts accord ill with current notions. Does poverty, for example, generate social revolution? The "social revolution" of Peron can hardly be explained in these terms. Though social services were poorly developed, the Argentine working class was one of the best-fed in the world.

Like most of the producing countries (it is not polite to mention this) Argentina did not do at all badly out of the war. Prices rose for her exports; her home industries were stimulated by lack of imports. Admittedly, the profits of neutrality were unequally distributed. As in Peru and Venezuela, it was in part the spectacle of this inequitable distribution that put left-wing governments in power after 1945. Still, it is undeniable that the most extreme "leftward" swing since 1930 coincided, not with economic distress, but with great economic prosperity.

Nor do economics explain the failure of the Argentine middle class to consolidate its triumph over the oligarchy in 1916. (Thirty per cent of Argentines were reckoned to be "middle class" as early as 1914.) No national bourgeoisie on Bismarckian lines came into being. Instead a fragmentation of the bourgeois parties occurred, not unlike that of their counterparts in Weimar Germany, a fragmentation that invited military intervention and paved the way for Peron. Still, the German analogy is of limited application. It cannot be argued that it was the Depression that demoralised the Argentine *bourgeoisie*. The tendencies towards fragmentation within the Radical party were evident much earlier, and had more to do with the "personalist" role played by President Irigoyen (a Radical splinter group came to be best known as the *anti-personalistas*) than with competing economic interests. Yet this "personalism" was only the expression of a deep-rooted lack of ideological and social coherence in the Argentine bourgeoisie. Irigoyen, indeed, summed up the faults of this new, post-immigrant bourgeoisie. His speeches were invariably high-flown and bombastic, in the worst tradition of Latin rhetoric. Yet he had no coherent conception of the kind of Argentine he wanted to create. Not surprisingly, when the Radical party came to power, its policies differed hardly at all from those of the Conservatives. Radicals, too, had to rely on foreign investment; they, too, were disinclined to attack the landed interests directly through land reform.

The Radicals, then, were an anti-party: once the oligarchy was overthrown, they had little to put in its place. They were militantly nationalist; but Argentina had no enemies. They were "anti-imperialist"; but they knew that Argentina's development was impossible without foreign capital. Arguably, if they had been faced from the start with a strongly organised working-class movement (the socialist and Anarchist parties were largely recruited from immigrants, and never struck root in the country), the Radicals might have become an anti-party of a different kind; an anti-labour party. But that challenge was a generation away. Or the Radical party might have developed an articulate ideology—like that of the Liberals in the nineteenth century—which would have given their movement a coherence in intellectual terms that it lacked in social and ethnic background. Instead, it was given the pseudo-ideology of an Irigoyen. We have remarked on the tendency of Latin American political parties to "personalist" leadership, and on the non-ideological character of most Latin American politics. If we look at the Radical party, or at Peron's party a generation later, we see that these tendencies are complementary. It is easy to criticise the ideological rhetoric of Latin American politics. And fashionable to conclude that what Latin America needs is greater pragmatism. But could not the opposite be true? Could it not be that Latin America needs not less, but *more* ideology, or at least better-articulated ideology? Whatever poses Latin American politicians may strike in public, their practice is usually highly opportunistic. A more coherent ideology might have saved Argentina's Radicals from the irresponsibility that characterised them once they were in power.

Sarmiento's "Facundo"

Economic explanations of Argentina's troubles do not take us very far. Economic failure has added to the malaise; but the malaise has deep roots in the history of the Argentine people. Why else should the failure of the Argentine middle class to assume national responsibility have been recapitulated in the history of the Argentine working class? What are the roots of the malaise? Argentina's writers—she is the most articulate, as well as the most literate, of Latin American nations—have spilt much ink on the matter. What strikes the foreigner is how little the terms of reference have changed over the past century and a half. To most Argentines these terms of reference are truisms; but they are little known outside, and therefore worth rehearsing. Whether apt or not, this is the way Argentines have seen themselves over many generations. For this reason, though we are not bound to accept the traditional self-analysis, it deserves our attention. The terms of reference are set out with un-Latin American strictness and brevity in the title of what is, indisputably, the greatest book to have come out of Argentina: Sarmiento's *Facundo, or Civilisation and Barbarism* (1845). Sarmiento, Liberal opponent of Rosas, himself later President of Argentina, is perhaps the noblest figure produced by Argentina in the century after Independence—indeed perhaps the noblest figure in modern Latin American history. Let us look, then, at Sarmiento's book, and sketch out Sarmiento's analysis of the Argentine character.

Facundo is as fundamental to the understanding of the Argentine, as *Rebellion in the Backlands* is to the understanding of Brazil, or *Don Quixote* to that of Spain. Ostensibly, it is an account of the life of Facundo Quiroga, a backlands *caudillo* of the Age of Rosas. But it is a great deal more than that. It is an evocation of the traditional life of the Argentine, outside the main cities, as it existed for more than three centuries. *Facundo*, then, is a seminal book. And it shares with da Cunha's *Rebellion in the Backlands* a quality that is given to few books: it sets up a system of coordinates that defines the subsequent literature, and indeed the life, of the nation as a whole. We shall look at da Cunha's masterpiece later; but it is useful, even at this stage, to point to the parallels between the books. Both were written by men committed to "civilisation". Da Cunha, though he wrote two generations later than Sarmiento, is his Brazilian equivalent: an army engineer, with a passionate faith in material progress, he was fascinated by the backland *sertanejos*, their suffering, their endurance, their fanatical religiosity. The *sertanejo*, though of much the same racial and social composition (both are abandoned remnants of the first *conquista*; both have an admixture of Indian blood), is a radically different type from the *gaucho*. His environment is altogether more harsh—hence his superstitious fanaticism—and he lacks those lordly airs, that concern with honour, which marks the South American *gaucho* as the descendant of the Spanish freeman or *hidalgo*.

Much of this is explained by the differing heritages of Spain and Portugal. But more striking to the foreigner is what these

books have in common: namely, their "Americanism".
Neither could have been written in Mexico, or Colombia, or
Peru. There, a different system of coordinates, European and
hierarchical, prevails. The marks of the older European order
—class system and ecclesiastical establishment—are clearly dis-
cernible. Of course, appearances are deceptive; these countries
are not as European as they seem. But neither are they "American" in the sense that *Facundo* or *Rebellion in the Backlands*
are. In these books, the European sense of hierarchy has fallen
away. A universal order exists for the people described in these
books no more than it did for the North American pioneer. Yet
the *gaucho* and the *sertanejo* are not to be equated with the
cowboy. They are lawless—"barbarian", Sarmiento would
have said—as the men of the West never were. Yet they represent a type that is American rather than European. We have
left the settled life of the highlands of Mexico, Central America
and the Andean *cordillera*, the home of the ancient Indian
civilisations, and returned to the Great Plains. New themes are
heard: the theme of American optimism, echo of the Utopianism that fired the European mind at the time of discovery; and
the theme of American tragedy. In Sarmiento's book, admittedly, there is little of the optimism of the prairie and the
pampas. But it was Sarmiento who—in an age when anti-
Americanism was not yet born—appealed to his fellow-
Argentines to "North-Americanise" their country. Latin
Americans often use the term "America" for rhetorical effect.
Applied to Sarmiento it is altogether appropriate. Sarmiento is
one of the greatest of Americans; his book among the greatest
of American classics.

One token of Sarmiento's Americanism is the tentativeness
with which he classifies this new race of South American
gauchos that found expression in the rule of Rosas and Facundo
Quiroga. The Spanish elements in this race cannot be ignored.
But Sarmiento, for obvious reasons, is reluctant to emphasise
the Spanishness of the Argentine *gaucho*. He is Spaniard enough
to wish to rank Spain with the civilising, European elements in
Argentine history. In the *gaucho* mentality he recognises something foreign to the European tradition. That something is new
and "American". Sarmiento, much travelled in Arab lands, seeks
a comparison with the nomadic peoples of Asia and North Africa:

Many philosophers have thought that plains prepare the way for despotism, just as mountains furnish strongholds for the struggles of liberty. . . . There is something in the wilds of Argentina which brings to mind the wilds of Asia; the imagination discovers a likeness between the *pampas* and plains lying between the Euphrates and the Tigris. . . . Pasturage being plenty, the means of subsistence of the inhabitants—for we cannot call it their occupation—is stock-raising. Pastoral life reminds us of the Asiatic plains which imagination covers with Kalmucks, Cossacks or Arab tents. The primitive life of nations—a life essentially barbarous and unprogressive—the life of Abraham which is the life of the Bedouin today, prevails in the Argentine plains. . . .

Yet Sarmiento does not find this comparison wholly satisfactory:

The Arab tribe which wanders through the wilds of Asia is united under the rule of one of its elders or of a warrior chief: society exists. Although not fixed in any determined locality, its religious opinions, immemorial traditions, undying customs . . . make altogether a code of laws and a form of government which preserves morality . . . as well as order and association of the tribe.

True progress, according to Sarmiento, is not possible: cities, industries and a settled agriculture are needed for this. But order and law do exist; and here the life of the *gaucho* compares unfavourably with that of the Bedouin. The *gauchos* are not "social nomads". They are a rural proletariat, ranging from *estancia* to *estancia* in search of work, with little loyalty to one another or to their *patron*:

Inevitable privations justify natural indolence; a dearth of all the amenities of life induces all the externals of Barbarism. Society has altogether disappeared. There is but the isolated self-concentrated feudal family. . . . Since there is no collective society, no government is possible . . . civil justice has no means of reaching criminals. I doubt if the modern world presents any other form of association as monstrous as this.

Interestingly, what Sarmiento condemns is less the cruelty and ignorance of the *gaucho* than the lack of "collected society". No doubt Sarmiento would concede that "collected societies" have been responsible for crimes far greater than those of his *gauchos*. But he insists that the cruelty and ignorance, the "barbarism" of the *gaucho*, stem from his anarchic way of life. What is the meaning of this "barbarism" of the *gaucho*? Is it a phenomenon of degeneracy? Or is the *gaucho* a lost child of nature, a cousin to Rousseau's Noble Savage? For W. H. Hudson, in *The Purple Land*, he is plainly the latter. The *gaucho* has become a romantic figure. Sarmiento's verdict is more ambiguous. In Sarmiento, too, there is a sense that Facundo Quiroga is a child of nature: "He is the natural man, as yet unused to repressing or disguising his passions; he does not restrain their energy, but gives free rein to their impetuosity. This is the character of the human race." Yet Sarmiento contrasts the *gaucho*'s way of life with that of the Roman municipality, the model for the *pueblos* of Spain and Latin America:

> It is the exact opposite of the Roman municipality, where all the population were assembled within an enclosed space, and went from it to cultivate the surrounding fields. . . . It differs from the nomad tribes in admitting of no social reunion, and no permanent occupation of the soil. Lastly, it has something in common with the feudal system of the Middle Ages, when the Barons lived in their strongholds and thence made war on the cities, and laid waste the country in their vicinity. But the Barons in their feudal castles are wanting. If power starts up in the country it lasts only for a moment, and is democratic; it is not inherited, nor can it maintain itself, for want of mountains and strong positions. It follows from this that even the savage tribe of the *pampas* is better organised for moral development than the *gaucho*. . . .

Sarmiento, then, sees the *gaucho* as the product of a degeneration. He puts the blame in part, as does da Cunha, on that intermixture of races which took place after the *conquista* ("for the American aborigines live in idleness"). But there is no escaping the fact that the *gaucho*'s character is basically Spanish. "The Spanish race did not show itself more energetic than the aborigines, when it was left to its own instincts in the wilds of America". "To its own instincts": a tell-tale phrase. Sarmiento seems to admit that the anarchic Spaniard is indeed father to the *gaucho*. Yet he stresses, rightly, that degeneration has taken place. Two forms of social order are characteristic of Spain: the feudal-Visigothic system of the Northern kingdoms, and the Mediterranean municipality system dating back to Roman times and before. Both have suffered shipwreck in the New World.

This is a point often overlooked. To describe the rural pattern of Latin America the term "feudalism" is often used. But from what Sarmiento says it is clear we should use it with care. Developed feudalism, in Europe, was a highly organised society. But the *encomienda* system in Latin America differed from feudalism in important respects. In many countries—on the sugar plantations of Cuba or the Brazilian North East—it was closer to the slave society of Virginia or the Carolinas. There was, indeed, a *patron*. But "feudal" rights and duties were in no sense reciprocal. On the *pampas* it was something different again. Here, too, rights and duties were not reciprocal. But the shoe was to some extent on the other foot. The *gaucho* was a free man, and had no fixed loyalty to his *patron*. Yet if it is wrong to equate the *gaucho's* way of life with feudalism, it is equally wrong to equate it with nomadism. For the nomad's is a closely-knit society as the *gaucho's* is not. It is tempting to seek a comparison with the Vandals and Visigoths of the pre-feudal age. But even that does not meet the case. For Sarmiento's point is that the gaucho's barbarism is not of the kind that can re-invigorate an enfeebled society. It is a regressive barbarism that civilisation must destroy.

It is only against the background of this way of life that the emergence of a Rosas or a Facundo is intelligible. What is Facundo's character? He is boorish, but not unintelligent; indolent, but no coward in the fight. His atrocities are unspeakable; yet he is no mass-murderer. He is a barbarian "who does not know how to control his passions". But this does not mean that his actions are not premeditated. When reproached with certain apparently arbitrary killings on a march across the *pampas* ("Is it not enough, General?"), Facundo replies: "Don't be a fool, how else can I establish my power?"

Sarmiento comments:

This was his one method—terror with the citizen, that he might fly and leave his fortune; terror with the *gaucho*, to make him support a cause in which he had no personal interest. With him terrorism took the place of administrative power, enthusiasm, tactics, everything. And it cannot be denied that terror, as a means of government, has much larger results than patriotism or belief. . . . Russia has made use of it from the time of Ivan . . . It is true that it degrades men, impoverishes them, and takes from them all elasticity of mind, but it extracts more from a state in one day than it would have given in ten years; and what does the rest matter to the Czar of Russia, the bandit chief, or the Argentine commander?

The truth is, Facundo's terrorism arises naturally in a society that recognises no natural or established authority. The *caudillo* is the product of an order that lacks legitimacy; terror is the weapon the *caudillo* uses to bind that society together. The terrorism of the Latin American *caudillo* is not the terrorism of the modern totalitarian. But it is terror none the less. Sarmiento describes the type of leader such a society throws up. A caravan of wagons makes its way across the trackless *pampas*:

> The head of each party is a military leader . . . the position can be filled only by a man of iron will, daring to the point of rashness, that he may hold in check the audacity and turbulence of the land-pirates who are to be directed and ruled by him alone, for no help can be summoned in the desert. On the least symptom of insubordination, the captain raises his iron *chicote*, and delivers on the mutineer blows which leave contusions and wounds; if resistance is prolonged, he leaps from his horse, grasps his formidable knife, and quickly re-establishes his authority by his superb skill in using it. If anyone loses his life under such discipline, the leader is not answerable for the assassination, which is regarded as an exercise of legitimate authority . . . from these characteristics arise in the life of the Argentine people the reign of brute force, the supremacy of the strongest, the absolute and irresponsible authority of rulers. . . .

Such, then, is the origin of the Argentine *caudillo*: of Rosas; of Facundo Quiroga; of those petty regional *caudillos* run to ground by President Sarmiento; and, in modern times, of that egregious neo-*caudillo*, Juan D. Peron. Where legitimacy is in doubt it is to the quickest man with a knife men look for authority.

"Gauchos" and Citizens

None the less, there is a curious dialectic underlying Sarmiento's great work. If Sarmiento's thesis is Barbarism, and his antithesis Civilisation, his synthesis is an Argentina fit to rank with the great nations of Europe. In putting the matter in this way

I have given a twist to Sarmiento's argument that, if seldom explicit, is certainly implicit in his book, and indeed in his life. On the face of it, of course, there is no doubt what *Facundo* is about. It is the biography of a bloodthirsty backlands *caudillo* of the age of Rosas; and Sarmiento is telling us that Facundo is Barbarism incarnate. What the Argentine needs is its opposite, Civilisation; and Civilisation is gas lighting, steam engines, and the electric telegraph. Equally, there is little difficulty in identifying this programme. It was the programme of all Latin American Liberals in that age of *Caudillos*. We have, then, what appears to be a straight opposition. The Barbarism of the Age of *Caudillos* must yield to the Civilisation of the new, frock-coated apostles of *positivisme*. But a second look suggests there is more to it than that. For history played an ironic trick on these champions of *orden y progreso*. What, after all, were Juarez and Sarmiento but *caudillos* to end all *caudillos*? Contemporary descriptions of this energetic, bull-necked, frequently ruthless man suggest that Sarmiento had *caudillo* characteristics in full measure. Sarmiento was not a professorial Liberal in the modern mould. But nor was he a loose-mouthed rabble-rouser like Irigoyen. Sarmiento, like Juarez, was that rare thing in Latin America, a principled man of action. And in that age to be a man of action required the qualities of a *caudillo*. Of course, Sarmiento's ruthlessness is not hard to justify. The country had to be pacified before the forces of progress could do their work. The regional *caudillos* had to be smoked out and destroyed.

Still, it is a sobering thought that Sarmiento's ascendancy coincided, not only with the virtual annihilation of the Argentine's Indians, but also with the hugely destructive War of the Triple Alliance (in which three-quarters of the male population of Paraguay is said to have been wiped out). "Don't be sparing with the blood of *gauchos*", Sarmiento instructed his generals. And, from all we hear, it seems they were not. At any rate Sarmiento, the Liberal, shed more blood than that much-deplored and much-derided *caudillo* of modern times, who fancied himself Rosas's successor, Juan D. Peron. That Sarmiento and his friends did introduce Civilisation into Argentina is not to be denied. They gave her, among other things, the best educational system in Latin America. But it is no accident that

Sarmiento, like Juarez, had to turn *caudillo* to do it. In the light of this, the ambivalence often detectable in *Facundo*—the sense that Facundo, after all, represents certain forces at the basis of the Argentine way of life—becomes easier to understand. It is only by drawing on these forces that the order and progress of Europe can be made actual in the context of Argentina. A synthesis of Barbarism and Civilisation must be brought about. And Sarmiento himself must preside over the shot-gun marriage.

We are now a little further. For it is clear that this Argentine dialectic is a variation on a theme that runs through Latin American history. Who are these *caudillos* and *gauchos*? We have met them already. The *caudillo* is the Cid, Cortes and Pizarro, Bolivar and San Martin; he is Sarmiento and Juarez, Peron and Fidel Castro. He is the chieftain of his band, the charismatic leader who, when legitimacy is in doubt, establishes his own legitimacy by force of personality. And his band? We have met them too. The men who followed the Cid, or Cortes, or San Martin were not serfs or slaves; they were freemen who, to achieve the purpose in hand, required a strong leader to impose order on their anarchy. The *gauchos* of the Argentine *pampas* are of the same breed. From Sarmiento and W. H. Hudson to Borges, they have found a measure of ambivalent admiration. Proud, hard-fighting, free-living men in an age of conformity, they represent something civilisation has repressed or rejected—to its own impoverishment. Their Spanish origin is evident. Their broad-brimmed hats proclaim them the descendants of the cattlemen of Extremadura, where so many of the *conquistadores* were born.

In the passage from *Far Away and Long Ago* (the greatest evocation in English of old, rural Argentina) which stands at the head of this chapter, Hudson draws a poignant picture of the decline of an energetic, agricultural people into a race of tough, but easy-living and improvident *gauchos*. That is part of the truth. The horses and cattle the Spanish brought with them in the sixteenth century were left behind when the Indians destroyed their first settlements. They bred so abundantly that future generations had only to catch and slaughter them to provide themselves with the food and clothing they required. But the link with Spain is really closer than Hudson suggests.

The pattern of Castilian society—and Castile alone counted in the age of the *conquista*—was pastoral and military. There are parts of Spain that belong to a different culture, agricultural and mediterranean: the *huertas* of Valencia, the *vega* of Granada, the hills and valleys of Catalonia. But Castile is not mediterranean. Harsh, hot, and dry, it belongs to Africa rather than to Europe. We say, loosely, that "Spain" reconquered her territory from the Moors. It would be more accurate to say that Castile, Spain's Prussia, reconquered Spain and, in reconquering it, imposed on it the values of Castile. While it is true that the *gaucho* represents a reversion to barbarism, it is also true that he represents something intensely Spanish. He is the liegeman of the Cid, the small-town adventurer who followed Pizarro to Peru from the dusty market-squares of Extremadura. He represents that anarchic, destructive love of freedom that has often erupted in Spanish history: in the *comunero* revolt of the 1520's, in the *Dos de Mayo* uprising against Napoleon, in the Anarchist movement of the years before Franco. No wonder, then, neither Sarmiento nor Borges can resist the charm of that free-ranging life. To deny its charm would be to deny something profoundly rooted in the Argentine and the Spanish character.

In this light, the ambivalence towards *gaucho* Barbarism shown by such champions of Civilisation as Sarmiento and Borges begins to make sense. In the past, we Anglo-Saxons have been treated to much propaganda about "Spanish Civilisation". It is a good line to take with North Americans who, as often as not, feel insecure about their own cultural values. But we must not be intimidated. I have quoted the late Mariano Picon-Salas's charming admission that, though *individualismo* might be the greatest gift of Spain to her children, it was also the root of all their troubles. As a comment on the Argentine *gaucho* it seems appropriate enough. The wild, pastoral life of the *gaucho* is one of the most Spanish things in the Argentine. Nor is it difficult to see how this gaucho way of life came to assume an ever more romantic quality, as it was displaced in the later nineteenth century by a city-bred civilisation and an increasingly non-pastoral economic pattern. (The figures are striking: in 1880, pastoral products made up 94 per cent of Argentine exports; agricultural products 2 per cent. By 1908, the roles were reversed: 30 per cent pastoral; 65 per cent agricultural.) It would be oversimplifying the Civilisation-Barbarism antinomy to see it as a struggle between town and the countryside. But that, of course, is the crux of the matter. Under the Viceroyalty, the backland *gauchos* and their masters had little say in the running of the country. At Independence, it was the burghers of Buenos Aires, having repelled two British invasions, who took matters into their own hands and formed a *cabildo abierto*. Nor is it surprising that the political thinking of town-bred liberators like Moreno and Rivadavia should have been moulded by the Enlightenment and the French Revolution.

This conflict between city-bred Enlightenment and rural traditionalism ran its course in all Latin American countries. That it was most acute in the Argentine is easily explained. Nowhere was the backland way of life more primitive than in this far corner of the Spanish Empire; nowhere was the merchant class so closely in touch with developments in the outside world as in Buenos Aires. The background to the conflict, then, is plain enough. Nor is it difficult to see why the Europeanising *Unitarios* of Buenos Aires, after their initial triumph, failed to assert themselves against Rosas and his *Federales*. Their ideas were ill-adapted to Argentine reality. Their power-base, Buenos Aires, could not dominate a countryside that was still largely self-sufficient. But by mid-century this had changed. The Argentine had become an exporting country; the needs of the backlands population had grown. The power of Buenos Aires could no longer be resisted. The rule of the *gaucho* was broken.

Yet the triumph of Sarmiento, and the huge influx of immigrants, did not wipe out the *gaucho* tradition. These newcomers to Buenos Aires only served to emphasise the foreignness of the city, compared with the primitive, but Hispanic backlands. In more recent times, another shift of population has taken place from the backlands to the industrial cities. Between 1933 and Peron's triumph in 1945, a million "internal migrants" were added to Buenos Aires' proletariat. These "new proletarians" were resentful, not only of the established oligarchy, but also of the "foreign" complexion of their economic betters. They played a big part in bringing Peron to power, and have remained the most loyal of *peronistas*. The wretched descendants of the once-proud *gauchos*, they yearned for a new *caudillo* to save them from the foreign devils and their *vendepatria* agents, the Oligarchy and bourgeoisie of Buenos Aires. That Peron should flatter himself in the role of a second Rosas was not wholly illogical. Argentine intellectuals saw him in this role as well. But they were less flattered. The most important intellectual group over the past thirty-five years has been that around Victoria Ocampo, founder and editor of the magazine *Sur*. Many of the writers she published are now famous: in particular, the novelist and essayist Eduardo Mallea, the poet Silvina Ocampo (Victoria's sister), the novelist and essayist Bio Casares (Silvina's husband), and—by far the best-known to the outside world—Jorge Luis Borges. Many of this group suffered under Peron. Victoria Ocampo was imprisoned; Borges was dismissed from his librarian's post. Nowadays, the group is staunchly conservative. Writers of a younger generation—Ernesto Sabato and David Viñas—regard it as obsolescent and reactionary. But the group's attitudes are more complex than that. Though Borges's generation hated Peronism when it came, and suffered under it, their opposition was not unambiguous. The attitudes adopted by the Argentine intelligentsia between the wars contributed to that undermining of confidence in the Argentine's public institutions that prepared the way for Peron. I am not implying that these courageous men and women connived at the vulgar demagogy of Peron and Evita: they were the first to suffer. I wish only to point to the complexity of the apparently straightforward antithesis between Barbarism and Civilisation.

Thus, in the thirties, it was a writer of this group, Eduardo Mallea, together with the radical *pensador*, Ezequiel Martinez Estrada, who published the most cogent and devastating self-criticism of the Argentine. Mallea's thesis was one few could deny: that the quality of Argentine public life had declined alarmingly since the turn of the century. The theme of Martinez Estrada's *Radiografía de la pampa* was likewise the decadence of the Argentine. But Martinez Estrada saw a way out in a programme of social reform and national regeneration designed to "integrate" the Argentine people, and help them to discover their destiny. To argue from this that Martinez Estrada and Mallea were working towards a *peronista* solution would be as absurd, of course, as to argue that the intelligentsia of Weimar

Germany desired a Hitlerian solution to Germany's ills. Still, the similarities between what the intellectuals had been saying, and what Peron told his *descamisados*, are not coincidental. They had proclaimed the moral and spiritual bankruptcy of modern Argentina. They had demanded national self-examination and regeneration. Like the Weimar intellectuals, they found their prayers answered in a form they did not care for.

There were other respects in which they, the cosmopolitans, found their cherished ideas stolen and parodied by the new Rosas. It would be hard in any country to find intellectuals of the breadth and range of experience of a Borges or a Victoria Ocampo. Yet it would be quite wrong to see their group as "un-Argentine". They were eager to assist at the birth of a "national" literature, where the best of the native tradition would be married with the best of European writing. Most of the group came from old-established Spanish families: Victoria Ocampo herself from one of the oldest, and wealthiest, branches of the oligarchy. In the early years of the century, as we saw, Latin America experienced a continent-wide revival of "nativism". A search began for those indigenous sources of vitality still allegedly alive under the crust of French *positivisme* or Spanish clericalism. Argentina was not unaffected by these currents. But what "native traditions" had the Argentine to turn to? With her Indians destroyed, and her cities flooded with non-Spanish immigrants, there was only the *gaucho* tradition to look to.

The romanticisation of the *gaucho* began at the moment his actual power went into decline—in the fifties and sixties. But it was present, in germ, even earlier. The "generation of '37" was the name given to a group of young intellectuals—Echevarria and Alberdi—who later became the champions of Liberalism in the Argentine. Their beginnings were different. Echevarria, returning from five years' in Paris, initiated his friends into the romantic nationalism, inspired by Herder, then fashionable in Paris. True, the honeymoon was soon over. But the incident offers a curious parallel to the position of the *Sur* group a century later:

> Following Herder, they concluded that Argentina must work out
> its national destiny within the terms prescribed by race and soil
> and revealed by history. This was the theme of an important paper

read by Alberdi in July 1837 at the first meeting of a literary salon which some of them had just founded; in it, Alberdi spoke slightingly of Rivadavia as doctrinaire, while calling Rosas not only 'great and powerful', but also 'eminently representative', as evidenced by his popularity, 'the most undeniable sign of the legitimacy of governments'.

The generation of '37 soon dropped their flirtation when its implications became apparent. But it is easy to see why they thought as they did. The "doctrinaire" Liberalism of Rivadavia was obviously unsuited to Argentine conditions. Their conclusion that Argentina must seek her destiny "within the terms prescribed by race and soil" was not unreasonable.

The *gaucho*, then, had his intellectual admirers from an early period. The most famous of all exercises in *gaucho* romanticism is Fernandez's *Martin Fierro*, published in 1872. Is *Martin Fierro* the "great Argentine epic" Argentine nationalists claim it to be? Probably not. The poem has a fine swing to it, and some powerful evocations of life on the *pampas*. But it is as essentially "literary" as any epic of the period. It belongs with *Hiawatha* rather than with Homer. Not that it matters; the poem became a symbol, not least for those who wished to build a "national literature" in the Argentine. Not by chance, then, were Borges and his generation known as the *martinfierristas*. Not by chance did they put so high a value on a novel still more literary than *Martin Fierro*, Ricardo Guiraldes' *Don Segundo*. The tavern-brawls, the stabbings and the shootings, found in the stories of Borges have a similar origin. Borges may not have cared for lawless violence in practice; but his literary fascination with it is undeniable. His admired Norsemen are the *gauchos* of the Northern Seas. They represent an attempt to redeem the *gaucho* spirit by imputing to it something of that sense of honour that it may once, in its Spanish homeland, have possessed. Undeniably, in his awareness of the underlying lawlessness of his society, Borges is a profoundly Argentine figure.

Jorge Luis Borges

Borges has always insisted on his *argentinidad*. It is his foreign admirers who take him out of context. Of course, Borges is also a figure of international stature. He is as international, and at the same time as rooted, as W. B. Yeats or Franz Kafka—the two modern writers with whom he may most usefully be compared. At first glance this may seem an unequal triangle. Is Yeats not one of the most "national" of modern writers, and Kafka one of the least so? And Borges—for all his obsession with violence— is he not far more like Kafka, with his puzzles and labyrinths, than the poet who spoke of his generation as "the last Romantics"? No doubt. Yet the comparison brings out points that might otherwise be missed. The first, in regard to Yeats, concerns the relation of the "alienated" modern artist to the society of his birth; the second, in regard to Kafka, concerns the technique such an artist should adopt. Borges is an "alienated" writer in at least two senses: he is both socially alienated, as was Yeats; and metaphysically alienated, as was Kafka. Borges, of course, never made Argentina the theme of his poetry as did Yeats. Borges has little of the bardic and, unlike so many Latin American writers, nothing of the rhetorician in him.

Yet, if we look closer, the position of the two poets is not dissimilar. Borges, like Yeats, belongs to the displaced ruling minority. The families of both are old-fashioned, though they are not themselves of the oligarchy. In Yeats' case, the minority is Anglo-Irish; in Borges' Hispanic, pre-immigrant Argentine. Both are aware of the threat "democracy" poses to the way of life of the class they admire. The triumph of Catholic Ireland, as of immigrant Argentina, cannot but mean the downfall of the oligarchy and its values. Both, again, are men of cosmopolitan culture: Yeats a Pre-Raphaelite and a Symbolist; Borges, French-educated and a friend of the Spanish *ultraistas* of the twenties. Each is to some extent a stranger in his own country. Their reactions to social alienation are similar. They drew deliberately on the resources, historical and mythical, of the country of which they find themselves so incongruously a part. A quotation, I think, will make the point. The following poem —referring to the Death of Colonel Francisco Borges (1835–74) —could almost be mistaken for a Yeatsian celebration of some real or adoptive ancestor:

> I leave him on his horse, and in the grey
> And twilit hour he fixed with death for a meeting:
> Of all the hours that shaped his human day
> May this last long, though bitter and defeating.

The whiteness of his horse and *poncho* over
The plain advances. Setting sights again
To the hollow rifles death lies under cover.
Francisco Borges sadly crosses the plain.
This that encircled him, the rifles' rattle.
This that he saw, the *pampas* without bounds,
Had been his life, his sum of sights and sounds,
His every-dailiness is here and in the battle.
I leave him lofty in his epic universe
Almost as if not tolled for by my verse.

The similarity of mood is startling. The modern city-bred poet, at his "sedentary trade", confesses admiration for a vanished life of freedom and violent action, where death—death-in-honour—had a meaning it has lost in the modern world, just as life—heroic life—has lost any meaning it once had. It is easy to make fun of such a pose. Neither Yeats nor Borges would have been much at home in the company of the gentlemen whose virtues they admired. One may doubt, also, whether the gentlemen possessed the virtues imputed to them. The Irish gentry were a loutish lot; and the *gaucho* of history was not the honest *hidalgo* the *martinferristas* thought him. But there is one element in the myth that has an unmistakably modern ring: the element of violence.

In Ireland, you are told that Yeats' *The Second Coming* is about the Irish troubles. Biographically, this is quite correct. This is what Yeats had in mind when he wrote the poem. Yet it is also, and plainly, nonsense. The poem is integral to Yeats's vision of the modern world: he foresees man's growing violence to man, but he hints, beyond that, at some mystical redemption of man through violence. It is the same, I think, with Borges. The violent life of his *gauchos*, his dockland brawlers, his military ancestors, reflects the violence of the modern world. Neither Yeats nor Borges offers a satisfactory resolution—their espousal of heroic values remains essentially literary. And both, at times, are tempted by another solution altogether. In this mood they are Platonic Idealists, able to prove by art that this "pig of a world" has no reality to it, that life and death are symbols of a reality that can never be apprehended. Still, neither Borges nor Yeats, for all their skill, seem to find their elaborate systems of correspondence finally convincing—and they do not convince us. But, of course, it does not matter. These playful constructions, like their historical romanticism, are not significant for themselves, but for the vision of chaos and violence underlying them. Of both writers we may say: in their violence is their modernity.

And the same is true—who will dispute it?—of the work of Franz Kafka. The parallels between Borges' and Kafka's work have often been noted. (Since Borges translated Kafka into Spanish we may legitimately speak of influence.) Consider the following fragment which Borges, with mock-pedantry, ascribes to Suarez Mariana, *Viajes de Varones Prudentes* (Book Four, Chapter XLV, Lerida, 1658):

ON RIGOUR IN SCIENCE

. . . In that Empire, the Art of Cartography reached such Perfection that the map of one Province alone took up the whole of a City, and the map of the Empire, the whole of a Province. In time, those Unconscionable Maps did not satisfy, and the Colleges of Cartographers set up a Map of the Empire which had the size of the Empire itself and coincided with it point by point. Less Addicted to the Study of Cartography, Succeeding Generations understood that this Widespread Map was Useless and not without Impiety they abandoned it to the Inclemencies of the Sun and of the Winters. In the deserts of the West some mangled Ruins of the Map lasted on, inhabited by Animals and Beggars. In the whole Country there are no other relics of the Discipline of Geography.

One would be not at all astonished to come across such a fragment in Kafka's diaries. Yet the anecdote is *ur*-Borges; it contains, in germ, the substance of his larger fictions (*Tlön, The Circular Ruins, The Babylonian Lottery, The Library of Babel*). The story might appear no more than a pleasantly ironic *denkspiel*. And it is easy to see why this kind of writing, which Borges perfected in the thirties and forties, should have aroused the impatience of younger Argentines. In Buenos Aires today, you will hear Borges denounced by the young as an antediluvian poetaster, an aesthete in an ivory tower, a man of genius who has turned his back on his native land—and thus betrayed both talent and country. These criticisms are not new. It so happens that Borges first became internationally known in the 1950's.

But his gifts were recognised in the Spanish-speaking world when he was scarcely out of his teens. Yet, as early as 1933, he found himself attacked by younger, nationally-minded critics who found his work too cosmopolitan, too precious, too little concerned with the Argentine of his day. Despite the fact that he took up a militantly pro-Allied position in 1940 (hardly the act of an ivory-tower artist), despite the fact that Peron persecuted him in petty ways, and Borges never concealed his contempt for the *peronista* régime, the old cry was taken up after the war by critics who blamed him (with strange inconsistency), both for having contributed to the rise of Peron, and for foisting an ivory-tower contempt of literature on the Argentine.

Borges, then, could do no right. Yet why should Borges, most peaceable and retiring of men, arouse such fury in his critics? There were many reasons. After 1930, the younger generation of Argentina were looking for an ideology, a programme of action; they were looking for someone to explain the Argentine *malaise* to them, and offer a remedy. Borges refused this role (it would not have been in character); and the young turned against him. He became that contemptible thing: a failed father-figure. The young were not unaware, for all the attempts of Mallea and Martinez Estrada to fill this role, that Borges' talent was of a different order. With Neruda, Borges was the most gifted writer of his generation in Latin America. But the young did not want an Argentine Kafka. They wanted a second Sarmiento, a statesman-cum-liberator, with a touch of the *caudillo*, to set the Argentine on the right path. These criticisms of a younger generation may sound trivial. Yet they cannot be wholly dismissed. There is in Borges a wilful fragmentariness, a shyness of contemporaneity, a preciousness and mock-pedantry (a mock-pedantry that can come perilously near to the real thing) which can irritate. Of course, Borges' genius is undeniable. But that only makes it worse. It aggravates the impression that Borges is an inhibited, even a crippled talent: a talent promising more than it achieves. But that, negatively, is as far as criticism can go. We cannot construct an imaginary Borges: we must take him as he is. Which is to say that the criticism of the Argentine *anti-borgistas*, in the last analysis, is unintelligent and not a little provincial. What his critics overlook is that this fragmentary, tentative quality is characteristic of all the writings of "Modernism": of Eliot and Rilke, Valéry and Proust and Beckett. Perhaps we shall come to regard the writings of Modernism as inferior, for this reason, to the work of other literary epochs. But we know why modernist writing took this form: it was the fragmentary, tentative writing of a fragmentary, tentative epoch. Certainly, if we take this argument too far, we fall into the "imitative fallacy": a confused work is not less confused because it is the product of a confused epoch. But I am not arguing for or against Modernism as a literary movement. The point is that the verdict young Argentines pronounce on Borges is a verdict on the Modernist movement as a whole.

Borges' work can be defended in more aggressive fashion. Indeed, the tables can be turned on his critics with relative ease. The criticism of Borges' work has been that it lacks reality, that it is pure *denkspiel*. But is this true? If the work of Borges is remote from reality, why should Peronist and Communist and Fascist combine to denigrate it? Here, again, one is reminded of Franz Kafka. Communist and Fascist alike have damned Kafka's writings. Yet if they are no more than the fantasies of an alienated neurotic, why should men of power, and their literary henchmen, concern themselves about them? With Kafka, of course, we know the answer. Kafka's fantasies are altogether too realistic for the totalitarian. In saying this, one is not insisting on a "political" interpretation of Kafka's work. Rather, in setting up his abstract model of human existence Kafka put his finger on that in man which lays him open to the totalitarian disease. Borges' work infuriates in the same way. His enemies profess not to know what he is talking about. In fact, they know all too well. There are, to be sure, *ficciones* which seem to be no more than clever intellectual exercises. But there are others of which this cannot be said, where the dimension of reality is explicit. There is the story *Tlön, Uqbar, Orbis Tertius*, apparently one of Borges' more fantastic tales, in which a group of scholars come together to construct a new language, and finally a new universe, on Idealist principles:

> The metaphysicians of Tlön are not looking for truth, nor even for an approximation to it; they are after a kind of amazement. They consider metaphysics a branch of fantastic literature. They know that a system is nothing more than the subordination of all the aspects of the universe to some one of them.

Borges, once again, is poking fun at Idealism. To make a map of the Empire—by map-making we must understand all intellectual activity—the geographers are compelled to ever greater pedantry and absurdity. Starting with a map as large as a province, they end with a map as large as the Empire. The joke is well taken. And the point is existentialist; man transcends any concept of his nature he may choose to devise. Beneath man's labyrinthine hypotheses, there is no all-subsuming theory of the universe; there is only raw human contingency. We are brought back to reality with a bang: to the kind of reality—the tavern brawl, the *gaucho* duel—Borges depicts in his stories, but also to that vision of modern violence Borges shares with Yeats. I have said that neither the solution offered by a Romantic concept of honour, nor the solution provided by Idealist metaphysics seems to satisfy Borges any more than it satisfied Yeats. Borges provides no solution. Nor, for that matter, does Kafka. Yet to call Borges a nihilist would be to ignore, not only the stand he has taken in politics, but also that explicit repudiation of certain aspects of the modern world contained, for example, in the closing passages of *Tlön*. Borges describes how the last forty volumes of the *First American Encyclopedia of Tlön* have been discovered in a Memphis library. The international press is enthusiastic:

Manuals, anthologists, summaries, literal versions, authorised reprints, and pirated editions of the Master Work of Man poured and continued to pour out into the world. Almost immediately, reality gave ground on more than one point. The truth is it hankered to give ground. Ten years ago, any symmetrical system whatsoever which gave the appearance of order—dialectical materialism, anti-Semitism, Nazism—was enough to fascinate men. Why not fall under the spell of Tlön and salute the minute and vast evidence of an ordered planet? Useless to reply that reality, too, is ordered. It may be so, but in accordance with divine laws—I translate inhuman laws—which we will never completely perceive. Tlön may be a labyrinth, but it is a labyrinth plotted by men, a labyrinth destined to be deciphered by men. . . . Contact with Tlön and the way it is planned have disintegrated this world; captivated by its discipline, humanity forgets and goes on forgetting that it is the discipline of chess players, not of angels. Now, the conjectural "primitive language" of Tlön has found its way into the schools. Now, the teaching of its harmonious history,

full of stirring episodes, has obliterated the history which dominated my childhood. Now, in all memories, a fictitious past occupies
the place of any other. . . . English, French, and mere Spanish will
disappear from this planet. The world will be Tlön. I take no
notice. I go on revising, in the quiet of the days in the hotel at
Androgue, a tentative translation into Spanish, in the style of
Quevedo, which I do not intend to see published, of Sir Thomas
Browne's *Urn Burial.* . . .

The Appearance of Order

"The truth is, it hankered to give ground . . . ten years ago, any
symmetrical system which gave the appearance of order was
enough to fascinate men." These are not the words, whatever
younger Argentines may say, of a writer uncommitted to
politics. Nor should it be forgotten that while this sniping was
going on Borges had taken up a public position—and suffered
for it. Though his work, like that of Sarmiento, is shot through
with Argentine ambiguities, there is no doubt where he stands:
like Sarmiento, he is a friend of "Civilisation". In Buenos Aires,
Borges told me that he remembered wealthy pro-Axis Argentines swarming to the German Embassy, while London burned
in 1940, and drinking to the success of the *Luftwaffe*. It was not
nationalism that excited them, but the idea of violence. The
anecdote confirms, I think, not only Borges' insight into the
mood of those years but his hatred of the age's gathering
violence. In the Argentine context, this meant that Borges was
strongly pro-Allied, anti-Fascist, anti-Communist and—when
the time came—anti-Peronist. These attitudes were shared by
the *Sur* group as a whole. Victoria Ocampo generously supported a Free French journal during the war; and she made no
bones of her loathing for the Argentine's post-war *caudillo*.

Yet, as far as the Argentine is concerned, the first part of the
above-quoted statement is truer than the second. By the end of
the thirties, as much a "low, dishonest decade" for the Argentine
as for Europe, reality was indeed "hankering to give ground".
But Borges was wrong in thinking that "the appearance of
order"—which so many, on the left as on the right, now craved
—would take the form of a "symmetrical system". Here,
perhaps, Borges was thinking too much in European terms. The

nemesis did not come in the form of the ideologies Borges specifies: dialectical materialism, anti-Semitism, or Nazism. It would be easier to analyse *peronismo* if it had. There is little doubt that *peronismo* must be considered a phenomenon *sui generis*. Borges and his friends had not expected this resolution to the malaise of the thirties. Nor had anyone else. Yet *peronismo* lasted ten years, and still commands the votes of a third of the electorate. Analysis of it tells us a great deal, not only about the Argentine, but about the general political *malaise* of Latin America.

The sequence of events is easily set down. The "Revolution" of 1930 was the immediate forerunner of the "Revolution" of 1943. On both occasions the military intervened in politics in "the national interest". They had some justification. Both interventions were popular, though for different reasons. The first intervention, against the corrupt, do-nothing Irigoyen Radicals, was popular because the Radicals appeared to be more interested in perpetuating their hegemony, and in lining their own pockets, than in solving the problems brought on Argentina by the Depression. Admittedly, the Army's popularity was short-lived. In elections announced for the following year it was evident that the Radicals would make a comeback. To prevent this the Army plumped for an alliance with the Conservative oligarchy and the right-wing, anti-*personalista* Radicals. But by 1943 the Army could see that this neo-Conservative solution was no more popular or viable than that offered by Irigoyen's Radicals. This second intervention, then, was also welcomed with relief. The incumbent President Castillo seemed determined to nominate Patron Costas, an unreconstructed oligarch, as his successor. An Army coup would prevent that. But what did the military conspirators of 1943 want? In 1930, General Uriburu had entertained certain quasi-Fascist notions, derived from Mussolini and Spain's Primo de Rivera. He put few of these notions into practice; they were of little relevance to modern Argentina. And the Army, as we have seen, fell back on an alliance with the oligarchy.

But by the forties, however, the Army could no longer be considered a branch of the traditional oligarchy. Its officers were now largely of middle-class origin. They had developed, partly as a result of their German training, considerable professional self-regard and *esprit de corps*. The moving element in the "Revolution" of 1943 was the *Grupo de Officiales Unidos*, prominent among them a certain Colonel Peron (he had taken part, as a junior officer, in the Uriburu coup). Peron's hand is evident in a manifesto circulated by the GOU in May 1943. It is a strange and revealing document:

Comrades!

The war has fully demonstrated that the nations are not able now to defend themselves alone. The era of the NATION is slowly being substituted by the era of the CONTINENT. Yesterday the feudals united to form the nation. Today the nations join to form the continent. That will be the end achieved by this war.

Germany is making a titanic effort to unite the European continent. The strongest and best equipped nation should control the destinies of the continent in its new formation. In Europe it will be Germany.

In America, in the north, the controller will be, for a time, the United States of North America. But in the south . . . there are only two nations that can fill this role: Argentina and Brazil. The first step to be taken, which shall lead us towards a strong and powerful Argentina, is to get the reins of government into our hands. Civilians will never understand the greatness of our ideal, we shall therefore have to eliminate them from the government and give them the only mission which corresponds to them: WORK and OBEDIENCE. . . . With Germany's example the right spirit will be instilled into the people by the RADIO, the CONTROLLED PRESS, by LITERATURE, by the CHURCH, and by EDUCATION. Only in this way will they forego the easy life they now enjoy! Our generation will be a generation sacrificed on the altar of a high ideal! VIVA LA PATRIA!

Now this is heady stuff. It suggests that GOU intended to impose a full-blown Fascist programme on the Argetine. The borrowings from contemporary Europe are obvious. It is plainly to the point that the group's leading spirit, Colonel Peron, should have served from 1939 to 1941 as Argentine military attaché in Mussolini's Rome. Still, we have learnt to treat the rhetoric of Latin American "revolutions" with scepticism. Nor is it out of place here. We learn that the document was intended for *internal* circulation. Subsequently, for public consumption, a different maifesto was issued: it promised respect for the Constitution, early elections and loyal inter-American co-operation.

It was this second manifesto that secured immediate recognition for the government by the Supreme Court, and gave the régime that air of legitimacy so important in Latin America. It could be argued, of course, that the second manifesto was an exercise in public relations; and that the key to the intentions of the group lay in the first, secret manifesto. But this imputes to the military revolutionaries a consistency of purpose they plainly lacked. The officers who engineered the revolt were as lacking in unity of purpose as their predecessors of 1930, or their successors of 1955. They knew what they did not want; but when it came to a positive programme, they were as divided as the parties they had displaced. Nor is this surprising. They themselves came from the middle and upper classes. The divisions among the Argentine's civilian groups, therefore, were reflected in her armed forces. The "monolithic" character of the military existed only in a technical sense; they owned the apparatus of coercion. Many senior officers inclined to Constitutionalism; without conciliating them it would have been impossible to secure the régime. Others were prepared to override Constitutional principles; their conception of the new state was "reactionary", not in a Fascist, but in a Conservative-Catholic sense. They looked to Primo de Rivera, General Franco, or *Action Française* rather than to Hitler or Mussolini. Others again—these were the younger men—were "Fascist" in the style of the secret manifesto. They were radical revolutionaries of the right, totalitarian and nationalist in their thinking, prepared to break with entrenched Catholic or Conservative interests if the nation could be mobilised for its "historic destiny" in no other way.

A Catholic-Conservative alliance constituted the Army's first bid for civilian support, as it did after the fall of Peron twelve years later, and after the fall of Dr Illia. It was not a viable policy. Within a year, a realignment of forces brought Colonel Peron—now political boss of the trade unions as Minister of Labour—to the Vice-Presidency. By the summer of 1945, Peron had become the object of violent criticism from Conservative elements. His popularity with labour was a clear threat to the establishment. The Army, dismayed at their growing unpopularity, decided to drop him. But now something happened that had never happened before in Latin America: a working-class demonstration compelled a military régime to change course. The organiser of this demonstration was a young actress, of questionable antecedents, Eva Duarte. It was a brilliant success. Hundreds of thousands of *descamisados* flooded into Buenos Aires. The Army hurriedly brought back Peron from his place of confinement, and proclaimed him their candidate for the forthcoming elections. Three weeks later, Peron married Eva Duarte. Together, they won the Presidential elections by an overwhelming majority. An element in Peron's triumph was the clumsy interference of the American ex-ambassador to the Argentine, Braden. Washington attempted, in a White Book, to smear Peron as "pro-Axis". This rebounded in the most damaging way. It fanned anti-Americanism in a country previously inclined to be anti-British rather than anti-American, and it sealed Peron's victory. In the following year, Eva and Juan Peron began to build their *"justicialista"* party, in alliance with the Army, into a passable imitation of the dema-gogic-nationalist movements of pre-1945 Europe. They did not impose a totalitarianism comparable to that of the Nazis or Communists. As long as the régime could count on popular support it was not notably illiberal. Only after 1949, as the economic situation worsened and popular support began to fail, did their régime become seriously repressive. The essence of Peronism was a marriage of nationalism with social demagogy, under benevolent military auspices. While boom conditions lasted, it throve. When the going got rough, its opportunistic character proved its undoing.

Still, Peronism cannot be dismissed as easily as that. For one thing, it has left a disastrous legacy in its wake. One third of the Argentine people remains *peronista* in its loyalties. And this solid base seems as irremovable a feature of the Argentine political scene as the Communist share of the electorate in post-war France or Italy. Yet what is *peronismo*? If we take the secret manifesto seriously—there is no doubt it reflected Peron's ideas at the time—Peronism must be considered a "right-wing" movement. Yet comparison with the working-class parties of other Latin countries suggests that, whatever the *origins* of *peronismo*, it ended up as a movement of the Left. It is arguable that there is no inconsistency here. Sorel influenced both Syndicalism and early Fascism. Both Doriot and Mussolini were renegades from the Socialist camp; Spengler appealed for a "Prussian Socialism". Hitler actually called his movement "National Socialism". It has never been easy to define Fascism. But it is clear that a line must be drawn between Fascism and right-wing Conservatism. Fascism, in effect, was an attempt to find a social basis for traditional values more effective than that offered by the old ruling upper class. Confident that it would bolster their position, establishment groups in Germany, France and Italy connived at the rise of Fascism. In Germany, at least, they later had reason to regret this attitude. The old élite saw that Fascism was directed at their left-wing enemies. They did not see that it was also directed at themselves.

In so far as Peron wished to inculcate an authoritarian nationalism in the Argentine masses he stood in a Fascist line of descent, and his ideas were acceptable to the establishment. He said that "he wished to do what Mussolini did, without his mistakes". He seems to have been impressed by the danger of a "Spanish situation" arising in the Argentine, with the working class bitterly alienated from the traditional structure of society. There is no reason to doubt that Peron was sincere in these beliefs. He had learned, from General Uriburu's failure, that an "élitist" Fascism would not work in the Argentine. Peron is commonly thought of as a loud-mouthed buffoon, who brought on his country only ridicule and disaster. This is not wholly fair. From all accounts, before he was corrupted by fame and power, Peron was a studious man. He was a shrewd judge of men and affairs, and had a remarkably retentive memory. The vulgar theatricality of his régime—where his own *macho* good looks, and those of Eva Duarte, stood him in good stead—should not blind us to the fact that Peron was a mature and travelled man by the time he came to power (he was then 50). He was no student hero, no Fidel Castro. Peron's weakness seems to have lain less in his intellect—though ignorance of economics was a disastrous handicap—than in his character. It was Eva Duarte who saved her lover when the Army locked him up in October 1945. And it may be that had Eva not died in 1952 his régime would have lasted longer. Like all Latin American dictators, Peron liked to play the strong man. But, like so many of them, he was also a playboy. He lacked the resolution and stamina of a Hitler or a Franco. For all that, Peron was no fool. What he learnt from his early political experience points to powers above the average.

Still, neither in 1943 nor later did Peron work to a preconceived plan. Like all the Fascist dictators Peron was an opportunist. But after 1943 he saw, as his colleagues did not, the logic of the Army's situation. The Army was always popular at the moment of intervention, since nothing could be worse than the prevailing *impasse*. But its popularity seldom lasted, for it had no solution of its own to offer. Since the Army could not rule alone, without incurring increasing unpopularity, it was imperative to find civilian allies. But where? Peron saw that neither the Conservative oligarchy nor its Radical satellites, nor the Catholic-Conservative alliance of the first post-revolutionary months, offered a firm foundation. These groups were not only too weak, they aroused too much antagonism. But there was one group in society which, though as yet unorganised, was a promising reservoir of political power: the *descamisados*. As Minister of Labour, Peron proceeded to reorganise the trade union movement (CGT), removing its existing leaders and replacing them with his own men. This policy proved fantastically successful—and, incidentally, beneficial to the workers. New labour laws and insurance schemes were introduced. Firms were compelled by government order to pay higher wages. We saw that European-style Communist, Socialist and Anarcho-Syndicalist movements had failed to strike root. Not only were they "foreign", they failed to deliver the goods. Here was an organisation, backed by state power, which was in a position to deliver the goods. There was no effective resistance, then, to Peron's *gleichschaltung* of the CGT. Within two years the labour movement, under Peron's control, had become the second most powerful social force in the country. Peron had found what he wanted: an effective civilian grouping with which the Army could ally itself—an ally which, by sheer numbers, was certain to sweep the polls. By no means all the military leaders were happy at this outcome, as their arrest of Peron showed. But once Eva Duarte had demonstrated the power of her *descamisados*, there was no going back. A new alliance of forces had come into being.

Two points should be made. If the new alliance was in one sense in accord with the logic of the situation—the Army needed civilian support of some kind—it was also *accidental*. The second and striking point is that the new alliance represented a deviation from European Fascist norms. This was not an alliance between various élite groups and a labour-threatened lower middle class, but an alliance between one élite group and the working class, directed *against* the upper and middle classes. Peron's Fascism, therefore, had a far more "socialist" look from the start than any of the "national-socialist" movements of Europe. Indeed, the term "Fascist" begins to seem inappropriate. Not that it matters what name we give Peron's invention. But the implications are interesting. It seems that Fascist ideas suffered a sea-change in crossing the South Atlantic; and this transmutation sheds light on the politics, not only of Latin America, but of the Third World in general. For the alliance was *accidental* in two senses: it was pragmatic, not pre-conceived; and it represented—as subsequent events showed—no real conjunction of interests between the parties involved.

We have expressed doubt as to whether Latin American politics are as ideological as they sound. Is the rhetoric no more than a cover? The origins of Peronism lend support to this view. For Peronism was invented to solve a practical problem. Indeed its rise parallels the rise of a similar, if more stable, political alliance: Mexico's PRI. The PRI is a more integrated political movement than Peronism ever was. But its coming into being, as we have seen, was equally accidental. For all the similarities neither the PRI nor Peron's party were simple copies of a Stalinist or Fascist model. And the two parties have much in common. The role allotted to labour in the Mexican system is uncommonly like the role it played in the *peronista* state. Though formally very powerful, the labour movement in Mexico is not autonomous; though state-pampered, it is also firmly state-controlled. Neither system can be described as democratic. But integration into the state machine not only won the workers greater social security, it removed a potential element of political instability. Both "revolutions" gave the working class a sense of participation in the political process. Both were attempts, however fumbling, to solve the perennial problem of Latin America's political instability.

Nevertheless, there is a logic to the Peronist modification of Fascism that is of great interest. Latin American Fascism, like

Latin American Communism, was essentially a fringe movement, a foreign importation that failed to strike root. Not, of
course, for lack of trying. Most Latin American countries had
primitive Fascist movements. Christian democracy, as we saw,
began as an imitation of the Spanish *Falange* or of *Action
Française*. Indeed, few countries escaped its influence entirely;
from Vargas' proclamation of his *Novo Estado* in Brazil to
the élitist notions of President Uriburu. Yet Fascist movements
remained weak or, where they prospered—as under Vargas and
Peron—were transformed into something else. Why was this?
The explanation, I think, lies in a paradox. To the foreigner
Latin America often looks backward and provincial. There is a
time-lag, sometimes of a decade, sometimes of a generation,
between her thinking and that of Europe or North America
(some Latin Americans would put the time-lag at three hundred
years). Yet Latin America is in thrall to "modernism", whether
in art, engineering or political ideology, like nowhere in the
world. Lévi-Strauss noted in São Paulo that his students were
only concerned with "new" theories: right or wrong, a new
theory was always more interesting than an old. This explains,
in great measure, the appeal of Marxism. Marxism is the latest
thing; in the nineteen thirties Fascism was the latest thing. Of
course, it is easy to understand this attitude. The very backwardness of Latin America generates a desire to be up to date,
to own the latest theory or the latest equipment. To the outsider, of course, it often seems that Latin America plumps for
the wrong bandwagon, that she confounds the modish with the
modern. Peron's "Fascism" is only another example: his
"secret manifesto" has exactly this modish note. Of course, Peron
and his friends were convinced the Axis would win the war. The
pro-Axis sympathies of the GOU are significant only because
they reflect the GOU's conviction that their neo-nationalist,
authoritarian ideas were the latest thing. (This, at a moment
when the rest of Latin America had prudently decided that
democracy was the thing to support.) Peron and his friends, of
course, had jumped on the wrong bandwagon. The style of '39
was old hat by '43. Once more, Latin America had got hold
of the wrong end of the stick.

Yet that was not the end of the story. For Peron went on
to create a movement that dominates and bedevils Argentine

politics to this day. The alliance between the Army and labour came about accidentally. Yet, once in being, the alliance proved formidable. What is more, it prefigured political developments in the Third World in the fifties and sixties. Paradoxically, then, what appears to be the fag-end of an outworn theory is at the same time the model of a specifically postwar phenomenon. All the political attitudes with which we have subsequently become familiar in Egypt, or in Indonesia, are present in germ in Peron's Argentina. It was Peron who launched the slogan of a "Third Force". It was Peron who discovered how to weld anti-imperialism, welfare-statism and nationalist militarism into a satisfying ideology. The interest, and the paradox, of Peron's rise to power is that he is both the last of the old and the first of the new. His triumph represents the point of transition from European-style Fascism to the nationalist authoritarianism of the Third World.

Despite its accidental arrival, then, the inner logic of Peronism is compelling. We have seen that the Catholic "Falangist" groups of the thirties soon cut adrift from their Conservative moorings and evolved into centre-left parties. Similarly, Vargas's movement had evolved by the nineteen-fifties into the left-wing nationalism of Kubitschek and Goulart. What Peronism shows is that political generalisations, customary in the developed world, may have to be revised, or even reversed, in dealing with the Third World. In Europe, conservatism and nationalism seem natural allies. Fascism, which combines the two, appears as a right-wing movement. But in the semi-colonial conditions of the Third World, where the conservative interest is often identical with that of the foreigner, there is a natural alignment between radicalism and nationalism. In Latin America, this has been evident at least since the Mexican Revolution. Porfirio Diaz, who cosseted the foreign investor, was overthrown by elements as anti-Conservative as they were anti-*gringo*. Successive Argentine governments, from Irigoyen to Frondizi, have stumbled over the same problem: How do you invite foreign investment without opening yourself to the charge of conniving at *gringo* infiltration? Peron, at the end, was also caught in this dilemma. What is the answer? Mexico's answer has been to pursue Porfirio Diaz's policies more rigorously than he would ever have dared, while proclaiming devotion to the

I

left-wing ideals of the Revolution. This may not be a feasible, let alone a desirable, solution to the problems of other countries. But, as India shows, it is one possible solution to an instability that is endemic, not only to Latin American politics, but to the politics of the underdeveloped world.

Anarchy and the Middle Class

Still, the point about Peron is that he did not last. And the reasons for Peron's failure to consolidate his régime are clear. He did not, like the *caudillos* of the Mexican Revolution, succeed in building up a monolithic party. Despite the bravado of the "secret manifesto" Peron was too little of a totalitarian. But perhaps the task was beyond him. Like Sukarno's, Peron's power depended on playing off one section of society against another. Peron was never really the master of the situation. He could only maintain his position, once the fat years were gone, by manœuvering precariously between the Army and the Frankenstein monster he had created out of his *descamisados*. To have survived longer he would have had to apply his techniques of *gleichschaltung*, not only to the trade union movement, but to the whole of Argentine society. In the years of his triumph he did not think this necessary. When his luck turned it was too late. Attacks on the remaining pluralist elements in Argentine society merely increased the resistance. In the end, these elements won the ear of the Army and he found himself supported neither by the military nor by his disillusioned *descamisados*. If he had been less of an opportunist, if he had eliminated potential sources of opposition, if he had shown greater resolution in the face of crisis, he would have lasted longer. But it was not in his character. Being what he was, Peron could no more have given the Argentine a stable political system than Sarmiento's Facundo.

What could? Why should the Argentine, with her economically powerful middle class, be so unstable? Or is the reason to be sought in the character of the Latin American middle class in general? We have seen that Argentina stands apart from the rest of Latin America by reason of the strength of her middle class. In 1914, the middle class made up 30 per cent of the population; by 1940, no less than 40 per cent. Now these are high figures. They are comparable with the figures for Europe and North America rather than with the figures for the Third World. Yet they are not untypical of Latin America. In this respect Latin America differs from the ex-colonial societies of Afro-Asia. Latin America has always been highly urbanised. She has inherited a powerful bureaucracy from her Spanish overlords, and this remains an important element in her society. (Part of the attraction of political power is that it enables politicians to fill these jobs on a "personalist" basis.) Over the past two generations an influential industrial and professional bourgeoisie has grown up. Not powerful enough—or not willing—to form a "national bourgeoisie", Radical parties, as in Argentina or Chile, have expressed the aspirations of this middle class. There are few countries, of course, where their presence is not indispensable to the functioning of society— it was these groups, we noted, that were the real legatees of the Mexican Revolution. A large middle class, then, is not untypical of Latin America. It is rather that the Argentine is in advance of her sister nations. In certain respects she differs from her neighbours. But this does not mean that she is an anomaly. On the contrary, the difficulties she has run into give us an idea of the difficulties that may confront her less developed neighbours in the future.

What, then, is the character of the Latin American middle class? A middle class, according to current notions, is a guarantee of political stability. The stronger your middle class, the more stable your country. The Argentine gives the lie to this conception. And the implications are not happy. What assurance have we that other, less-developed nations, when they reach the Argentine level of development, will not show the same instability?

Let me quote what a Chilean, Dr Claudio Veliz, has to say on the subject (in his introduction to *Obstacles to Change in Latin America*). What is interesting about Dr Veliz's analysis of the middle class, and its failure to develop into something analogous to the bourgeoisie of nineteenth-century Europe, is that it corresponds to what we have seen of the psychology of *mestizaje*: namely, that Latin America is a profoundly con- servative society. Dr Veliz writes:

In spite of its reputation for frequent and violent political upheaval, perhaps the principal contemporary problem of Latin America is excessive stability. . . . There exists in the region a resilient traditional structure of institutions, hierarchical arrangements which has survived centuries of Colonial government, movements for independence, domestic revolutions. . . . More recently, it has not only successfully resisted the impact of technological innovations and industrialisation but appears to have been strengthened by it.

Dr Veliz is arguing from a different point of view from that which we have adopted. His criticism of the middle classes is that they have allied themselves with the traditional structure, and helped to freeze Latin America in the traditional mould. I would go some way with Dr Veliz. He is right in saying that the aspirations of the middle and, later, of the lower middle and working classes (and even of the *lumpenproletariat*) have been directed towards assimilation to the *criollo*-oligarchic norm. Dr Veliz argues from this that Latin America suffers from "excessive stability". The truth is, I believe, that while Latin America is conservative, it is important to distinguish conservatism from stability. It could be that Latin America is both highly conservative and highly unstable. Still, the reasons Dr Veliz gives for the characteristics of the Latin American bourgeoisie are most interesting. He points to the pre-existence of a "sophisticated pre-industrial urban civilisation", and to the "uniqueness of the region's first decades of import-substitution industrialisation". This sounds somewhat technical. But it comes near, I think, to the heart of the matter. We noted that the *conquistadores* were pre-eminently town-builders. Latin America was an attempt to transplant Mediterranean-Roman civilisation to the soil of the New World. This explains what on the face of it appears contradictory: that in Latin America the rise of the urban middle class *precedes* the coming of industry by a century. It explains why, in many Latin American countries, 50 per cent of the population lives in three or four major cities; why in Uruguay, Chile and Argentina, one third of the population lives in the capital. It explains why Latin America is more highly urbanised than Europe, America, or the Soviet Union. This cannot be put down to the industrial revolution; it is the way Latin America has been designed from the start.

One consequence was that the *Reforma* was carried through, not by an industrial bourgeoisie but by an urban professional bureaucratic middle class. In Britain, too, the rise of the middle class preceded the Industrial Revolution. But the vigour and self-confidence of the Victorian middle class owed much to the industrial revolution it had brought about. The middle class deferred to the Establishment; but it was also eager to reform it. And in this it was not unsuccessful. The achievements of the Latin American middle class in the nineteenth century were considerable. But the triumph of the *Reforma* can hardly be compared with the repeal of the Corn Laws (there are still countries in Latin America where the land-owning interest is wholly exempt from taxation). And the main reason for the difference lies in the self-confidence of the British industrialist, and in the dependent, deferential attitude of the Latin American *bourgeoisie*. It is not surprising that when industrialisation came it did not reproduce the British situation. Not only was the economic motivation different, it bred different values in its protagonists:

> Industry came to South America not as the outcome of a deliberate policy of modernisation on the part of a reformist urban middle class, or as the marginal consequence of the distinct way of living of a rising industrial class on the European model . . . but as the direct result of a historical accident. Unable to implement their projected reforms, the leading groups of the urban middle class were drawn to industry . . . because they had a vague hope that industrialisation would perform painlessly and automatically the social transformation they had not been able to bring about. Industry became a gigantic *deus ex machina* expected to solve social and industrial problems, change attitudes, and bring prosperity. . . . To support industry was not only to act on the side of history but was—and still is—patriotic.

The Latin American bourgeoisie, then, was not "revolutionary". In this light, we can understand better why the Argentine Radical party lost its impetus after 1916. The Radicals did not come to power to reform the social structure, but to manipulate it for their own purposes. Socially, their ambition was to be accepted by traditional society:

> In the absence of an alternative set of cultural values and prestige symbols . . . the only possible way of attaining at least a measure of

social prestige is by association with the traditional aristocracy. This the urban middle classes have done systematically and successfully.

Industrialism, for the Latin American middle class, was a soft option. The new industrialists did not have to compete with Europe and North America. On the contrary, they owed their success to the fact that foreign imports were too dear or too scarce. As a result, it became fantastically profitable to invest in manufactures for the home-market. The coffee planters of São Paulo, and the cattle-owners of the *pampas*, discovered that it was more profitable to put their money into manufacturing than into pastoral or agricultural schemes. Is it surprising that they, and their ex-peasant work-people, carried into these activities many characteristics of that feudal *patron-campesino* relationship they had known in the countryside?

We must not press the analogy too far. But that there are analogies between this middle-class mentality and that of the *mestizo* is evident. There is a common need to identify with traditional values. Neither group has developed a class- or caste-consciousness that would have enabled it to transform the life of the nation. Both groups may be said to be "revolutionary", in the sense that they feel themselves to be underprivileged, and contain the seeds of instability and social violence. Yet neither *bourgeois* nor *mestizo* is a true revolutionary. Not only does he lack the political stamina, and the requisite ideology; he lacks also the will. The deepest desire of both groups is to be accepted into the system that has for four centuries dominated Latin America. Reformist aspirations are there too. But while these aspirations cannot be ignored, and may be the cause of great trouble in the future, neither the Latin American *bourgeois* nor the Latin American *mestizo* represents the stuff of which revolutions are made.

Men on Horseback

There remains the problem of militarism. In her better days Argentina was little plagued by this curse of Latin American politics. Argentines were proud of the fact; theirs was no banana-republic, a prey to the Marines, with picturesque, *opera buffa* generals ever ready to "do their patriotic duty".

True, Rosas and Facundo were a blot on the national escut-
cheon. But all that was in the past. Civilian rule, and respect
for law and order, had taken root at last in the land of the *gauchos*.
Sarmiento had won. At the glittering Independence Celebra-
tions of 1910—the youthful Victoria Ocampo was the *belle*
of the ball—statesmen made the pilgrimage to Buenos Aires to
render homage to this most prosperous and peaceful of Latin
American states. Yet, within a generation, the idyll was
destroyed. Whereas Mexico—Argentina's rival among Spanish-
speaking states—had found a way out of her troubles, Argentina
had fallen into economic stagnation and become the fief of her
armed forces. There seemed no way out. Her intellectuals,
Martinez Estrada and Mallea, had begun to write of the
"Argentine malaise". Fascist ideas began to spread among
the once-confident, but now increasingly nervous upholders
of the *status quo*. On the Left, there was growing unrest, a sense
that something radical must be done. Yet the old Socialist and
Anarchist movements, like the various Radical groups, seemed
to have lost all sense of purpose. There was a political vacuum;
and into it the Army was ineluctably drawn. To ask why the
Argentine succumbed to militarism is to ask why the civil
polity admired by foreign statesmen in 1910 should so quickly
have gone sour.

Gratefully, then, we find our question half-answered before it
has been asked. The problem of militarism in Latin America is
the problem of the weakness of her civil institutions. In his
The Man on Horseback, Professor S. E. Finer has correlated
nations' susceptibilities to militarism with their levels of "political culture". Thus Britain and America, and even the Soviet
Union, which have "mature" or "developed" political cultures,
seldom experience direct military intervention (though the
military make their influence felt behind the scenes). These
countries possess political and civil organisations of a robustness
that makes military intervention problematic. Why is this?
We should note that Dr Finer does not assume that civilian
rule is "normal", and military intervention "abnormal".
Rather he asks how it is that these well-disciplined organisations
ever let civilians alone. There are almost no countries where
the armed forces could not take over the apparatus of the state
were they so minded. They have a monopoly or near-monopoly

of modern arms (the police, too, are a factor to be considered). They possess a necessarily higher degree of organisation than civilian institutions, including an independent signalling and supply system. And, psychologically, they possess a highly developed caste-consciousness and *esprit de corps*. It is not that Latin America's armies are especially efficient or well-equipped. The question is whether her armed forces are *better* organised than her civilian authorities. In countries of "developed" or "mature" political culture this is only doubtfully so. In the case of the Soviet Union, the Party itself is a kind of civilian army, highly-organised, and disposing of a secret police force of its own. The Army can exert pressure; but it seldom has the last word.

But in countries of "low" or "minimal" political culture the armed forces enjoy an overwhelming superiority. They are the best-organised of national institutions. They are the respository of "national honour". They despise the corrupt and muddling politicians, whose authority is not in any case—as in "developed" or "mature" political cultures—legitimised by ideology or tradition. The people have little respect or affection for their new rulers. They may be disenchanted into the bargain once the euphoria of the Independence struggle evaporates. The politicians can neither satisfy the aspirations they have awoken, nor command the respect of the people. They may well be administratively incompetent and lacking in constructive ideas for the post-Independence period. The result is a rapid decline in civilian authority. Armed intervention is popular, since the Army's claim to be the repository of national honour is by no means implausible. True, its popularity does not last. But once the Army is in power its rule is likely to be prolonged, since no combination of civilian groups is strong enough to displace it.

This, then, is the situation in countries of "low" or "minimal" political culture. The New States of the post-war world mostly exhibit "minimal" political culture. But this is no new phenomenon. It is the situation Latin America has known for a century and a half. Indeed, much of the interest of Latin America stems from this fact: the Latin American states are merely the earliest of the New States. Still, it would be wrong to assert that all Latin American states exhibit "minimal" political culture. Few countries exhibit "mature" or "developed" political culture in the sense that the military have the last word: only Mexico, Uruguay, Costa Rica, and Chile fall into this category. On the other hand, fewer countries belong in the "minimal" category than people think. (Haiti and Paraguay are the exceptions that prove the rule.) But the picture is more complicated than that. Argentina, in Dr Finer's terms, is a country that has fallen from "developed" to "low". In other words, nations can rise from a lower to a higher level of political culture (though they can also fall). In practice, Dr Finer considers that most Latin American countries belong to his middling group ("low"), rather than to either of the extremes. The characteristic of this middle group is that the military, while able and willing to intervene, are deterred by certain factors that are absent in countries of "minimal" political culture. Clearly, it is important to know what these factors are. Only by encouraging their development can long-term political stability be attained.

Let us look at Dr Finer's definition of a low political culture, and see how far it corresponds to our analysis of the Argentine polity. To this low political culture he reckons: the Argentine and Brazil, Turkey and Spain, Egypt and Venezuela, the pre-war Balkan countries, Syria, Iraq and the Sudan. Most of these are post-colonial countries: successor-states to the Habsburg, Turkish, or Spanish Monarchies. Each has a tradition of political activity, an experienced bureaucracy, and a rich cultural past. Yet all have fallen prey to military intervention over the past forty years:

> In any other sense than the level of political culture, the Argentine and the Sudan are poles apart. Yet they fall into the category because, like the rest, they suffer acutely from the absence of consensus, and from the feebleness of organised attachment to the régime.

Dr Finer, too, is surprised that Argentina should belong to this category:

> At first sight, Argentina possesses most of the objective pre-conditions of political stability. There is no *patria chica* here but, on the contrary, a xenophobic and arrogant nationalism. Her institutions have been developed since the Constitution of 1863. Her population is well-fed and literate.

What, then, is the trouble?

> The three main sections of society have been at cross-purposes,
> each opposing the other two. Furthermore, up to 1943, no party
> rooted itself among the masses. The traditional Radical and
> Conservative parties came into being only at election time.
> Additionally, the Radicals were split into three factions based on
> personal loyalties. The only powerful party Argentina has known
> was that of Peron, and it was an official creation. The Argentine,
> despite her high level of material and literary culture, is afflicted
> with a kind of *anomie*. Her society is compartmentalised. . . . The
> situation resembles the situation in Spain in the twentieth
> century.

A grim comparison. But one made with circumspection.
Countries of low political culture are countries where peoples
have little attachment to, or comprehension of, their political
institutions. They are countries of latent opposition to the ruling
group, in which no clear political legitimacy exists. Here,
military intervention is popular:

> In the first place, the existing institutions are either discredited or
> incomprehensible. Secondly, these institutions have usually
> resulted in a situation of deadlock, where change cannot be
> brought about constitutionally. Thirdly, in such circumstances
> the deposition of the government is widely welcomed because,
> initially, the military coup means all things to all men. The army
> is not popular because of what it stands for . . . but because of
> what it has fought against.

We have seen that the Argentine coups of 1930, of 1943 and of
1955, were indeed greeted by popular enthusiasm. But a distinction must be made between the states of "minimal", and
those of "low" political culture. In the former the Army can
do what it likes. But in the latter the Army, though popular at
first, becomes progressively less so:

> If civilian organisation happens to be strong in countries of low
> political culture, this condition produces two contradictory
> effects. It both engenders resistance to military attempts to pass
> from simple deposition to a complete supplantment of the
> civilian authorities, and yet impels the military to attempt this
> very thing. The result is a history checkered by short-lived
> military interregna as in Argentina. The reason is this: the
> previous supporters of the displaced government may be strong

enough to stage a return to power, and then the military must reckon with the possibility of their vengeance. It therefore takes steps to prevent such a return to power and is thus impelled to take full powers to itself. But when it does so it runs into increased resistance, not merely from the ex-supporters of the government but from all sides. This induces the military either to give way and call for some kind of elections, or alternatively to go into politics itself as a sort of political party, in order to legitimise itself by some plebiscitary or electoral procedure.

This is what the Argentine Army did in 1930 and 1943: they allied themselves first with the Conservatives, then with the *descamisados*. The logic of this is interesting: in countries of low political culture the Army is often on the point of intervention. But intervention does not lead to the relative stability of an all-out military régime. It leads rather to a new instability, an oscillation between open, but in the long run unpopular military rule, and civilian rule which ends by being equally unpopular, yet has to live with the constant threat of military intervention. In most respects, then, this type of polity is in advance of what we find in Haiti or Paraguay. But it is, paradoxically, more unstable; for it both frustrates military intervention and invites it. The military, once they have regained power, act according to their own political interest. They are often anxious to give up political power, for which their experience and organisational talents are not suited. But they cannot do so to a party that will take its revenge once it is back in power. This has been the situation in Argentina more than once. Indeed, it is the situation in much of the Third World. The charge against the military is not that they intervene arbitrarily and brutally—their motives are often genuinely patriotic—but that by the fact of intervention they constitute themselves a "party above politics" which, while it may not itself be criticised, holds a veto over any government.

Militarism, traditionally, is an obscene word in the Liberal vocabulary. But we must get the thing in perspective. "Militarism"—in the Latin American sense—lacks two component that are associated with it elsewhere. First, Latin American militarism is rarely expansionist; in this it differs from militarism of the Napoleonic or Hitlerian type. Secondly, it has seldom set itself the aim of forcing society into a "militaristic" mould.

Latin Americans will tell you that their continent has an excellent record in international relations, that its disputes are rarely settled by resort to arms. This is not entirely true. Chile's war against Peru and Bolivia, to gain control of the mineral wealth of the Atacama desert, was a piece of outright imperialist militarism. And for sheer savagery it would be hard to beat the Paraguayan war of the 1880's. Nor have their civil wars been as bloodless as Latin Americans like to assume: the Mexican civil war was comparable to the Spanish in atrocity. Yet, on the whole, Latin Americans' indignation at such charges of immoderate violence is justified. There is in Latin America a subliminal violence, which we may put down to Spanish *individualismo* or to *mestizo* instability according to taste. But Latin America's record of political violence compares well with that of Europe since the French Revolution. The traditional *golpe de estado*, far from leading to excessive blood-letting, is like a game with chocolate soldiers. A general "pronounces"; some army corps follow him, some do not. After negotiations, the incumbent President offers his resignation. Alternatively, the coup collapses because the bulk of the armed forces have remained loyal. In either case it is conventional for the "pronouncing" general or his Presidential opponent to be allowed to go into exile once a decision has been reached. Large-scale violence is the result of a hitch, a misreading of the situation. Thus General Franco supposed that his *golpe* would lead to victory for the military and nationalist forces within a few days. He did not forecast violence on the scale of the Civil War. By nature a prudent man, Franco would probably not have acted had he known for certain that his *golpe* would meet with such resistance.

Intervention or Non-intervention?

None of which excuses Franco or his fellow-*caudillos* of Latin America. But it suggests that our picture of military intervention is inaccurate in certain respects. Latin American generals are not especially bloody-minded. Many have never heard a shot fired in anger. They seldom share the ideological fanaticism that has its origins in the armies of the French Revolution and of Napoleon (Napoleon is important in Latin American history; but as a *caudillo*, not as the bearer of a universal ideology). One of the troubles with the Latin American military, perhaps, is that they have too little fighting to do: idle hands make mischief. One of the errors of US policy has been to give support to the thesis that the Latin American military have a contribution to make to "hemispheric defence". For this is nonsense. If the Latin American contribution to the defeat of Germany and Japan was marginal, what importance has her military effort in the nuclear age? The truth is different. The Pentagon has managed to unload quantities of semi-obsolescent equipment on Latin America over the past twenty years; and Latin Americans have been persuaded, partly out of vanity, that this military hardware increases their prestige. In the old days this would have been called "dumping". Now it is called "hemispheric defence", and is apparently beyond criticism. But the serious defence of "the hemisphere" is now, of course, entirely a US concern. The contribution of Latin America is even less significant than it was in the 1939–45 war (when a Brazilian contingent fought in Italy). In the Korean war, Colombia alone was prepared to send troops to fight against Communist aggression, though the majority of Latin American governments were anti-Communist. But then the reasons behind Washington's indulgence of these military pretensions are political, not strategic.

As such they may be criticised. Still, we must get the thing into perspective. Latin American militarism is a game, an indigenous game in which the United States, from questionable or muddled motives, has come to play an important part. It is easy to criticise the US for encouraging the ambitions of military men in Latin America. They are being indoctrinated with an anti-Communism as doctrinaire as it is irrelevant; the sub-continent is being used as a dumping-ground for obsolescent weaponry. But how far can the dozen military interventions of the past decade be attributed to the action, or inaction, of the United States? Would they not have taken place had the US supplied no arms, and undertaken no indoctrination? There are cases where the facts of US intervention are well-known. There is the case of Guatemala in 1954. And, from what is known of the antecedents of the 1965 Dominican crisis, it is clear that US military attachés played a crucial role in precipating US intervention. Should we go beyond this and argue, with the demonologists of the Left, that US policy is decided entirely by the Pentagon and the CIA? Nobody who knows Washington politics could take this very seriously. Yet it contains a grain of truth. It reflects a dichotomy in American policy that has its roots less in administrative than in intellectual confusion: a dichotomy that has done harm in the past, and may do greater harm in the future.

What the United States has done is to take out a double insurance policy. She hoped, naturally, that the two policies would reinforce one another. But the Dominican crisis has shown that the two policies may be contradictory. The strategy runs as follows: Latin America is threatened by Communist subversion. The strongest weapon against subversion is a régime dedicated to reform and economic progress. The US must therefore support régimes that are stable and effective. This policy is not only dictated by *raison d'état*, it is also the clear moral obligation of the US. Let us note that this policy was not invented by Kennedy any more than the "hard line" policy was invented by Johnson. (The Eisenhower administration had supported the Bolivian revolution of 1952, the Betancourt régime in Venezuela, and even Fidel Castro in the early days.) But it is not always possible to find a reforming government for the US to support. In the early days the State Department looked favourably on Castro's rebellion. It took a good deal of provocation to persuade it that Castro was not the man it was looking for. After Castro's success it became necessary to prepare a second line of defence. In every Latin American country there exists one institution that is indubitably anti-Communist: the Army. And it is the Army, traditionally, that has had the last word in the making and breaking of governments. A fortunate conjunction! Let us build up democratic governments where they exist. But let us at the same time build up the armed forces as a second line of defence. The political stability of countries like Betancourt's Venezuela, Bosch's Dominican Republic, Frondizi's Argentina will then be doubly sure. For should democracy falter, the military will be there to make sure that nothing unpleasant can occur.

Is this a travesty of US policy towards Latin America? I think not. The point is that the United States, though Latin

Americans paint her as the chief demon of *imperialismo*, is not imperialist in the traditional sense. The relations of the United States to Latin America are analogous, not to the relations of Britain or France towards their Empires, but to the relations of Britain and France towards their ex-empires. That is to say: the limitations on US policy towards Latin America are like those imposed on Britain and France in the treatment of their ex-colonies. Most Britons would prefer to see democratic régimes in Africa and Asia. But what can they do? Very little. The truth is, Britain and France will be compelled, in the coming decades, to pursue the same policy towards the New States for which many Britons and Frenchmen criticise the US in Latin America. Since democracy cannot be imposed, *raison d'état* dictates that we go for a second-best: stability. Crises will arise where the ex-colonial power can tip the balance: France has intervened in Gabon and Biafra; Britain has put down military rebellions in Kenya and Tanzania. Should the ex-imperialists intervene on the side of "democracy", or of "stability"? There is no general, only an empirical, answer to this question. But there will be cases where treaty obligations oblige a metropolitan government to intervene *against* a "democratic" revolution, where non-intervention would be tantamount to favouring the forces of rebellion. At this point, non-intervention and intervention become difficult to distinguish.

What course will in fact be taken depends on many factors: on the metropolis's assessment of the viability of the régime under assault; on its assessment of the nature of the revolutionary forces opposing it; on its assessment of its own national interest; and on its assessment of the effects of intervention (or non-intervention) on regional and world opinion. The answer can only be empirical. It will often have to be arrived at in haste, and it will often be mistaken. It is, certainly, a gloomy prospect. The more so since these New States may well be moving, now the glamour of Independence has worn off, into an ever deeper instability. But the friends and allies of the US, however censorious she may have been about their colonialism in the past, have no reason to repay her in that coin. The situation she faces is neither unique, nor of her own making. It is the same situation that faces all the ex-colonial, industrialised powers of the northern hemisphere. Their power is growing faster than that of the Third World; yet never has intervention been so politically tabu. One reason for studying the history of Latin America since Independence could be to learn something of the history of the New States of Afro-Asia over the coming decades.

If this sounds like a counsel of despair, it is not intended in that spirit. Militarism is a disease, and I believe that there are ways in which the US could mitigate its effects. But we must be realistic: militarism is an *indigenous* disease, and it can only be cured within the national polity itself. The size of the problem is formidable. In 1954, twelve of the twenty Latin American states were ruled by military dictators; by mid-1961 only one of these remained in office—General Alfredo Strössner of Paraguay. This was, then, the heyday of democracy in Latin America and, under Kennedy's auspices, of the Alliance for Progress. Yet by late-1963, at the time of his assassination, six of these democratic régimes had been toppled. And between 1964 and 1968 came still heavier blows: military intervention in Bolivia, in civil-minded Brazil and in Dr Illia's Argentina, and finally in Panama and Peru. By late 1968, then, Latin America seemed to be back to square one. Still, one point emerges from these figures: if there is a historical rhythm underlying these events, it is *indigenous*, not foreign-inspired. It was indigenous Latin American anti-militarism that chased out the dictators of the 1950's—not any change of view in Washington. But, equally, it was the indigenous political weakness of Latin America that led to the renewed military interventions of the sixties—though, during the Kennedy years, Washington had come to regard military régimes with disfavour. It is perhaps mistaken, then, to blame Washington for falling back into old habits by supporting military dictatorships. Is is rather that Latin America has fallen back into old habits, and that Washington has followed her lead.

It is apparent that this alternating rhythm of militarism and anti-militarism in Latin America does not always coincide with the ups and downs of politics in the outside world. Washington was directly responsible neither for the post-1945 leftward wave in Latin America, nor for the rightward wave that came in its wake. (This is not to deny that the allied victory in 1945,

like the axis victories of 1940–2, had an important demonstration effect in Latin America.) The past decade has seen a
repeat performance: a leftward, anti-militarist wave in the late
fifties has been followed by a rightward, interventionist wave
since 1961. We must be careful, of course, not to be over-
schematic. An important group of countries—Mexico, Colombia, Chile, Costa Rica, Uruguay—seem to be exempt from
this pattern. But it seems justifiable, alas, to regard these as
exceptions to the rule, since the countries which do conform
(Brazil, Argentina, Venezuela, Peru) not only display close
parallels, but are among the most influential in the hemisphere
and contain a majority of its inhabitants. If we grant these two
points—that these political oscillations are essentially indigenous, and that foreign influence is essentially marginal—what
conclusions do we draw? Can we read in these swings of the
pendulum a general tendency towards more democratic,
civilian forms of government? Or is the situation deteriorating,
and the likelihood of military rule increasing? If the disease is
indigenous, can Latin America hope to cure herself over the
next generation? Finally, if we accept that foreign influence is
essentially marginal, what is there that advanced nations—
and in particular, of course, the United States—can do to
help Latin America?

First, one general point. In an earlier chapter I argued that
the popular, cyclical view of Latin American history was not
strictly correct. I argued that Latin America had a dialectic of
her own, not simply identical with that of Europe, North
America, or the Third World, but reflecting similar tendencies
in an indigenous form. Thus, looking closer, we see that the
leftward swing of the fifties was significantly different (except,
of course, in Cuba) from that of the forties: APRA and *Accion
Democratica* had ceased to be revolutionary parties and had
espoused a social democratic reformism. There was less rhetoric
now, and more pragmatism. During the same period, however,
the parties of the Right had also shifted their position. In most
countries Conservatism as such was a lost cause. The new
leaders of the Right—in Chile, say, or Peru—had begun to see
that they could only retain control by "an opening to the left".
Both Right and Left, therefore, have shown a tendency to move
towards the centre. Whereas Castro and the Communists have

set their hopes on a polarisation of forces, the actual pattern seems to have been one of convergence.

If the two leftward swings were significantly different, the subsequent swings to the Right were no less so. And this is true even in the military sphere. The early fifties brought forth a crop of dictators as repulsive as any in Latin American history. The US could not have prevented this; though she might have refrained from showering honours on these men (conduct that brought its nemesis on Richard Nixon during his humiliating trip in 1958). Yet we can see now that the new type of military dictatorship had begun to diverge from the traditional pattern. Military men were no longer creatures of the Oligarchy; more and more they understood that *caudillismo* of the old type was no longer tolerable. Thus General Odria initiated an energetic welfare-state programme for Lima on *peronista* lines—and has been rewarded ever since with the votes of grateful *Limeños*. During the recent wave of military interventions, it is notable that it is the moderate, Constitutionalist elements (not the extremist *gorilas*) who have had their way. Responsible officers are aware that they must either initiate reform programmes of their own, or ally themselves with a party that will do the job for them—as has happened in Venezuela and Peru. If the consensus of opinion in the armed forces has moved towards the centre, the reason is evident. Apart from nationalism and a preference for efficiency, the armed forces do not have many opinions of their own—except in so far as they are anxious to retain their own privileges. Essentially, they reflect the range of opinion to be found in the classes from whom they are drawn. The tendency to move towards the centre, which we have seen at work in civilian life, appears to have penetrated the ranks of the warriors.

This should be excellent news. But it has a darker side which we should not blink. According to Professor Finer's hypothesis, a nation can move from a "minimal" to a "low" level of political culture, and from a "low" to a "developed" or "mature" polity. In Latin America the obvious example is Mexico, where civilian institutions are so strongly entrenched that a military coup is highly improbable. But a corollary of Professor Finer's hypothesis was that as the level of political culture rose military intervention might become more frequent.

For the military would now face much stronger civilian resistance and thus have more reason to fear a civilian comeback. In so far as this is true—and it is plainly true of contemporary Brazil and Argentina—the situation may be said to be actually worsening in the short run, but improving in the longer run. For, in the long run, it is only the growth of strong civil institutions that is going to deter the military from intervention.

But there is a third possibility that is, arguably, even more alarming: it is that the armed forces in Latin America may be tempted towards "*nasserismo*" as a solution to the problems of their society. The same leftward shift that has weaned the military from their traditionalist past may persuade them that, in the absence of a political party to implement their aims, they themselves are called upon to do the job. Despite the lead given by Peron in Argentina, or by Odria in Peru, it is far from clear how strong these tendencies really are. They appear to be widespread among younger officers in Argentina and Peru and Venezuela, and possibly elsewhere. Here again, it looks as if US policy-makers have not thought out the implications of what they are doing. The US has done much to improve the efficiency of Latin American managers, soldiers and bureaucrats. But the end-result may not be what Americans would wish. MIT and CALTEC are fine schools; but they are not necessarily schools of *democracy*. Because *yanquis* who graduate from these schools turn into law-abiding, liberty-loving democrats, it does not follow that students from a society with different premises and problems will react in the same way. The truth is that technocracy and authoritarian government can go well together. By transmitting her own developed technology, the US may simply be preparing the ground for régimes where, as under Mussolini, "the trains run to time". Again, there is little the US can do to prevent this. But Americans should at least be aware of this possibility: that if there is a race in Latin America, it may not be a race between Communism and democracy, but between democracy and authoritarian technocracy.

What, then, can be done? What can we, the developed countries, do to help Latin America in mastering these problems? I have compared the situation of the U.S. *vis-à-vis* Latin America with that of France and Britain *vis-à-vis* their ex-colonies. If the analogy fits, it follows that we can do very little directly. But there is one kind of influence that is too easily discounted: the influence of example. It is fashionable in Britain today to make light of "the Commonwealth". But this is less realistic than it sounds. It is said that the countries of the Commonwealth will grow up, and Britain will be left with no baby to hold. But growing up does not necessarily mean growing away: it may mean growing into the vacant parental role. In other words, the psychology of Prospero-and-Caliban may be prolonging metropolitan influence where that influence has apparently long been rejected. Both Britain and France still play—and cannot help playing—Prospero to the Calibans of their respective communities. As long as Britain upholds the rule of law, free speech and democratic principles, the violators of these principles will enjoy an uneasy sleep, and their opponents, equally, will be comforted. I believe that much the same is true of the United States. The tremendous, even exaggerated response to President Kennedy's charisma is proof enough that Latin Americans are as responsive to the "American" idealism he embodied as North Americans themselves.

It is my judgment, as the reader knows, that Kennedy's ideas for Latin America met with little success—though the reasons for that failure lay as much in Latin America as in Washington. But the episode shows that beneath the predictable denunciation of the US as the arch-exponent of *imperialismo*, there exists a hidden concern for the values that the US, in her best moments, has always represented. It follows, I think, that the tendency in certain circles in Washington to argue for a purely pragmatic policy towards Latin America is mistaken. A policy of this kind, deliberately pursued, would represent not only a betrayal of the US's own best instincts, but a betrayal of all those in Latin America who wish to rid the continent of the evils that have plagued her for so long. I have said that the US role cannot be more than marginal. But there is no reason why the US should not openly profess towards Latin America those principles she professes towards the Communist world and which she strives to practise, however imperfectly, at home. Certainly, she can only work with the material in hand; a degree of diplomatic pragmatism is inevitable. But she should not hesitate, I believe, to make her displeasure known to those who flout the principles of democracy, just as she should not hesitate to encourage, as far as she can, those who have the principles of democracy at heart. She should do these things, not because they are expedient, but because they are right. America will not find, and should not look for, quick and spectacular success in this course; this was one of the faults of the original Alliance for Progress conception. But she may find that modified idealism will bring better rewards than either the immoderate hopes raised by President Kennedy or the do-nothing pragmatism into which disappointed idealists too readily relapse.

9

BRAZIL:

or Life in the Future Tense

Europeans and foreigners, who, hastening to make fortunes, hate every excitement which can interfere with the money market, are very severe upon the "arid and acrid politic" of the land. They never think that the excitement of partisanship is a phase through which all juvenile societies and governments must pass, like the hot youth of the individual. *Un peuple nouveau, positif par conséquence,* has to provide for its physical wants, to establish civil order, and to secure life and property: it will indulge in wars, and other calamities must occur: the breathing time is necessarily spent not in science and philosophy, the highest aims of its later life, but in religious functions, and in adjusting its political questions. And indeed these are the two noblest exercises of youthful human thought, thus embracing all interests between heaven and earth. . . .

I find in Brazil another symptom of strong and healthy national vitality. Men wage irreconcilable war with the present; they have no idea of the "Rest and be thankful" state. They balance "Whatever is, is good" by the equation "Whatever is, is bad"; yet they are neither optimists nor pessimists. They have as little idea of "finality" as have New Yorkers. They will move and remove things quiet, and they will not leave well or ill alone. . . . There is everything to hope from a race with prepossessions for progress towards such a high ideal.

It is said that the first words learned by the stranger in the Brazil are *"paciencia"*, *"espere un pouco"*, and *"amanhaa"*— Patience, wait a wee, tomorrow. I may add that some foreigners learn the lesson better than their teachers.

Brazil: Richard Burton (1869)

Spain, Portugal, and America

DOES LATIN AMERICA REALLY EXIST? Or is it merely a geographical expression? We asked ourselves this question in an earlier chapter. And we decided that on the whole it did. There was a simple test: despite huge distances, despite national rivalries, a major happening in one quarter of Latin America is seldom without repercussions in another. When Guatemala is pricked, Chile bleeds. A coup in the Argentine starts ripples; soon it will be Peru's turn, then Honduras, and then the Dominican Republic. And it has always been so. Bolivar, Andres Bello, Rodo, Peron, Fidel Castro are truly inter-American figures: they speak not for a nation, but for a continent. Certainly, the particularist tradition, the tradition of the *patria chica*, is also strong. The chances of a political union of Latin American states are as slight now as they were in the years after Independence. True, the chances of political union in Africa are scarcely more hopeful. But an underlying cultural unity persists; and, unlike in Africa, it is a cultural unity that becomes more striking the deeper one goes. That point we may take as established. Up to now we have been speaking, however, of "Latin America" without regard to its specific Spanish and Portuguese components. How far can they be lumped together? The stock answer runs roughly as follows: Brazil is to Spanish America as Portugal is to Spain. Most educated Portuguese speak or understand Spanish; but not vice-versa. Brazil is now by far the largest country in Latin America and the most populous. Its potential is immense. It is the traditional "land of the future" ("The land of the future—and always has been", say the cynics). But it has adopted many of the attitudes that characterise the Portuguese *vis-à-vis* Spain. Equally, Spanish Americans inherit many of the traditional attitudes of Spaniards towards Portuguese.

What are these attitudes? Spaniards think:

We are more *macho* than the Portuguese because the Spanish

bullfight, like much else in Spain, is fought to the death—to the "*momento de la verdad*".

Portuguese reply:

We are more human (but not less brave) than the Spaniards. We have made the bullfight a test of skill rather than an *auto-da-fe*. Spaniards are bloody-minded, fanatical, inflexible. They confuse vanity with honour. They go to extremes—each is Don Quixote or Sancho Panza, nothing in between. They lack our Portuguese sense of compromise.

To which Spaniards (and Spanish-Americans) reply:

You call it compromise; we give it a ruder name. Do you want to be Anglo-Saxons? When you Brazilians won independence, you didn't have to fight for it; the Portuguese just ran away. Later, you got rid of your Empire; your Emperor ran away. You got rid of your Peron, Getulio Vargas, in 1954; the fellow obligingly committed suicide. And Janio Quadros, the great and incorruptible Janio, who was going to clear up the mess when you made him President in 1961: why, he ran away too—that is, he *compromised*. . . .

And so on. But the foreigner had better not intrude. For the quarrel is ancient and intimate: a quarrel between a couple who have shared the same house for as long as they can remember, squabble incessantly, have never married and yet seem to the outsider strangely at one. Still, the Iberian house is a constricting one. After that explosion of energy under Portugal's Henry the Navigator and Castile's Catholic Monarchs, the fires quickly died. Spain and Portugal returned to what they had been in the dark ages, to what geography has so often condemned them to be: a vestigial tail, a phantom limb of Europe. So Spanish and Portuguese America became doubly alienated from post-Renaissance, post-Reformation Europe; they became, as it were, the appendage of an appendage. The Spanish and Portuguese world had a distinct culture of its own—that of the counter-Reformation in its rigid, Iberian stance. But it was cut off from the new world of ideas springing up in Holland and in Britain, in France and Italy, in the still fecund womb of the old world, the dialogue with which soon became a conversation through a double thickness of glass. This constriction, this impoverishment, Spain and Portugal had in common, as had their colonies in the New World. True, their former colonies later drank deep—too deep!—of the new ideologies of post-1789 Europe. But these modified ancient patterns of thought and behaviour only superficially. And what is true of Latin America is true of the Iberian nations themselves: they remain on the margins of Europe. Salazar ruled a compliant Portugal for a generation and more; Franco, at the time of writing, is still *Caudillo de España*.

I am not sure that there is a convincing analogy for the Luso-Hispanic relationship at hand. England and Ireland, or England and Scotland, are examples of nations shut up in a box together. But at bottom these are convergent cultures, not cultures in parallel that never meet, like those of Spain and Portugal. Take, again, Prussia and Austria in the German-speaking world. Prussia certainly has something of Castile in its steely, austere, disciplined—but also somewhat bleak and barren—attitude to life. Austria has something of Portugal: she is softer, more easy-going, more moderate—but also less resolute, less *charaktervoll*. And these differences have profound historical roots. Prussians look down on the softer, South-German type as a degenerate species; South Germans regard Northerners as barbarians from beyond the *limes*. Much the same can be said of the view Portuguese (and Brazilians) take of Spaniards (and Spanish-Americans)—and vice versa. The cruelty, courage and harshness of Castile is still part of the Spanish American make-up. The mellower Atlantic-melancholic airs of Portugal still mould the Brazilians of Rio, Bahia, and Recife. There is not perhaps much mutual respect or liking for each other's way of life. But that is no less true between Mexico and Argentina, or between Venezuela and Peru. It is only when you bore deeper that the unity of the Spanish-Portuguese, Iberian world becomes apparent.

Nevertheless, the Iberian is only one strand in the make-up of Iberian America. I put forward, in an earlier chapter, the hypothesis that between the cultures of the two Americas, Anglo-Saxon and Iberian, there is a difference in quality; a difference in kind rather than degree. The Anglo-Saxon American has made himself, or has been made by his environment, into something radically different from the European. This was not intended in a mystical, but in a severely practical sense. The world the North American inherits, the world he has constructed for himself, is not that of even the most "Americanised" European. This has nothing to do with intelligence, artistic creativity, or cultural superiority. Few would deny that North America has proved herself over the last generation more creative in many respects than Europe—and than Latin America. Probably this situation will not endure. But even now "cultural" anti-Americanism of the French and Latin American variety is untenable because it flies in the face of the facts. For all that, the North American is a different animal from the European: he is a universalist, a meliorist, a Pelagian. And he is these things by birth. His pessimism is not a self-sustaining tradition—though it may have been that in Puritan days—as was Jansenism or Nietzscheanism or even Burkean conservatism. American pessimism is the obverse of American Utopianism. It springs from the despair of the lonely individual; it is not the product of original sin.

Now, as I see it, the distance between Iberian America and Europe is altogether less formidable. It is an old-fashioned kind of European arrogance that sees the United States as an extension of Europe. De Gaulle, in that celebrated remark to Churchill quoted in his *Memoirs,* made no such claim, "Britain is an island; France is the cape of a continent; America is another world." *America is another world.* That is the point. North America is a new civilisation, sprung from the West and belonging to the West; but not European. Or rather: no longer European. Between the world of Jonathan Edwards, Franklin, Jefferson, and Hawthorne, and the world of Mark Twain and J. P. Morgan, Theodore Dreiser and Teddy Roosevelt there falls a caesura. We need set no arbitrary date for this sea-change that took place in American culture. But we cannot doubt that it took place. And the test must be empirical. We can say: reading X's work we feel that it could have been written by a European; reading Y's we know that it could not. In the eighties Mark Twain boasted: "The English language is a joint stock undertaking, and we have the majority of the shares." That could not have been said thirty years earlier—by Hawthorne or Washington Irving or James Fenimore Cooper. They would have considered it rather vulgar. But it is the conscious vulgarity of it that makes it a perfect expression of its age. I do not intend "vulgar" in a pejorative sense: who would not prefer the vulgarity of Huck Finn to the gentility of latter-day Boston? The point is that this was a new America. It was the America Henry James found when he returned to the country in middle age and wrote his *American Sketches*. It was the new Caliban-America of Twain, Rockefeller and Roosevelt that so alarmed Rodo and Dario in Latin America.

It was a materialistic and acquisitive society. But Latin Americans cannot criticise the United States for its materialism and acquisitiveness without hypocrisy. If ever a society was founded on the principle of "get rich quick", it was the America of the *conquistadores*. And it is precisely the crude materialism of the upper classes of Latin America that shocks the Anglo-Saxon observer today. They lack the conscience of the rich. This difference is apparent in the attitude to the Playboy. To the heirs of the Puritans, the Playboy is basically a contemptible, degenerate, unmasculine creature. Mr Hugo Hefner's delights, for example, are reserved for those who earn their bread by honest toil: a hard day's work deserves a fair night's play. But that is not the Latin American idea. To the heirs of the *conquistadores*, the Playboy stands for the fulfilment of man's desires. To conquer woman and fame and to flaunt one's wealth are not sins: it is the *virtus* of the rich man to live as fully as he can; honour demands no less. Like so much in Iberian culture, it is a highly individualistic concept. It is also a profoundly worldly one; and, therefore, to the unworldly Anglo-Saxon, a stumbling block. But we must not forget that Seville was the city not only of the *conquistadores*, but also of Don Juan, the acquisitive man *par excellence*. Don Juan is the Faust of the Latin peoples. The Playboy, therefore, is an archetypal figure. To us he is the man-with-the-brilliantine, flashy smile concealing spoilt child's sulky pout, haunter of the nightspots of Miami or St Tropez till the last photographer goes home. That is how the Anglo-Saxon sees him. But, we must remember, he has a tradition to live up to: he has the blood of Don Juan and Pizarro in his veins.

What differentiates the America of the Latins from the America of the Anglo-Saxons, I suggest, is that the latter underwent this sea-change and the former did not. Latin America has remained Colonial-European. North America has evolved into something which, if not rich and strange, is at least strikingly *different*. Whether Latin America has benefited by preserving its traditional values, or has lost by not cutting free from Europe's apron-strings, is something that only Latin Americans can decide. Certainly, it is one of the main reasons for Latin America's provinciality. But the defects of this provinciality must be balanced against the fact that access to the parent culture is often available to Latin Americans in a way that it is not to the Anglo-Saxon American. The Peruvian feels himself at home in Madrid or Paris; the North American seldom feels at home in London, let alone in Paris or Madrid. It is a moot point, again, whether the aristocratic vulgarity of Latin America is preferable to the democratic vulgarity of the United States. Most intelligent Latin Americans would probably regard both with equal distaste (that is one reason why Communism, at a distance, makes so great an appeal; it looks so much more spiritual than either). But approval and disapproval are perhaps beside the point: Latin America has a relationship to Europe different in kind from that of the US, and that relationship is unlikely to change. Having said this, we would be defining Latin America imprecisely if we put all the emphasis on "Latin", and none on "American". Nothing irritates Latin Americans more about North Americans than their innocent, yet very arrogant, appropriation of the term "American". The traveller has to be wary about this. However awkward it may sound in English, he must learn to say "North American" when referring to the United States. At first, I admit, I resented this usage. But I came to realise that, as a mental tripwire, it had something to be said for it. It pointed to the fact that the English language, in defining what is "American", leaves the Latins out of it. Our disregard of Latin America is built into the English language.

What, then, is "America"? Here is a negative definition: it has nothing to do with plumbing. True, industrial civilisation was not invented in North America. Until the time of Edison, America was a technological borrower rather than a lender. Right up to the Second World War, in technology and science —if we consider radar, rocketry, splitting-the-atom, penicillin —Europe was the equal of North America. North America's technological pre-eminence is more recent than many Europeans think. Yet we cannot ignore the plumbing definition

entirely. Even early nineteenth-century European travellers
were impressed by North American gadgetry. But there are
other, more fruitful definitions of Americanism: there is, for
example, a specifically American attitude to nature, and a specifically American solitude—phenomena to be found equally
in Latin and in Anglo-Saxon America. Nor is it difficult to
show that Americanism, so defined, has an inner coherence:
both the gadgetry and the solitude are American man's
response to the wilderness that surrounds him. Technology is
the weapon with which man attempts to discipline nature, to
re-create in the New World the settled order of the Old, to
exorcise the terror of the open frontier and the flat horizon. Yet,
when technology has done its work, when the wilderness has
been reduced to an imitation of a French or a Japanese garden,
the result is disappointment: solitude remains. Americans, for
all their exertions, inhabit a land of existential bareness, of
terrifying solitude and emptiness. (True, most Americans—
Latins as well as Saxons—are city-dwellers today; but it is
notorious that the American city, whether São Paulo or
Chicago, provides no comfort: it is the wilderness reproduced
in ferro-concrete.) This, then, is the American tragedy. Technology is the wand by which solitude should be exorcised. Yet
the solitude remains. In America, Don Quixote and Sisyphus
are one.

São Paulo

São Paulo, they say, is the Chicago of Latin America. It is not
a bad description. Like Chicago, São Paulo is a city that grew
overnight from a market town into a metropolis. Like Chicago,
she is a temple devoted to commerce. There is nothing Imperial
about her, as there is about Rio or Lima or Mexico City. There
is something of the *bourgeois Belle Epoque*, of that weary *fin-de-
siècle* ostentation that is the charm of Buenos Aires. But where
Buenos Aires has the appearance (though not, alas, the reality)
of ordered civility, São Paulo is what it seems. She is a bustling
commercial metropolis that grew rich on the coffee of São
Paulo State, as Chicago grew rich on the meat and grain of
the Middle West. Coffee, since the Depression, has ceased to be
her commercial *raison d'être*. After 1930, the profits that the

coffee planters made (and thanks to Government protection in the famous coffee-burnings of the thirties, these profits often came out of the tax-payer's pocket) went into consumer production for the Brazilian market, since, in the post-Depression world, this had become more profitable than coffee production itself. São Paulo now has six million inhabitants: her industrial potential is said to be growing at the rate of a factory a day. From a distance, set in the rich, red, coffee-bearing plain, São Paulo's cluster of skyscrapers seems to rival Chicago's or New York's. Closer to, the effect is less grandiose, perhaps, than Caracas' uprush of concrete against the green backcloth of the Andes. But then Caracas has so far "Americanised" herself that little of the older city remains. São Paulo still has a rather ponderous Edwardian core that will disappoint the traveller who has heard tall tales of her modernity.

"The cities of the New World have one characteristic in common: that they pass from first youth to decrepitude with no intermediary stage." Thus Lévi-Strauss. São Paulo, where he taught for a while in the thirties, was only a station on his journey into the interior. Yet not only is Lévi-Strauss's account of São Paulo masterly, as a sketch for a phenomenology of the Latin American intellectual it cannot be bettered:

> One of my Brazilian girl-students returned in tears from her first visit to France: whiteness and cleanness were the criteria by which she judged a city, and Paris, with its blackened buildings, had seemed to her filthy and repugnant. But American cities never offer that holiday-state, outside of time, to which great monuments can transport us; nor do they transcend the primary urban function and become objects of contemplation and reflection. . . . The older a European city is, the more highly we regard it; in America, every year brings with it an element of disgrace. But they are not merely "newly built"; they are built for renewal, and the sooner the better. When a new quarter is run up it doesn't look like a city, as we understand the word; it's too brilliant, too new, too high-spirited. It reminds us more of our fairgrounds and temporary international exhibitions. But these are buildings that stay up long after our exhibitions would have closed, and they don't last well: façades begin to peel off, rain and soot leave their marks, the style goes out of fashion, and the original lay-out is ruined when someone loses patience and tears down the buildings next door. It is not a case of new cities

contrasted with old, but rather of cities whose cycle of evolution is very rapid as against others whose cycle of evolution is slow. Certain European cities are dying off slowly and peacefully; the cities of the New World have a perpetually high temperature, a chronic illness which prevents them, for all their everlasting youthfulness, from ever being entirely well.

As a description of modern Brasilia—but Lévi-Strauss is writing about a Brazil on which Le Corbusier had not yet made his famous descent—this must seem all too apt. As a comment on Americanism, it neatly dovetails with Henry James's dictum that America moves in one stage from adolescence to deca-dence. "American", too, and of a piece with the city's furious pace of architectural advance, was the mentality of the students Lévi-Strauss taught:

> Our students wanted to know everything: but only the newest theory seemed to them worth bothering with. Knowing nothing of the intellectual achievements of the past, they kept fresh and intact their enthusiasm for "the latest thing". Fashion dominated their interests: they valued ideas not for themselves but for the prestige they could wring from them. That prestige vanished as soon as the idea passed from their exclusive possession; there was great competition, therefore, for the magazines and handbooks and "popular" studies that would empower them to get a lead over their fellows, and my colleagues and I suffered much from this. Ourselves trained to respect only those ideas which had been fully matured, we were besieged by students who knew nothing at all of the past but were almost always a month or two ahead of us in the novelties of the day. Learning was something for which they had neither the taste nor the method; yet they felt bound to include in their essays, no matter what their nominal subject might be, a survey of human evolution from the anthropoid apes to the present day. Quotations from Plato, Aristotle and Auguste Comte would be followed by a peroration paraphrased from some egregious hack—the obscurer the better, for their purpose— since their rivals would be the less likely to have happened upon him.

This may sound unkind. But it is not intended so. Lévi-Strauss admired the eagerness and charm of his young pupils and adds, apologetically, "this characterisation is to be understood as a period piece of little relevance to the Brazil of today". We are

K

entitled to take this tongue-in-cheek. For, of course, what Lévi-Strauss says of the young people he taught in São Paulo in the thirties is true of their successors today—in Brazil as elsewhere in Latin America. Provinciality, and its complement, the urge to some all-embracing, universal theory, are still potent factors in the mental development of young people. Marxism, as we have seen, is attractive because it is a universal theory, permitting the spirit to transcend the narrow confines of the *patria chica*. But it is the *Americanism* of these attitudes that strikes the foreigner today, as it struck so self-consciously European an observer as Lévi-Strauss a generation ago.

The Psychology of Inflation

São Paulo stands for one aspect of Brazil's Americanism—for a Utopian faith in man's power, through technology, to overcome the wilderness. So vast are São Paulo and Rio—with some twelve million inhabitants between them—that it is easy for the traveller to overlook the complementary reality of the *sertão*: the blank, barren space of the Brazilian backlands. It is not until he has seen something of the vastness and desolation of these backlands—if only from the aircraft on the day-trip to Brasilia—that the traveller can grasp their significance for the Brazilian imagination. Admittedly, if he were left to his own devices, the foreigner would find the going hard. The cityfied Brazilians he encounters are as unlikely to have met a *sertanejo* from the backlands as New Yorkers are to have met a Red Indian brave. The gap between the city-dweller and the countryman is very great. Fortunately, literature is able in some degree to make good the deficiency. For the *sertão* is the subject of the greatest book that has come out of Brazil, Euclides da Cunha's *Rebellion in the Backlands*—to which we shall return in a moment. First let us look at Rio, most famous and most spectacular of Latin America's cities. The reader will have detected a note of sourness in this traveller, I dare say, when exposed to a barrage of Latin American superlatives: these intolerable *-isimos*! I remain unapologetic. What looks like Anglo-Saxon curmudgeonliness is merely a defence reaction. Should the reader doubt this, let him try the same diet: caviar and foie gras, as it were, for breakfast, lunch, and dinner. After some weeks, I assure him, he will crave Puritan bread and water. To savour this continent you must take it with a pinch of salt. Rio, then, presents something of a problem. Brazilians like to call it *"a maravilhosa cidade"*. To prevent misunderstanding, let me say that I agree: Rio is indeed a marvellous, an extraordinary, a unique city. With its dark-green, sugar-loaf hills, its beaches and its dazzling sunlight, its grey granite Colonial churches and shining-white, stilted apartment blocks, Rio is certainly beautiful. But the *cariocas* will not leave it at that. An English journalist of my acquaintance told the following sad tale: when he first arrived, *cariocas* would ask how he liked their city. Oh, he liked it *very* much. Had he seen anything as beautiful in South America? No—no, on reflection he didn't think he had. Had he in fact seen any city so beautiful anywhere—anywhere at all? English shyness overtook him at this point. But the incident had taught him, he declared, a valuable lesson: Latin America is not a place for comparatives.

It does not take long to discover that inflation, monetary or otherwise, is the motor of modern Brazil. Prices in the cafés are chalked up afresh on a board every morning according to the shifting mood of the *cruzeiro*. This, one reflects, must be what it was like to live in Berlin in the twenties. But that does not quite catch the mood. Such palpable evidence of the world's disrespect for Brazil's national currency ought, surely, to have a depressant effect on the *cariocas*. These years of galloping inflation ought to have undermined the morale of the middle classes. Inflation, after all, lay at the root of the collapse of German middle-class morale that made Nazism possible. But this is not what has happened in Brazil. The functioning of Brazil's wildly inflationary economy is something of a mystery to the professional economist (the situation was at its worst under Kubitschek, builder of Brasilia, and under Goulart: it is now a good deal steadier). But Brazil does seem to show that it is possible to live with inflation over a very long period. My guess is that the damage is done on a different level. Certainly, Brazil's reckless inflationism in the fifties gave a lift to the national economy, though it was perhaps the kind of lift the drug-addict experiences, and suffers for later. Still, its expansionist effect on the national economy cannot be denied. However precarious the financing, Brazil has in twenty years far outstripped

Argentina as an industrial producer. The building of Brasilia, for example, was seen to be speeding the inflationary spiral. But that never dissuaded Brazil from going ahead with the project. The building of Brasilia kept the wheels of São Paulo industry turning, even if it aggravated Brazil's foreign exchange problems. Brazil's economy is one that generates more heat than light. It seems to feed, and at the same time feed upon, that euphoric strain in the Brazilian character to which Kubitschek's Great Inflation gave suitably operatic expression.

The outsider, I think, has two choices. He may join the chorus of self-congratulation to which this euphoria gives rise. Or he may react with some violence against it (in the depressive phase of their manic cycle—those political suicides!—Brazilians react against it with still greater violence). This makes it more difficult to write fairly about Brazil than about any country in Latin America. For this her self-appointed friends are partly to blame. Brazil has been promoted in recent years more zealously, I suppose, than any other Latin American country. She has been tipped as a future Great Power, an industrial Colossus of the South. Is she not as large in area as the United States? Will she not soon be as populous as Japan and, in a generation's time, as Britain, Germany and France together? The reader will have acquired by now a proper scepticism about such predictions. But the myth of Eldorado has not lost its power: it lurks, once again, behind these prophecies for Brazil. Brazilians, or so they will tell you, are an easy-going lot, lacking the immoderation of the Spaniard. Yet Brazil is the victim *par excellence* of that fecklessness, that gambler's euphoria which is the mark of the *conquista*. Brazil has always been a country of boom and goldrush. It has never taken thought for the morrow. The sugar boom of the seventeenth century; the gold-and-diamond boom of the eighteenth; the coffee boom of São Paulo; the rubber boom of Amazonia at the end of the nineteenth century; the consumer boom of the forties and fifties: Brazil's economic cycle has always had the same hysterical, manic-depressive character. "Brazil is the country of the future, and always has been." But while it is exhilarating to live in the future tense, it is also precarious. Nothing seems quite real; nothing *is*, all is becoming. And American euphoria ends in American cynicism. Scepticism would be quite a different matter. But

America is as little a continent for scepticism as for comparatives.

A Brazilian Mythology

If it is difficult to write fairly of Brazil, it is for this reason: too
much is claimed and too little delivered. Her admirers point,
for instance, to Brazil's present burst of architectural creativity,
to her racial harmony, or her tradition of political moderation.
If true, these things are of no small importance. The modern
world groans in the toils of racial intolerance: if Brazil has
found the answer, it is something we should know about. Latin
America's politics is bedevilled by political violence; if Brazil
knows a way out, let us hear of it. As to her architecture: where
could we find a better setting than the New World's virgin
wastes for Auden's "new styles of architecture, a change of
heart". These are the claims that are made by foreign admirers,
and by Brazilians themselves. Nowhere are they so eloquently
set out as in Gilberto Freyre's *Brazil: an Introduction*. The book
does not, of course, rank high in the Freyre canon. But it is a book
that many travellers to Brazil will have in their luggage.
Abroad, Freyre is perhaps Brazil's best-known intellectual
figure. He is a literary sociologist-cum-historian whose fame
rests on the famous study of life on the sugar plantations of the
north-east, *Casa Grande e Senzala* (*The Masters and the Slaves*) he
wrote in the nineteen-thirties. *The Masters and the Slaves* is a
work in the tradition of da Cunha, an erudite, passionate
reconstruction of patriarchal Brazil, a Brazil remote from the
commercial bustle of São Paulo. But Freyre is much more than
a sociologist. A spry, white-haired old gentleman, he is the very
model of the benevolent patriarch he would have the old sugar
masters of the north-east to have been. The air of old-world
charm is beguiling. But it may set the Northerner on his guard.
Where has he met it before? It seems reminiscent. And indeed
it is. Freyre's charm is that of a Southerner, telling you how the
ante-bellum South was the only real civilisation America has
known. Freyre, in fact, is the interpreter, apologist, and high
priest of what one might well call "the Brazilian way of life". It
is as if Faulkner, or Allen Tate, or another of the Southern
generation of the twenties, had devoted his life to a massive,

detailed reconstruction of the *ante-bellum* way of life. In their case, too, the result would not have been sociology, it would have been rather a manifesto, a gauntlet thrown down to the money-minded, philistine Yankee. Freyre's work is the equivalent of that literary Declaration of Independence, "I'll Take my Stand". The difference is that Freyre claims to speak, not for a depressed and aggrieved region, but for the Brazilian nation as a whole.

The views we find expressed in *Brazil: an Introduction*, then, are not unrepresentative of Freyre's general argument. By the younger generation Freyre is seen now (not unlike Borges in the Argentine) as something of a back-number, a feudal relic who has no place in modern Brazil. But, of course, this is unfair. It ignores the part Freyre played in evolving that neo-Brazilian mythology which, far from being for foreign consumption, now informs the thinking (though not necessarily the practice) of most educated Brazilians. How does Freyre phrase his claims? On Brazil's new architecture and music he has this to say:

> Brazil is a pioneer also in modern functional architecture. Office buildings, factories, private residences recently built in São Paulo and Rio are considered by foreign architects to be examples of a really new method of building and happy solutions to a number of problems facing a modern architect in the tropics.

Of the famous hedonism of the Brazilians he writes:

> Brazilians, being Latin, are free—perhaps too free—from the Protestant conception of leisure as a vice, and recognise, apparently instinctively, its importance as an antidote to those money-making activities which reduce man to a mere economic entity ... In this happy combination of toil and leisure, an optimist might see that Brazil has a contribution to offer to the happiness of mankind.

Or, again, of the Brazilian "genius for compromise":

> The secret of Brazil's success in building a humane, Christian and modern civilisation in tropical America has been her genius for compromise. While the British, as no other people, have had this genius for compromise in the political sphere ... the Brazilians have been successful in using the same power of compromise in the cultural and social sphere. Hence their ethnic democracy, the almost perfect equality of opportunity for all men regardless of race or colour.

Of slavery in the North-East Freyre writes:

> The student of the Brazilian plantation system is tempted to compare it with the plantation system in other areas of America, especially the South of the United States. The system in Anglo-Saxon America probably had a more rigid aristocratic structure, from the point of view of race superiority and inferiority, than in Brazil where race prejudice was never so strong as among Anglo-Saxons. There was race prejudice among plantation area Brazilians; there was social distance between master and slave, between white and black, just as between young and old, man and woman. But few Brazilian aristocrats were as strict about racial purity as the majority of Anglo-American aristocrats of the Old South were. Family pride was stronger than race pride.

What are we to make of this? Let us, to begin with, set against these speculations of Freyre what Darwin has to say of *fazenda* life in *The Voyage of the Beagle*. On the voyage out, Darwin stayed at a friend's *fazenda* in the neighbourhood of Rio de Janeiro. His description of life on a Brazilian gentleman's estate in 1832 could be drawn from *The Masters and the Slaves*:

> This profusion of food showed itself at dinner, where, if the tables did not groan, the guests surely did: for every person is expected to eat of every dish. One day, having, as I thought, nicely calculated so that nothing should go away untasted, to my utter dismay a roast turkey and a pig appeared in all their substantial reality. During the meal, it was the employment of a man to drive out of the room sundry old hounds, and dozens of little black children, which crawled in together at every opportunity. As long as the idea of slavery could be banished, there was something exceedingly fascinating in this simple and patriarchal style of living: it was such a perfect retirement in independence from the rest of the world . . . and on such *fazendas* as these, I have no doubt that the slaves pass happy and contented lives.

But the idyll is soon broken. On this same *fazenda* Darwin is involved in the kind of incident that "can only take place in a slave country":

> I was crossing a ferry with a Negro, who was uncommonly stupid. In endeavouring to make him understand, I talked loud, and made signs, in doing which I passed my hands near his face. He, I suppose, thought I was in a passion, and was going to strike him; for instantly, with a frightened look and half-shut eyes, he dropped

his hands. I shall never forget my feeling of surprise, disgust and shame, at seeing a great powerful man afraid even to ward off a blow directed, as he thought, at his face. This man had been trained to a degradation lower than the slavery of the most helpless animal.

Interestingly, while Darwin's testimony contradicts Freyre's in one respect, it confirms it in another. Brazilian slavery was often cruel; but it cannot be compared with the sufferings of the "free" Indian who worked the mines of Mexico or Bolivia. This was not a society dominated by the cash nexus; older, feudal ties, and a sense of mutual obligation are still operative. Historically, this is what we should expect. The Masters of Freyre's Brazil lived, not as their own ancestors had lived (for they were often of Portuguese peasant stock) but like the feudal lords of medieval Portugal; indeed, that is why, like Cortes and Pizarro, they had come to the New World. But there is another factor, also implicit in Darwin's account. The fertile, well-watered coastal strip between the desolate *sertão* and the Atlantic was a land of abundance. In this respect it was not unlike the Africa from which Brazil's Negroes had originally come (most slaves came from Guinea, the Congo basin, or Angola). The sugar planters made large profits, until they were undercut by their West Indian rivals in the eighteenth century. But this surplus was spent on luxuries from Europe. With the necessities of life they were well provided; and most planters, Brazilian-style, were too short-sighted to plough back the surplus and become more efficient sugar-producers. Under one aspect, then, Freyre is obviously right: Brazil's virtues are rooted in the feudal life of the coastal *fazendas* he describes. But so, one is bound to add, are Brazil's vices. If the easy tolerance, the grace and charm of *fazenda* life are part of modern Brazil's inheritance, so are the casual cruelties, the simmering racial resentment, the archaic patriarchal structure that form the reverse of the coin.

What is the truth, then, in the claim that Brazil is "colour-blind"? One point that needs to be made is that Brazil is by no means—as *Orfée Nègre* might suggest—a country where "colour" predominates. There are many countries in Latin America where the proportion of non-whites in the population is much higher. Statistics show that 15 per cent of Brazilians are pure Negro; that 3 per cent are Asiatic or aboriginal

Indian; and some 20 per cent are of mixed White-and-Negro, or of mixed White-and-Indian blood. (Indian-Negro crossing has also taken place, but is rarer.) On the other hand, the majority of the population (some 60 per cent) are more or less pure White; and the European stock is concentrated in the urban areas and settled agricultural country of São Paulo, Rio, Minais Gerais and the Brazilian South. And these areas are the heartland of modern Brazil. (This represents, incidentally, a remarkable reversal of the ratio at the time of Independence. Humboldt calculated that Brazil had then 900,000 Whites, two million Negroes, and over one million Indians: Brazil's Whites were therefore outnumbered at that time by something like three to one.) But the figure I have given for "Whites"—60 per cent—may well be misleading. There is no hard and fast barrier. Not everyone will tell the truth about the proportion of coloured blood in his veins; most people wish to appear "whiter" than they in fact are, and may get away with it. Many people of mixed blood can "pass" as White in some social contexts. And more and more are acquiring the means to do so —whether through education or the hair-straightening arts of the Brazilian coiffeur. In the literature about Brazil the Indian often looms large: Brazil was the original home of the Noble Savage. Yet this, too, is misleading. Pure-bred Indians are almost wholly confined to the Amazonian forest, and those remote regions of Mato Grosso Lévi-Strauss describes in *Tristes Tropiques*. Brazil's colour problem, in other words, is a good deal more marginal than either her admirers or detractors assert. It is only a minority of her population that cannot "pass". This minority, moreover, is to be found in the most backward and sluggish areas of the national life. It is not just, then, to compare Brazil with South Africa or with the American South. For the domination of Brazil's economic, social, and political life by the White is assured—at any rate for a long time ahead. There is no real threat to White domination; and since the White birth-rate is among the highest in the world such a threat is not likely to develop for a long time. It is because there is no such threat that you do not hear talk of "White Supremacy" in Brazil. It is taken for granted.

How far, then, is it possible for the man of mixed blood to "pass" in White society? And how far—to put the question the other way round—is colour a cause of social injustice in Brazil? Brazilian apologists argue that it is only lack of education that disqualifies. With education, with the acquiring of the externals of the Portuguese-Brazilian way of life, even the darkest Brazilian may hope to "pass". It is pointed out that many important Brazilians—Brazil's great nineteenth-century novelist, Machado de Assis, is an example—have been of Negro or Mulatto stock. There is no doubt that Machado de Assis— founder of the Brazilian Academy of Letters—was thoroughly accepted in Brazilian society. And this, Brazilians will tell you, could not have happened in an Anglo-Saxon environment. Superficially, this is an attractive argument. But its weakness is evident: it puts too much emphasis on the exceptional case. For even in the Anglo-Saxon societies of that period it is possible to point to certain exceptional men—Negro, Jew or Hindu— who passed the race barrier with success. Today, a certain Uncle Tom element has to be allowed for: it is in Liberal Anglo-Saxon circles that the domesticated parlour-Negro is in demand. Interestingly, this is much less common in the less hypocritical Latin societies. Brazilians make little effort to put on a good front: The Navy and Foreign Service, for example, are still restricted to candidates of European stock ("Would we want a black man to represent Brazil at the Court of St James?"). The argument from the exceptional man does not prove much; though it is probably easier for the exceptional man of colour to establish himself in Brazil than in Britain or the United States. Nevertheless, it is striking that Machado de Assis's novels, for all his Mulatto background, are concerned wholly with the doings of the White aristocracy. *Orfée Nègre* romanticism belongs to a later generation.

There is another argument the traveller in Brazil is likely to meet, the truth of which is not easy to determine. It is admitted that discrimination exists, but it is said that this is simply social discrimination, and has no racial basis. It is hard to get at the truth of this, if only because almost all coloured people in Brazil are poor. According to a Brazilian saying "a rich man is White, and a poor man is Negro". But there is a good deal of evidence against a purely "social" interpretation of this discrimination. And the more concrete the evidence, the less does it support the thesis of Brazil's unique colour-blindness.

Thus a Brazilian Negro professor writes in an UNESCO report:

> It is said that the racial problem does not exist among us, that
> the Negro enjoys the same rights, the same prerogatives, as the
> White man. Unfortunately this is largely Utopian.

Thus, while in law no restriction may exist, it is a fact that there
are no Negro surgeons or dentists, and that coloured people are
seldom employed in banks or business houses. It is unfortun-
ately the case, whatever Brazilians may say, that blackness is
widely regarded as an inferior state—not least by Negroes
themselves. Consider, for example, what the Negress Carolina
Maria de Jesus has to say about being black—and she is speaking to a Brazilian, not to a foreign public—in her account of the
life in a São Paulo *favela*, *Beyond all Pity*:

> May 13th: At dawn it was raining. Today is a nice day for me, it
> is the Anniversary of the Abolition. The day we celebrate the
> freeing of the slaves. In the past the Negroes were the scapegoats.
> But now the Whites are more educated and don't treat us any
> more with contempt. May God enlighten the Whites so that the
> Negroes may have a happier life. . . .
>   June 16th: I write plays and show them to directors of circuses.
> They tell me, "It's a shame you're black". They forget I adore my
> black skin and my kinky hair. Negro hair is more educated than
> White man's hair. Because with Negro hair, where you put it,
> it stays. It's obedient. The hair of the White, just give one quick
> movement, and it's out of place. It won't obey. If reincarnation
> exists I want to come back black.
>   One day a White told me: "If the Blacks had arrived after the
> Whites, then the Whites would have complained and rightly so.
> But neither the White nor the Black knows his origin." The White
> man says he is superior, but what superiority does he show? If
> the Negro drinks *finga*, the White drinks. The sickness that hits
> the Black hits the White. If the White feels hunger, so does the
> Negro. Nature hasn't picked any favourites.

Let us add that the racial problem in Brazil is many-headed.
Carolina writes of a certain Senhor Alcides, "he is not Japanese
yet he is as yellow as rotten butter". Carolina Maria de Jesus
witnesses, of course, to the "social" discrimination from which
the lower-class Brazilian suffers. But since her book has become
a best-seller, she put the pullulating, anarchic life of the *favela*
behind her. She has, in fact, succeeded in "passing".

Today I had lunch in a wonderful restaurant and a photographer took my picture. I told him: Write under the photo that Carolina, who used to eat from trash cans, now eats in restaurants. That she has come back to the human race and out of the garbage dump.

Carolina's diary, a best-seller in Brazil, is a touching and terrible document. But there is no mistaking that it is the lot, not just of "the poor", but of the *Negro* poor that she so bitterly, yet so unsentimentally laments. If there is any doubt on this point, the following remarkable Negro litany, discovered by an American anthropologist in Bahia, should serve to remove it:

The Negro came from Africa and has spread throughout the whole world. He is descended from Cain, not from Abel. The Negro is an ass and a brute. He is the cousin of the orang-outang, the monkey and the chimpanzee. He is not a human being, and all he is good for is to make black magic. Here in Brazil they want to be God, but they are not even good enough to wash the feet of the White men:

> The Negro has a jam pot instead of a face.
> He has headlights instead of eyes,

> His mouth is a cave
> And his nose is a tunnel.
> He has holes instead of ears,
> And he walks on planks, instead of feet.
> His lips are rubbery tyres,
> His beard is like a goat's,
> And his whole face is Satanic.

These extraordinarily revealing lines are quoted in M. Pierre Joffry's excellent Vista book on Brazil. M. Joffry concludes that the inferiority association of blackness is as strong in Brazil as anywhere in the world. While agreeing that social and economic inferiority are bound up with colour prejudice in Brazil, he suggests that the coming social and economic emancipation of the Negro may serve to increase racial tension. Today, Brazil is a more tolerable country for the Negro to live in than any other country of the White world. But this may be because Brazil is behind the rest of the world, rather than ahead of it. Far from her possessing the key to the colour problem, her troubles may simply be in store.

We are prudish about race: plain speaking is not the mode.

But in Brazil the difficulty is compounded because the Brazilian, when speaking to a foreigner, tends to adopt his angle of vision. Among themselves Brazilians are a great deal less prudish. But in behaving like this Brazilians are only exhibiting that tendency to take on a protective European colouring, whether or not appropriate, traditional to Latin America. The irony is that whereas modern opinion sees virtue in a racially mixed society, an earlier generation took a contrary view. It is no secret that the contempt of Argentines for Brazilians in the nineteenth century (and even today) had a racial basis. The political and social corruption of Brazil was notorious, and Argentines saw a connection between Brazilian social immorality and racial miscegenation. No doubt this was unfair. But it seems that Brazilians saw such a connection too. We have, for example, only to compare da Cunha's views on the subject with Freyre's. Writing at the turn of the century, da Cunha makes no bones about it: Brazil's Achilles Heel is racial miscegenation, which has produced "an inferior race". Freyre, commenting on this aspect of da Cunha, writes that he was guilty of "ethnocentric exaggerations" and that his positivist upbringing made him "the victim of scientific preconceptions with the appearance of anthropological truth". Freyre is plainly right. Da Cunha's "scientific preoccupations" are derived from Comte and Darwin. It so happens that da Cunha's views are unfashionable—so unfashionable as to be beyond discussion in liberal society. Equally, it is the case that Freyre's views correspond to current "preoccupations" of European and American Liberals: here is a multiracial society that actually works.

But the point that must strike the European or North American is the extent to which *both* views seem to be tailored to his predilections. Both da Cunha and Freyre are exceptional men. But their views are typical of their age. And it is hard to avoid the impression that both men—their sincerity, of course, is not in doubt—are really looking at Brazil *through European eyes*. One might wish that the psychology and sociology of *mestizaje* could be discussed as frankly as they were in the time of da Cunha. There seems little doubt that the *psychological* situation of any mixed blood group, torn between an admired, but unapproachable white-skinned élite and a despised, dark-skinned helot caste is profoundly pathetic. And this is what commonsense would suggest. What da Cunha writes of Brazil's miscegenation may not be "scientific". But much of what he has to say—in his "irritating parenthesis" in *Rebellion in the Backlands*—gives uncomfortable food for thought:

> An intermingling of races highly diverse is, in the majority of cases, prejudicial. According to the conclusions of the evolutionist, even when the influence of a superior race has reacted upon the offspring, the latter shows vivid traces of the inferior one. Miscegenation carried to an extreme means retrogression. The Indo-European, the Negro, and the Brazilian *guarani* or the *tupi*, represent evolutionary stages in confrontation; and miscegenation, in addition to obliterating the pre-eminent qualities of the higher race, serves to stimulate the revival of the primitive attributes of the lower; so that the *mestizo*—a hyphen between the races, a brief individual existence into which are compressed age-old forces—is almost always an unbalanced type. . . . The fact is that in the marvellous competition of peoples, all of them evolving in a struggle that knows no truce, with selection capitalising those attributes which heredity preserves, the *mestizo* is an intruder. . . . The tendency towards regression towards the primitive race is a mark of his instability. It is an instinctive tendency towards a situation of equilibrium. The play of natural laws appears to extinguish little by little the anomalous product which violates those laws, by sending it back to its own generative sources. The Mulatto has an irresistible contempt for the Negro, and seeks with the most anxious tenacity such inter-marriage as may extinguish in his progeny the stigma of a dark brow. The *mameluco* becomes the inexorable *bandeirante* and hurls himself fiercely on the conquered native villages. . . .

A reminder is in order at this point: the writer of these lines is no Nazi or Southern racialist, but the fallible, scrupulous witness of an age franker than our own.

The ambiguity of Brazil's claim to a greater degree of racial, social and political harmony than other nations is now apparent. The inferiority complex educated Brazilians once felt about their racially-mixed society has been transformed into a claim that racially-mixed Brazil is a beacon of sanity in a world of racial strife. From what we have said it is clear that this claim is a little disingenuous. Yet there is surely a grain of truth in the claim. Brazil is indeed more tolerant in her day-to-day racial practice than most societies in the world today. The mistake has been to sentimentalise this to a point where the ugly reality, which Brazil shares with other race-divided nations, vanishes beneath the sugar-icing. If there is any basis for the claim that Brazilians are less colour-conscious than Anglo-Saxons, it must lie in the imponderables of colour relationships, not in any ambitious claim that the problem has been solved. And there is indeed such a basis. It is clear that the almost physical revulsion from the Negro that is found in most Anglo-Saxon societies is lacking in Brazil. It is true that an upper or middle-class Brazilian does not want his daughter to marry a Negro. But it is also true that his feelings would be mollified if the man possessed wealth and position. Again, living in a society where few are of entirely unmixed blood, the Brazilian likes to flirt with the idea that Negro blood makes for sensuality and sexual attractiveness. Afrikaners, too, are susceptible to the sexual charms of colour; but in that puritanical ambience all such tendencies are sternly repressed. In Brazil, least puritanical of societies, the opposite is the case.

It seems, therefore, that the *permissiveness* of Brazilian society is an important element in her reputation for tolerance in racial and social matters. But how far can modern Brazil legitimately draw moral dividends from this ambiguous heritage? This is not, perhaps, a question that an outsider can answer. But caution seems to be demanded. It happens that both sexual permissiveness and colour-blindness are favoured by modern liberal opinion: in combination, therefore, they are likely to be irresistible. It is evident that Brazil's racial permissiveness owes a great deal to the extreme sexual permissiveness that has pervaded Brazilian society from its earliest days. Her racial tolerance, then, is as much a by-product of concupiscence as of any deliberate pursuit of Christian virtue. More tragically, it is the by-product of that exploitation of the Indian and Negro—especially of their womenfolk—that mars the pages of Brazilian history. But much the same may be said of Brazilian tolerance in other fields. What we are pleased to call "tolerance" our ancestors might have called laxity. Morally, Brazil cannot really have it both ways. She has inherited both the good and evil of the old *fazenda* system described by Freyre. The ease, charm and tolerance of her ways go back to that system. But so do the graft, the indolence, the permissiveness and the cruelty that

characterise her society, and that are among the real obstacles
to her becoming that "land of the future" she is so ambitious
to be thought to be.

Into the Wilderness

Statistics are the plague; up to now we have taken them in
homeopathic doses. But there is one statistic I must now give,
because it says more about Brazil than acres of grey prose: 90
per cent of Brazil's vast territory can be cultivated, but after
400 years of colonisation Brazil still cultivates *no more than 5 per
cent* of that territory. The implications of such a figure are staggering. Brazil is in many respects an underdeveloped country.
But Brazil is not over-populated, like India or South East Asia;
on the contrary, she is under-populated. Her ninety millions
are a fraction of what her land is able theoretically to support.
Three-quarters of this population live in the three south-central
states of Minas Gerais, São Paulo and Rio Grande do Sul; and
three-quarters of the cultivated land is to be found in these same
states. Thus it would be true to say that apart from this central
bloc, the heartland of modern Brazil, and the highly populated,
but poverty-stricken North-East, Brazil is almost empty. Of
course, much of this soil is poor: either too dry, like the drought-
ridden *sertão*, or too wet, like the great basin of Amazonia. But
the same might be said of much of North America: there, too,
are vast infertile deserts, barren mountains and frozen tundra.
To judge by the reaction of some observers, one might think
that any comparison with North America was unsporting: it's
not fair! But why is it not fair? Did the North Americans have
unfair advantages? Where do they lie? Hardly in geography,
or in climate, or in antiquity. Colonisation began a century
earlier in Brazil, and was quickly successful. By the 1630's, when
the New Englanders were still struggling to maintain a foothold
in the New World, Brazil's sugar-growing North-East was rich
enough for the Dutch to attempt invasion and occupation. In
the eighteenth century, the newly-discovered gold and diamonds of Minas Gerais made Brazil the most valuable of all
Europe's overseas colonies. Later, when that precious stream
dried up, came the coffee and rubber booms of the nineteenth
century. Wealth poured into Brazil over many centuries, as it

poured into few Spanish-American nations. What was done with the wealth is another matter. But it is only half-true to say that Brazil, compared with North America, is ill-favoured by nature. It would be truer to say she was spoilt.

Comparison with North America is tempting for another reason. The topography is uncannily similar. In Brazil, as in North, the colonists clung to the Atlantic seaboard for almost two centuries. At their back lay a rugged, highland barrier, lightly peopled with hostile Indian tribes; difficult but not impossible of access. Beyond that lay the great river systems of the Amazon and the Parana, and, in North America, of the Mississippi. Beyond that, the mountain ranges of the Rockies and of the Andes; beyond that, the Pacific Ocean. In the North-East of Brazil, a wealthy north-Portuguese, sugar-planting, slave-owning aristocracy ruled the countryside—a society not unlike that of Virginia and the Old South. In the Brazilian south, a tougher race of southern Portuguese, of pioneering "Paulistas"— with their offshoot, the marauding *bandeirantes*—had emerged; the complement, in many respects, of New England's hardy pioneering stock. The comparison with North America, then, has substance. Brazilians, it is true, are inclined to object that the mountains and the rivers are in the wrong places. The Amazon was never as useful an island waterway as the Mississippi. Other rivers, such as the São Francisco, are not navigable upstream from the populous seaboard because they are interrupted by steep falls at the points where they descend from the highlands. Still, it would not be difficult to think of similar reasons why geographical conditions should have made it impossible to develop continental North America. The fact remains that North America has been successfully developed and inhabited, whereas Brazil's population still clings to the coastal regions where it was to be found at the time of Independence. I have spoken of the sea-change that came over North American society in the middle decades of the nineteenth century. Its literary landmark is Mark Twain. But its physical correlation was the *conquista* of the American West. In Brazil that *conquista* never came to completion.

The tragedy that is implicit in this analysis is evident; let us not rub salt into the wounds. Let us recognise, again, that this is only one face of Brazil. There are others—the faces more usually turned to us—that are so attractive and so charming that the most hard-bitten ideologist must relent. There are Rio's Carnival, Bahia's waterfront, and the bikini-strewn beach at Copacabana. There are Brazil's rivers and mountains, her sea and sun. Brazil is a gigantic tropical hybrid out of Kew Gardens and the Garden of Eden, whose people are pleased to boast that "God is a Brazilian". All this is true. Yet is such an approach really so flattering to Brazil? For Brazil, more than any country in Latin America, is a country of aspirations: a profoundly *American* country. The lizard-life of Copacabana is all very well. But man is not an animal well adapted to the rhythms of nature: he cannot come out of the water, have sex, and go back into the water, like some reptile or amphibian. Not, at least, in the long run. If Brazil is the most determinedly hedonistic country in Latin America, she is also the most determinedly American. The Brazilian is double-natured: he is both lotus-eater and pioneer. And this other, American face is essential to the understanding of Brazil—and, indeed, of the America of the Latins.

Who is the American? The American is the man who sets out to conquer the wilderness: with fire and sword, but also with Bible and sewing machine. The American is an adventurer; but he is also a civiliser. He is in the wilderness, certainly; but he is not *of* the wilderness. He is no plunderer, viking or tartar. Unlike the Arab, he has not learnt to make the wilderness his friend; it remains a foe to be reduced. And the yoke he would impress on it is civilisation. Not for nothing do lawyers enjoy such standing in the Americas; they are the priests of order, and their power rises in proportion to the disorder menacing society. The *conquistadores*, as we have seen, were no mere plunderers: they were founders of cities, hospitals, churches and universities. And it is in this capacity to civilise, to bring order into the wilderness, that we recognise them as the first Americans. The first act of the first White intruder on American mainland soil, Hernan Cortes, was the solemn proclamation and foundation of a *ciudad*. Much has been written of the differences between the Puritan founders of New England and the Spanish *conquistadores*. But the resemblances are seen less clearly—or misunderstood. It is as easy to play up the rugged individualism of a Pizarro as it is to point to the resemblances between Francis

Parkman's explorers of the Great West and the intrepid Spaniards and Portuguese who, in less than fifty years, had taken the measure of the New World.

But to present either the *conquista*, or the opening of the Great West, as individual achievements would be misleading. The American cowboy is rugged; he has to be that. But is he an individualist? To assert this is to make nonsense of that most powerful of all frontier myths: the Western. The Spanish bull-fight celebrates the triumph of man over nature; it is essentially anarchistic and metaphysical. The Western, on the other hand, celebrates the triumph of man over the wilderness and over his own lawless nature. The sheriff, after all, is simply the lawyer armed. It was because the *gaucho* represented that lawless individualism he feared that Sarmiento saw in him the incarnation of Barbarism. In Sarmiento's vision of America, the town meeting, or the *cabildo*, was the sole source of civilisation, the sole bulwark against the wilderness and its devouring solitude.

If this is true, it becomes less surprising that Latin America should be more highly urbanised than Western Europe. It is understandable that where organised society is so brittle, and nature so hostile, the *civitas* should be the focus of men's lives. It is logical that the chief symbol of man's defiance of the American wilderness should be the founding of a city—for preference in virgin territory, for preference as big and bold and handsome as human hand can build it. Need one look further for the making of Brasilia? Brasilia is the American myth in steel and concrete. These two great towers, soaring sheer out of featureless scrubland, may look like the latest thing in functional architecture, brashly transplanted from Manhattan, Tokyo or Milan to the wilderness of central Brazil. But their functionalism is misleading. It is not simply that Brasilia does not function very well as a city: that elevators get stuck; that façades are beginning to crumble; that surprisingly little thought has been given to making the city habitable for human beings. At bottom, Brasilia's architecture—indeed the very conception of the city—has little to do with functionalism at all. Brasilia is a gesture, a challenge, a figure of rhetoric. Her enemies say Brasilia represents a triumph of Latin bravado over rational common sense. But Brazilians do not take this as an insult: they see in it a triumph of Ariel over Caliban. The mistake foreigners make—and Brazilians give encouragement to this error—is to trumpet abroad that Brasilia is the authoritative expression of all that is hard, factual and quantifiable in the *zeitgeist*: that Brasilia is *modern*. It is a misunderstanding: Brasilia is not modern, she is Baroque.

Lest the reader accuse me of playing at paradoxes, let me add that I intend this statement in a quite literal sense. Historically, after all, the Baroque is Brazil's, and Latin America's, most profound aesthetic experience; and that experience has set her sensibility in a definite mould. We speak, loosely, of Latin America's "European inheritance". But Latin America's inheritance from Europe, like Russia's, is a partial thing—as, indeed, is her inheritance from Spain and Portugal. Traditional Latin American culture is often described as "medieval" or "feudal". But this is not quite true. The *conquistadores* were as much men of the Renaissance as of the Middle Ages. The Middle Ages proper, the spirit of Gothic art and architecture, have no place in Latin America. The Iberian Renaissance gave a handful of Renaissance-*plateresque* churches and palaces to the colonies of the New World. But it was the Baroque age that gave Latin America her great architecture, ecclesiastical and secular. And the Baroque bore the impress of a different age, the age of the Jesuits, of the Counter-Reformation, of the Inquisition. At Independence, it is true, this mould was rudely broken. Where the Spanish Habsburgs offered Latin America the Baroque, and the Spanish Bourbons at least the Rococo, what had the Europe of the nineteenth century to offer of equal vitality and invention? The answer is plain to see in the cities of Latin America: an overblown neo-Classicism or an incongruous romantic neo-Gothicism. To say that Latin America's basic aesthetic experience is Baroque is therefore to state a plain truth. That Latin America should have taken the materials and forms of modern architecture, and have given them a content of her own, is therefore far from surprising. Compared with Brasilia, that stark Iberian palace-city, the Escorial, is the quintessence of functionalism. But then, it is not the spirit of Castile that Brazil inherits. To appreciate Brasilia it is necessary to recall those luxuriant, flamboyant churches and palaces of the Manueline era, in which Portugal strove to express in architecture the exuberance of her great age of discovery.

Brasilia is for show. And showmanship is the essence of the Baroque. In this, Brasilia is merely the latest of a series. Brazil's cities are rich in Baroque churches and palaces; Bahia and Recife, like Quito and Cuzco on the west coast of the continent, vie with Salzburg or Prague as museums of the Baroque. But there are, in Europe, few Baroque cities as such, few cities where the medieval basis, as in Prague, is not present in the background. That is, necessarily, a Colonial phenomenon; and in the Portuguese empire it is to be found both in India (as at Goa); and in America—as in Brazil's Ouro Preto ("Black Gold"). Ouro Preto, then, is Brazil's first show-city. Built on the profits of the gold-and-diamond boom of the eighteenth century, it is a town breathtaking in its beauty. Like other boom towns of Colonial America—Potosi in Bolivia, Taxco in Mexico—its beauty has been preserved by the very completeness of its decline. At Ouro Preto, 400 miles inland from Rio, at 3,500 feet, twenty or more churches perch precariously among the convoluted hills and terraces of Minas Gerais. Wherever one glances, a sheer white-and-grey granite façade rears on the skyline. It would be tempting, such is the masterly *mise-en-scène*, to say that Ouro Preto was pure spectacle, pure show. But that is to forget that the Baroque mode is also didactic. Like the Jesuit theatre, its beauty does not exist for its own sake alone, but to body forth some greater truth, human or divine. This Ouro Preto does—unashamedly. And the men of that epoch would have seen nothing strange in this. For Ouro Preto bodies forth, not only her own material glory, but the greater spiritual glory of her Creator and Redeemer.

Ouro Preto is not, architecturally, more original than most of the Baroque art of South America. Like much else in Brazil, she is an importation. But she is a most charming, intelligent and successful importation. Her delicately gilded, blue-tiled, sunlit interiors are extraordinarily lovely. They have something of the charm, for all their provincial modesty, of that masterpiece of the Rococo, Franconia's *Vierzehnheiligen*. And, as is proper to the style, the worm in the flesh is not forgotten. It is poignantly there in the person of Brazil's strangest genius, Aleijadinho, the crippled Mulatto who toiled at his marvellous soapstone sculptures, hammer and chisel strapped to his wrists. These sculptures—especially the craggy, brooding stone Prophets, and the

cedarwood carvings of the Last Supper at Congonhas do Campo
—are Brazil's greatest contribution to the plastic arts, at least
until modern times. Aleijadinho is one of those Brazilian men of
genius—he belongs with Machado de Assis and Euclides da
Cunha—whose peculiar pathos is that they seem equally to spring
from nowhere and to lead nowhere. In this hedonistic, permissive, gregarious society, they are the great solitaries, the great
sufferers. They are the other face of Brazil: they express Brazil's
underlying *saudade*, the Celtic melancholy that is part of her
Portuguese inheritance. Still, appropriate to the Baroque as is
Aleijadinho's vision of suffering, it seems less at home in the
Rococo gaiety of the picturesque Brazilian Eldorado of Ouro
Preto. Humanly, of course, Aleijadinho gives poignant utter-
ance to the sufferings of the Negro or Mulatto man of talent in
White society. But that, of course, is to narrow his significance.
Aleijadinho is a true original, not specific to his own place and
age. Whether he is in fact the great sculptor he is claimed to be,
I am not sure; perhaps, again, too much has been claimed for
him. There is something rough and awkward—though that is
also the secret of his vigour—in those tortured Christs, those
dark forbidding Prophets staring blankly into the void at
Congonhas do Campo. If Aleijadinho belongs anywhere, it is
with the pious German craftsmen of the age of Luther—with
Tilman Riemenschneider or Matthias Grunewald. But Aleijadinho is at bottom a primitive; and fashionably sophisticated
comparisons reduce rather than add to his stature. Like Brazilians themselves, most writers of Brazil hug the coast; they rarely
get beyond Rio. And that is a pity. To come on these gaunt
Gothic figures among the green hills of Minas Gerais is one of
the experiences of a lifetime.

Brazil's leaders have waged a long campaign to wean Brazilians from the coast. The notion of building a new capital in the
interior has haunted Brazil since the eighteenth century. The
first rebels against Portugal—who hatched their conspiracy in
Ouro Preto, and were later executed there—had proclaimed its
necessity. The Constitution of 1891, after the fall of the Empire,
set aside an area for this new inland capital. Thirty years later a
foundation stone was laid. But the city remained unbuilt. It
was only in 1955, with the Presidency of Joscelino Kubitschek,
a populist leader out of Vargas's stable, that a design was com-

missioned and the political decision taken. Fortunately, one of today's most gifted architects, Oscar Niemeyer, was a personal friend of the President. Niemeyer and his former teacher, Professor Lucio Costa, were given *carte blanche*: few architects, in any period of history, can have had such an opportunity. I have said that the notion of Brasilia was not new. Nor is she in fact the first planned New City in the history of Brazil. Earlier in the century, Belo Horizonte had been built as Minas Gerais' new capital; Goiania, likewise, as a new capital for the State of Goia. But the most spectacular and disastrous of these projects —an ill omen for Brasilia, some would say—was not the work of any planner: Manaus, that extraordinary monument to capitalistic megalomania in the heart of Amazonia. She is not a city that attracts many visitors today. It is her fate to be on the road to nowhere. And she is of an interest so exotic that only the very rich, or the very adventurous, include her in their itineraries (I would have given much to have gone). There is today no access except by air or river to Manaus. Lying in the jungle, a thousand miles from the mouth of the Amazon, she is yet only a hundred feet above sea-level and swelters in an average temperature of 80 degrees. It is said that Manaus still does a flourishing trade in brazil-nuts, lumber, cocoa and rubber. But the great days of rubber are long over. Brazil, which got hold of the rubber tree from French Guiana by devious means, had it stolen from her by no less devious means a few years later. (A British explorer collected thousands of wild rubber seeds for Kew Gardens in the eighties; from these a better-yielding stock was bred. This was then planted in Malaya and drove Brazil out of the market.) But while the boom lasted Manaus bodied forth her wealth with an abandon that put Ouro Preto in the shade. Manaus became the first city in Latin America to install trams and electric street-lighting. Steamers made her a regular port of call, despite the thousand-mile haul up the Amazon. Opera singers—that great contemporary status symbol—were imported from Europe to sing at the vast, opulent *Teatro Amazonas* (Sarah Bernhardt is said to have played there). This legendary building, complete in 1896 and rebuilt in 1929, with its huge dome of green, yellow, blue and red tiles, survives in solitary grandeur. The singers are departed; the orchestras have fallen silent. The Amazon jungle has still to be tamed; another

Eldorado has proved to be a mirage. Defiantly, the *Teatro Amazonas* towers above the wreckage, a modern Babel, and bodies forth the frivolous, melancholy, indomitably Baroque spirit of Brazil.

Brasilia

The praises of Brasilia have been sung to the point of tedium. So brashly sold, so loudly trumpeted a project invites critical retribution. It is hardly possible, therefore, not to be disappointed with the thing itself. For this Brazil's foreign admirers are much to blame. We are told, for example, not simply that Brasilia is a well-designed modern city, but that Brasilia is *the* only modern city yet in existence. Brasilia is more than glass and concrete: she has a distinctly metaphysical dimension. Indeed, the accents of Utopia are unmistakable. Thus it is a city without traffic intersections or pedestrian crossings. In this Utopia the road death, most modern and most accidental of deaths, is to be eliminated by rational engineering. Indeed, it seems death itself is to be cheated—an un-Baroque touch, this—by a cunning contrivance. The city cemeteries are situated at the terminal points of the axial road dividing Brasilia into two. The reason? It will not then be necessary—explains the brochure—for funerals to pass through the inhabited quarter of the city. In life, as in death, nothing is to be left to chance. The inhabitants of Brasilia are to be housed in *"supercuadras"*: rectangular dwelling blocks arranged around a core of collective institutions—the primary school, the clubhouse, and the obligatory swimming pool. Shops are nearby; and each *supercuadra* is designed to be self-sufficient. The *supercuadras* are laid out on an extended arc, intersected at mid-point by the before-mentioned axial road. Seen from the air, therefore, the ground-plan resembles an airplane whose wings form the dwelling quarters, and whose fuselage the political-administrative axis of the city. The ground-plan has been criticised as something of a gimmick. One can see why. The airplane was evidently chosen, not for "functional" reasons, but because it was a symbol of the new age to which Brasilia bears witness—rather as a cruciform church bears witness to the crucifixion of Christ. Irreverently, we may wonder how this "modern" plan will look in half a century should the winged airplane be phased out in favour of a less archaic mode of transportation.

One need not be an expert, then, in the ways of modern architecture and town-planning to see that Brasilia is a very curious hybrid. It is even said by malicious *cariocas* that Brasilia is not thirty years ahead of her time, but thirty years behind. True, *cariocas* resent the removal of Brazil's capital from their graceful, cosmopolitan city and secretly hope that Brasilia may wither on the bough. Even now—so they tell you—the Friday evening planes from Brasilia are crowded with civil servants and politicians fleeing the boredom of a weekend in the sticks. The fleshpots of Rio are traducing the idealism of these new colonists of the *sertão*: and, given the Brazilian temperament, cynical *cariocas* say this does not point a bright future for Brasilia. But I doubt if the pessimistic view is correct: Brasilia will survive, as New Delhi and Washington survive, though some of her early aspirations may have to be modified.

For when *cariocas* wisecrack that ultra-modern Brasilia is really thirty years out of date, they are questioning, quite legitimately, the habitability of the place. True, it is emphasised that the *supercuadras* are "planned for people". But they are planned for people with legs and baby-carts, not for people with Volkswagens and Cadillacs. And this is hardly realistic. Without an automobile you cannot get round the city at all; and the automobile is not the most sociable of vehicles. No doubt, when the vast semi-subterranean opera house—a still potent symbol— is finally finished, together with the cinemas, theatres and other places of entertainment, these will provide a social focus of a sort. But the natural focus will remain the neighbourhood block. And whatever the merit of these blocks (they are certainly in no way original to Brasilia) the *supercuadras* will not do duty—if Brasilia is one day to be the capital of a nation of 200 million souls—for the Roman *forum* or the Greek *agora*, or for the traditional, Roman-derived *Plaza Mayor* of the Iberian town. What has happened is that the concept of the *unité d'habitation*—which has changed the face of Rio since Le Corbusier's lightning descent on the city in the 1930's, so that not a building worth its name lacks its stilts and *brise-soleils*— has been married to a quite different, monumentalist concept of what a capital city should be. This is where comparison with

Washington or New Delhi comes to mind. The *supercuadras* are, as it were, the suburbs of Brasilia. Each lives its separate life; none is integrated into the greater life of the new metropolis. Standing apart from them, equally unintegrated, are the buildings of state; the equivalent of the White House or the Capitol or of Lutyens's Moghul-Britannic New Delhi.

The marriage, then, is an unhappy one, and likely to remain so. And the fault lies, not in the counter-attractions of Rio, but in the basic conception. It follows, I fear, that the dream of using Brasilia to "open up" the *sertão* is unrealistic. Whatever their defects, Ouro Preto, São Paulo and Manaus were natural growths. Brasilia is an artefact. Her meaning is symbolic, not practical. But I think her defenders, were they willing to give up their extravagant claims, could fall back on a more defensible position. For Washington, and much-maligned New Delhi, are cities of great beauty. True, in neither city is the proportion of certifiably beautiful buildings very high. But that is not the point: it is not high in London either. The purpose of a capital is to express the statehood of the nation. Here, then, the monumental mode is in order; as are flamboyance, solemnity, or conspicuous waste—according to the national spirit, genius or soul. For old Prussia, *Unter den Linden* was exactly right. In Habsburg Austria it would seem cramped and frigid: Vienna needs her Prince Eugene riding high in the court of the Hofburg. Until recently, Washington must have been a dreary town; we cannot well imagine Virgil, Molière, or even Dr Johnson as a citizen of that pretentious pseudo-Roman capital. Yet Washington, since she came to world power, has subtly changed her character. This is not, I think, because President Kennedy brought fine music to the White House. This new Washington is like the actress of whom Brecht's Herr Keuner, correcting a friend who insisted she was successful because she was beautiful, remarked that, on the contrary, she was beautiful because she was successful. So it is with Washington: she has grown more beautiful as she has grown into her role as capital of the world's most successful nation. What once appeared hollow and grandiloquent now appears appropriate and harmonious.

We might say that Washington's beauty had been won in obedience to Nietzsche's admonition: become what thou art!

Possibly Brasilia too may grow into her appointed role as the
capital of America's second nation. That remains to be seen.
Earlier, I suggested that Brazil's genius was essentially Baroque.
It is not surprising, then, that Brasilia should have so much of
the Baroque in her conception. Indeed, we may combine the two
trains of thought. What Brazil needed to express her will to
statehood was Baroque monumentality in modern dress: and
that is what she has got in Brasilia. But once this is admitted,
complaints of Brasilia's oldfashionedness lose their force. It does
not matter that her *supercuadras* are no different from apartment
blocks in Chicago or Copenhagen; or that, as an experiment in
town planning, she is less relevant to modern needs than British
New Towns like Cumbernauld or Peterlee. Nor does it matter
that while some individual buildings—the "Palace of the
Executive Power" and the Presidential "Palace of the Dawn"
—are of great beauty, others are surprisingly pedestrian. This
is no less true of Washington or Paris, London or Rome. What
matters is the combination of the parts, the *gesamteffekt*. Brasilia
must be judged as an essay in monumental architecture. As
such, Brasilia may not always be successful. Her proportions
are not quite satisfactory. The horizon is too flat, the blue dome
of the sky too intimidating; as a result her buildings are often
dwarfed. Still, there are few more exhilarating experiences than
to let the eye follow those sheer, steel-and-glass towers soaring
above the saucer-and-dome roofs of the Parliament Building.
True, the experience is mildly vertigo-producing. For the eye
has no way of judging the dimensions of these towers; they
might be three hundred feet high, or three thousand. It is the
same with Brasilia's Crown-of-Thorns-shaped cathedral. Near
to, it is in fact rather humble and earthbound. But from a
distance there is no telling what its dimensions are; at one
moment it could fit into a matchbox, at the next it has the
scale of Machu Picchu. These are, I suppose, architectural
solecisms. Certainly they are anti-humanistic, not only in the
classical, but also in the modern sense. Man, or the "modulor",
is supposed to be the measure of Le Corbusier's architecture.
But the only parallel for what Costa and Niemeyer have done
is to be found in Gaudi's Barcelona or in Gilly's fascinating,
megalomaniac designs for buildings to express the glory of
Prussia. I confess to a weakness for romantic, monumental

architecture of this kind. And it has, surely, its legitimate place in the modern tradition. If Brazil has something to offer the world architecturally, it is not those broiler-house parodies of Le Corbusier endlessly and unimaginatively (and most unhygienically) repeated on the beach-front of Copacabana. Even the squalid, huddled, iron-roofed shacks of the *favelas*, hugging the contours of Rio's sugar-loaf skyline, seem more appropriate than those barren acres of rectangularity. Still more exciting, if one has a taste for such things, are these romantic, arbitrary buildings that stand on the lonely face of the *sertão*, and could as well be standing on the face of the moon.

"*Rebellion in the Backlands*"

If I have spoken harshly of Gilberto Freyre's opinions, it is because I have had a standard of comparison in mind. That standard, as the reader knows, is Euclides da Cunha's *Rebellion in the Backlands—Os Sertoes*. Compared with da Cunha's masterpiece, the works of Brazil's other great nineteenth-century writer, Machado de Assis, may seem no more than the productions of an effete, frenchified, coast-bound intellectual. I hasten to add that such an evaluation would be wide of the mark. Machado de Assis is certainly "Europeanised"; but he was no dilettante, aping the ways of an Establishment he could never hope to be part of. Indeed, Machado is so fine a writer that his affiliations with the European literature of his time, with Maupassant or, in a different way, with James, cease to be relevant. We have said a good deal in criticism of Brazil. But it is a kind of compliment in reverse. We criticise her because, with her endowments, we expect more of her. It must be said, then, that no Latin American writer of the first century after Independence approaches Machado de Assis. I cited, earlier, Mr Philip Rahv's essay, *Paleface and Redskin*. As I see it, Machado is the classical Paleface; and da Cunha the quintessential Redskin. Mr Rahv's point was that a dichotomy existed in North American writing between the refined, intellectual, Anglicised East-Coast writer—Hawthorne, James, Emily Dickinson or T. S. Eliot—and the tougher, frontier-bred, extravert, and more self-consciously "American" writer of the type of

Whitman, Dreiser, Sinclair Lewis, Sandburg or Steinbeck.
Mr Rahv defines:

> Consider the immense contrast between the drawing-room fictions
> of Henry James and the open-air poems of Walt Whitman.
> Compare Melville's decades of loneliness, his tragic failure, with
> Mark Twain's boisterous career and dubious success. At one pole
> there is the literature of the low-life world of the frontier and of
> the big cities; at the other the thin, solemn, semi-clerical culture
> of Boston and Concord. The fact is that the creative mind in
> America is fragmented and one-sided. For the process of polarisa-
> tion has produced a dichotomy between experience and con-
> sciousness—a dissociation between energy and sensibility,
> between conduct and theories of conduct, between life conceived
> as an opportunity and life conceived as a discipline.

One does not have to go all the way with Mr Rahv to appreciate
the distinction. It is not difficult to pick holes in the argument:
are Melville and Mark Twain really reducible to either
category? Do they not perhaps transcend, and subsume, both?
The dialectic informing these two modes of "American" experience is of the greatest interest. For every lunge into the
unknown interior, there is a shrinking back, a revulsion from
the wilderness, as it were, a clinging to the older bridgeheads of
European order on the Atlantic coast. The same argument is
applicable to Brazil; and, as we have seen, to Latin America
generally. If Neruda is an obvious Redskin, Borges is no less
obviously a Paleface. The *criollista* epicists of the early part of
the century were Redskins, with many of the same faults as
their North American cousins. Writers as various as Sister
Juana de la Cruz and Rodo, on the other hand, are clearly
identifiable Palefaces. Obviously, the distinction must not be
pressed too hard. But it is evident that Machado de Assis, with
his sensitive, elegant, ironic-melancholic tales of life on the
coastal periphery is the Paleface *par excellence*. And what Mr
Rahv says of the American Paleface's strength and weakness
is true of Machado de Assis—and, allowing for the time-
difference, of Borges:

> As to the Paleface, in compensation for backward cultural con-
> ditions and the loss of religious ethics, he has developed a supreme
> talent for refinement. . . . (In this connection it is pertinent to

recall T. S. Eliot's remark about Boston society, which he describes as "quite refined, but refined beyond the point of civilisation".) Now this particular excess of refinement is to be deplored in an imaginative writer, for it weakens his capacity to cope with experience and induces in him a fetishistic attitude towards tradition. . . .

Of the Redskin writer Mr Rahv has this to say:

> The Redskin writer in America is a purely indigenous phenomenon, the true-blue offspring of the Western hemisphere, the juvenile in principle and for the good of the soul. He is a self-made writer in the same way in which Henry Ford was a self-made millionaire. On the one hand he is a crass materialist, a greedy consumer of experience, and on the other a sentimentalist, a hard-baked mystic listening to inward voices and watching for signs and portents. Think of Dreiser, Lewis, Anderson, Wolfe, Sandburg, Steinbeck, Farrell, Saroyan: all writers of genuine and some even of admirable accomplishments, whose faults, however, are not so much literary, as faults of raw life itself.

Mr Rahv's aspersions on the work of these Redskin writers are similar to those of contemporary Latin American critics on the nativist epicists of a generation ago—the literary equivalents of Rivera and Portinari. For the work of the Redskin is

> ridden by compulsions that depress the literary traditions because they are compulsions of a kind that put a strain on literature, that literature more often than not can neither assimilate nor sublimate. He is the passive instead of the active agent of the *zeitgeist*, he lives off it rather than through it, so when his particular gifts happen to coincide with the mood of the time he seems modern and contemporary, but once the mood has passed he is in danger of being quickly discarded.

Yet there are points of comparison. Da Cunha's lengthy digressions in *Rebellion in the Backlands* on genetics and geology, ethnology, climatology and comparative religion, reveal the autodidact. Da Cunha is neither a "sentimentalist", nor a "mystic"; but he is certainly a materialist and "a greedy consumer of experience". The theories on which the book is based are mostly out of date; and da Cunha's "compulsions" do at times put a strain on literature, since they are not always of the kind that literature can "assimilate or sublimate". Yet it does not really matter. The strength of da Cunha's book does not reside in its intellectual structure—that is, in the intellectual structure he intended for his book. It is the "raw life" of the Brazilian *sertão* caught in his artist's imagination that makes da Cunha's epic probably the finest evocation of American man that has ever been composed—only *Huckleberry Finn*, in North American literature, approaching it in quality. In this sense, da Cunha is indeed a Redskin, possibly the greatest of them all. Nor is it untrue to say of him that his faults "are not so much literary, as faults of raw life itself".

"Raw life"! Hardly a phrase to the taste of modern critics! It has the wrong associations. It suggests—appropriately, in this case—those socio-Darwinist doctrines of "nature red in tooth and claw" whose modern extrapolations have not always been happy. It brings to mind, too, those interminable "baggy monsters" from which critics like Mr Rahv—Palefaces to a man—recoil in horror. However, there is no cause for alarm. *Rebellion in the Backlands*, for all its length and its occasional prolixity, is a remarkably well-disciplined monster. And it is precisely da Cunha's *positivisme*—in that age the Liberal religion of all Latin America—that provides the necessary discipline. It is only by courtesy that we call *Os Sertoes* a novel at all; had the genre a better name we might call it a "documentary" without hesitation. Indeed, it could be argued that *Os Sertoes* goes back to one of the historical roots of the novel itself—not to the Iberian chivalric-picaresque roots, but to the journalistic-documentary from which Defoe (a figure not unlike da Cunha) drew his strength. Two centuries separate Defoe's *A Journal of the Plague Year* from *Os Sertoes*; but in spirit they are close. Fact-fetishists as they are, both authors belong to the profane, inquistive, profoundly humane spirit of the Enlightenment.

Yet, if this were the whole story, *Os Sertoes* would rank only with the dozen or so narratives of South American life—with Humboldt's *Travels*, with Fanny Calderon or Maria Williams —which survive of the thousand-odd that have seen the light of day. What is it, then, that makes da Cunha's book essential reading for anyone who would understand modern Brazil? The plot is simple enough: it records the rise to fame in the bleak northern *sertão* of a certain false prophet, Antonio, known to his followers as "the Counsellor". The people of the *sertão*,

a prey to drought and to natural disasters of all kinds, respond
to his chiliastic preaching. Persecuted by authority, Antonio
and his followers fortify themselves at Canudos, like the Ana-
baptists at Münster. When the central government sends an
expedition against them, they resist to the last man. The tale is
told with strict objectivity—da Cunha himself accompanied
the expedition as a war correspondent. Antonio was not, da
Cunha insists, an exceptional man. He had a remarkable talent
for evil, but scarcely genius. Indeed, da Cunha's point is that
the man was completely the product of his extraordinary and
inhuman environment. If he was mad, it was with a madness
that spoke to something in the condition of the poor, semi-
nomadic, half-breeds of the north-eastern *sertão*:

> . . . filthy and battered in appearance, clad in his threadbare
> garments and silent as a ghost, he would spring up suddenly out
> of the plains, peopled by hobgoblins. Then we would pass on,
> bound for other places, leaving the superstitious backwoodsmen
> in a daze. And so it was that in the end he came to dominate them
> without seeking to do so.
>
> All the legends and conjectures which sprang up about him
> were propitious soil for the growth of his own hallucinations. His
> insanity therewith became externalised. Intense admiration and
> the absolute respect which were accorded him gradually led to
> him becoming the unconditional arbiter in all misunderstandings
> and disputes, the favoured "Counsellor" in all decisions. . . . The
> multitude created him, refashioning him in its own image. It
> broadened his life immeasurably by impelling him to those
> errors which were common 2,000 years ago. The people needed
> someone to translate for them their own vague idealisations,
> someone to guide them in the mysterious paths of heaven.

As da Cunha sees it, this story recalls a skirmish, an unremark-
able incident in the long contest between civilisation and
barbarism. *Civilisation and Barbarism!* We are close, here, to
the world of Facundo Quiroga. And the erudite da Cunha,
writing half a century later, certainly knew his *Facundo*. To
ask where da Cunha's sympathies lie in the contest may seem
absurd. His very language betrays the apostle of "Civilisation".
Yet that is not the whole story. Da Cunha, we remember, was
assassinated by a brother officer; and his book was long considered defamatory of Brazil. Clearly, then, da Cunha did not

regard the soldiers of the Canudos expedition—the point was not lost on his contemporaries—solely as bringers of light to them that sit in darkness. He describes the expedition at one point as a tragedy. He makes the curious remark that "we are condemned to civilisation". Gradually, we realise that da Cunha's attitude to the fanatics of Canudos is no less ambivalent than that of Sarmiento to Facundo Quiroga. What has been destroyed at Canudos, when the government troops— three times repulsed by the ragged backwoodsmen—finally bring their superior fire-power to bear, is not simply "Barbarism". Or, if it is Barbarism, it is necessary to admit that it is not something extraneous to the race, but of its essence, that is at issue here.

> It was the very core of our nationality, the bedrock of our race which our troops were attacking here, and dynamite was the means precisely suited. It was at once a recognition and a consecration.

Da Cunha, no friend of racial miscegenation, makes an exception of this Indian-Portuguese *mestizo* people of the *sertão*. Like São Paulo's *bandeirantes*, but unlike the inert, flaccid peoples of the coast, the *sertanejos* are "a strong race". In them are combined the cunning and stoicism of the Indian, and the doggedness and spirit of adventure of the Portuguese. What was destroyed at Canudos, then, by the self-appointed envoys of "Civilisation", was something more authentically Brazilian than the bureaucrats of the new republic could have realised. Still, for all their fantical courage, the followers of Antonio are doomed:

> One thing only they knew was that the *jagunzos* would not be able to hold out for many hours. Some of the soldiers had gone up to the edge of the enemies' last stronghold and there had taken in the situation at one glance. It was incredible. In a quadrangular trench of a little more than a yard in depth, alongside the new church, a score of fighting men, weak from hunger and frightful to behold, were preparing themselves for a dreadful form of suicide. . . .
>
> And fight they did. With the advantage relatively on their side still, at least they succeeded in halting their adversaries. Any of the latter who came too near remained there to fill the sinister trench with bloody, mangled bodies. . . . The terrible exploits that

followed are veiled in obscurity for all the time to come. Those who undertook them seldom returned. Standing above that ditch, the horror of it all overcame the fury of that attack. There before them, a tangible reality, was a trench of the dead, plastered with blood and running with pus. It was something beyond their wildest imaginings and they were paralysed by it.

The last scene of the book, after the total destruction of Antonio's followers, concerns itself with the mortal remains of Antonio the Counsellor. Here, da Cunha's bitter, bewildered irony comes into its own:

Previously, at dawn that day, a commission assigned that task had discovered the corpse of Antonio the Counsellor. It was lying in one of the huts. After a shallow layer of earth had been removed, the body appeared wrapped in a sorry shroud, a filthy sheet, over which pious hands had strewn a few withered flowers. There, resting upon a reed mat, were the last remains of the notorious and barbarous agitator. They were in a fetid condition. Clothed in his old blue canvas tunic, his face swollen and hideous, the deep sunken eyes filled with dirt, the Counsellor would not have been recognisable to those who in his life had known him most intimately. . .

Then they ·put it back in its grave. Later, however, the thought occurred to them that they should have preserved the head, that head on which so many maledictions had been heaped; and, since it was a waste of time to exhume the body once more, a knife cleverly wielded at the right point did the trick, the corpse was decapitated, and that horrible face, sticky with scars and pus, once more appeared before the victors' gaze.

After that they took it to the seaboard where it was greeted by delirious multitudes with carnival joy. Let science here have the last word. Standing out in bold relief from all the significant circumvolutions were the essential outlines of crime and badness.

Da Cunha's ambivalence then, like Sarmiento's, is the making of his book. A plain account of the destruction, by an overwhelming military force, of a *caudillo* like Facundo or a religious fanatic like Antonio would be of small interest. Such an account would be dull, not only because the outcome would be predictable, but because the element of tragedy would be lacking. If Facundo and Antonio had stood for nothing, their destruction would have at most a certain element of pathos. It is because both Sarmiento and da Cunha are convinced that they stand

for something deep in the national character that the story of
their destruction rises to the level of tragedy. Tragedy is the
conflict of good with good, not the predetermined victory of
evil over good, or of good over evil; and it is the good both
writers see in their protagonists that gives these books their
tragic note. Compared with these books, much that has been
written of the South American *gaucho* or *sertanejo* is the merest
sentimentality. Sarmiento's books are profounder than most
that have been written about America; this is not because they
pour scorn on the legend of the Noble Savage, or on the theme
of technology as man's weapon against the American wilderness. On the contrary, all these themes are present. Antonio is
only the latest, ironic incarnation of the Noble Savage, as
Canudos is the latest, ironic realisation of those heavens-upon-
earth that Europeans have looked for on American soil. And as
for technology, what is the new Army of Republican Brazil, in
which da Cunha was commissioned, but the embodiment of
those European principles of hygiene and logistics that will
enable semi-colonial Brazil to conquer the *sertão*? Da Cunha
does not exclude these themes. Indeed, he excludes nothing:
neither American man nor American nature, neither Brazil's
geology nor her religious history, neither Brazil's debt to the
Indian, nor her debt to the Portuguese conqueror. Of no
American writer would it be truer to say, in Mr Rahv's phrase,
that he had attempted "an open and bold confrontation of
reality". The sum of this may not add up to that best of all
possible worlds Dr Pangloss believed he had found in the
Andean fastness of Eldorado. Da Cunha's greatness, on the
contrary, is that in a country not given to tragic thought he saw
that what he had learned at Canudos must lead to profoundly
tragic conclusions, not only about his own country, but about
the human condition.

O My America!

Rebellion in the Backlands has been called Brazil's greatest book.
But it is more than that. Machado de Assis, the Paleface, is
acknowledged to be a universal writer. The epithet "Brazilian"
does not detract from his appeal; he belongs to Goethe's
Weltliteratur. With da Cunha, the Redskin, we are less certain.

To speak of *Os Sertoes* in the same breath as *War and Peace* may seem to invite ridicule; the expedition to Canudos, after all, is hardly the expedition to Moscow. For all that, I believe da Cunha is no less universal a writer than Machado. *Rebellion in the Backlands* has all the imperfections to which Mr Rahv draws our attention in the work of American Redskins. But it has one characteristic otherwise found only in the greatest works of world literature: in *Don Quixote*, in *Hamlet*, in *Faust*. I mean the character of inexhaustibility. *Don Quixote* is about the Decline of Chivalry, about the Ideal and the Real, or about Spain at the turn of the sixteenth century. Yet it is also about the human condition. But if *Don Quixote* and *Hamlet* and *Faust* are inexhaustible, it is not because of any spatial or temporal extension beyond the ordinary (significantly the boring parts of *Faust* are where Goethe attempts this). It is because there is something in these symbols that speaks to all ages and conditions of men. It is characteristic, perhaps, that these books should all have been attacked by modern critics at one time or another for their ambiguity and vagueness, for their sheer irreducibility, their offering of symbols that may be interpreted to mean everything or nothing. For this reason, T. S. Eliot spoke harshly, in his early criticism, of Shakespeare's *Hamlet* and Goethe's *Faust*. His irritation was understandable; the moderns thought art should be hard and precise. They did not care for those flapping, baggy monsters handed down to them by tradition. There was something irresponsible about free-floating symbols of this kind: Virgil and Dante would not have permitted it. Yet *Hamlet*, *Don Quixote*, and *Faust* survive. In its modest niche, *Rebellion in the Backlands* survives too. The bad science, the "irritating parentheses", the prolixity; none of this matters. Da Cunha's masterpiece lives, not in its apparatus, but in the web of symbolic themes it has to offer.

What are these themes? Of the most explicit, the theme of man's inhumanity to man, little needs to be said. What is startling is how many of the themes we have explored in this book are implicit in da Cunha. In examining Latin America it has been necessary to speak of the violence beneath the surface of her life: in Colombia, Mexico or Argentina. A Brazilian claim, it will be remembered, was that the Luso-Brazilian tradition lacked the violence of the Spanish-American. Brazil's coups were bloodless; Brazil had no Rosas, no Santa Anna, and Vargas—Brazil's Peron—was no man of blood. Yet there is a ferocity and fanaticism about the Canudos incident that is unmistakably Iberian. And da Cunha was clearly aware of the irony of this. For ferocity and fanaticism, courage and tenacity, are exactly the qualities lacking in "civilised" coastal Brazil. I suggested, earlier, that Brazilian tolerance in racial and political matters was not something that foreigners should take at face value. I do not think da Cunha would have disagreed. Tolerance can mean charity and sweet reason: but it can also imply lack of conviction, and the courage that goes with conviction. The latter quality Spaniards and Spanish Americans have in excess. Da Cunha clearly implies that Portuguese Americans have too little. That is how da Cunha can see in the crazed followers of Antonio those "aboriginal virtues of the race" which civilised Brazil is destroying, and yet cannot do without.

In a political sense, again, *Os Sertoes* remains remarkably relevant. At the centre of the stage da Cunha places the relationship—apparently straightforward, but in fact of a subtle reciprocity—between Antonio and his amorphous, fanatical following. At first sight there may appear nothing remarkable in this; all men desire to be led, and we know what a *Führer* of talent can make out of a motley following. It will not do, then, to speak of Antonio's relationship to his followers as "feudal" or "tribal". Something more like Max Weber's "charismatic leadership" is implied here. As we have seen, a relationship of precisely this kind between leader and following is fundamental to Latin American politics. This is as true on the local as on the national plane. In discussions of the politics of the poverty-stricken North-East a great deal was formerly heard (before 1964) of Francisco Julião's Peasant Leagues. These represented, it was said, a profoundly revolutionary element in Brazilian society; and Julião's trips to Havana and Peking appeared to confirm this. Yet Julião, the "Castro of Brazil", was at bottom an invention of *Time* magazine. In Brazil he was too traditional a phenomenon to be taken seriously (Brazilians read their da Cunha.) He was yet another of those spectres Americans invent to torment their Puritan conscience. What actually happened was that the oppressed—but not therefore "revolutionary"—peasants of the North-East followed Julião, the city-bred lawyer, because they saw in him a protector of their interests more effective than the feudal *patrão* to whom they customarily gave their allegiance. The peasants of the backlands transferred their loyalty from an authority both ineffective and unjust to a new *patrão* whose favours held greater promise. Shades of Antonio the Counsellor! To call such groupings "revolutionary" would be as inappropriate as to call Antonio's community at Canudos revolutionary. For the terminology of international politics is simply inapplicable. The ties binding leader and following are ties of mutual interest; once the leader is dead, or the interest satisfied, the ties are abrogated. But to say that such phenomena cannot be explained in the language of international politics is not to say that they are unimportant. As Gerald Brenan points out, in *The Spanish Labyrinth*, this kind of relationship between protector and *protégé* is deeply rooted in Iberian life. We saw, in the case of the Argentine, that to describe the relationship as "feudal" is to presuppose a more stable pattern than actually exists. We have seen, also, that it is not the European-style, disciplined, ideological mass-movements that succeed in Latin America, but the *caudillo*-led, personalist movements. And these movements follow the pattern da Cunha traces out in *Os Sertoes*. Bolivar, Sarmiento, Haya de la Torre, Vargas, Peron, Castro are simply Francisco Julião and Antonio writ large. Even about contemporary Latin American politics there is more to be learnt from *Os Sertoes* than from *Time* magazine.

I have argued that, while da Cunha was surely an erudite man, his strength was as much intuitive as intellectual. As it happens, there is interesting confirmation of this to hand. Since da Cunha's time a good deal of research has been done into such phenomena as the Canudos rising. (A comprehensive survey is to be found in Vittorio Lanternari's *The Religion of the Oppressed*, to which I am much indebted.) From a comparative study of such phenomena, in several parts of the world, certain conclusions emerge. The first, not unfamiliar to da Cunha, is that religious movements of this kind arise at a particular point in space and time. They are the product of the clash between the expanding civilisation of the Christian West and the primitive peoples of the non-European world. Da Cunha was almost certainly not aware of the extent of this clash. Yet what he wrote about Brazil (whose backlands population, as he saw, was really an alienated fragment of the nation itself) is no less applicable to North America, Africa, or Melanesia. The form taken by the confrontation may differ from place to place, but the underlying pattern is remarkably similar. Indeed, the assaulted, aboriginal culture, aware of its inability to resist "westernisation", reacts in a fashion that, for all its seeming irrationality, has a compelling logic. A society wounded in this way is a society requiring reassurance. Since it has become convinced of its own inferiority, it is unable to draw on its own resources. To regain self-confidence, therefore, it is necessary to borrow from the deeply-hated—but also deeply-admired—culture of the foreigner. But what is borrowed, while magically transferring the power of the invader to the aboriginal, must also protect the aboriginal from the invader's inroads. In other words, that which is borrowed must also exclude. Still better, it can try to turn the tables on the invader by using his own weapons. How can it do this? In the civilisation of the Christian West there is one element tailor-made for this purpose: Christianity itself. The Judaic-exclusive element in Christianity ministers ideally to the psychology of the down-trodden aboriginal. This fetish, stolen from the culture of the White Man, proves to him that it is really he, the victim, who should inherit the earth. The aboriginal and the invader change places: the former becomes the Jew, the chosen of God; the latter the outcast Gentile.

Except by intuition, da Cunha can hardly have been aware of the further ramifications of his theme. It is only now that we see how fitted was Christianity—neglected by a newly rich and sceptical Prospero—to become the religion of Caliban, at least in one phase of their complex relationship. Still less can da Cunha have been aware of the ramifications of his theme in regard to the aboriginal inhabitants of America. For it appears that there was an indigenous millenarianism in America, pre-dating the introduction of Christianity by the *conquistadores*. We have seen how profound was the effect the Eldorado and related legends exerted on the European and American mind. How did the legend of Eldorado arise? It began, it seems, as a tall tale told to the Spaniards at Chichapoyas, in Peru, about the year

1549, concerning a land in the interior of South America abounding in gold and precious stones. It appears that this tale was told to the Spaniards by some members of the Tupinamba tribe. Originally settled on the Atlantic Coast of Brazil, they had been displaced by the Portuguese invader and determined to migrate inland, in search of the earthly paradise of *Maran-im*. These Indians appear to have spent nine years travelling up the Amazon before meeting with the Spaniards in newly-conquered Peru.

Now this is a tall tale in itself. Yet the evidence for it is good. Moreover, from Lanternari's researches it is clear that the pursuit of the millennium was endemic among the Indians of South, as also of North America. It is not always easy to separate this Indian millenarianism from later, Christian accretions. Thus in the *peyotl* cult of the North American Indian it is evident that a fusion has taken place. The Indian believes that "when all tribes have eaten it, then will come the end of the world". Yet these promises are ascribed to Jesus Christ: "when all the Indians have eaten this, the world will be made over, then all will be as God wills it". It is known that the use of *peyotl* originated south of the Rio Grande (*peyotl* produces, according to Lanternari, "a peculiar sensation of levitation, a vision of brilliant coloured images, and an inordinately sharp perception of sounds and shapes". One of its ingredients is the alkaloid mescalin, whose effects Aldous Huxley described in *The Doors of Perception*). The Dominican Sahagun had described, in 1560, the ritual use of this cactus by the Chichimeca of Mexico. Its use, therefore, is certainly pre-Christian. As it spread north from these ancient centres of Indian civilisation, the properties ascribed to it seemed to have merged, among the Plains Indians of North America, with the half-apprehended doctrines of the Christian missionaries. "The Bible", according to John Wilson, founder of the cult in the nineteenth-century United States, "was given to the White Man because he had been guilty of crucifying Jesus. The Indians had no responsibility for this act and therefore the Bible was not intended for them. The Indians know God's truth from the *peyotl* spirit, but the White Man needed Christ's Word in order to learn it." Or, again, also of *peyotl*: "It was given exclusively to the Indians and God never intended that the White Men should understand it." By the end of the century, the *peyotl* cult—and the related "Ghost Dance"—had spread to Indians across the whole extent of the United States and Canada. The "Great Spirit" of Indian tradition had merged with the monotheism of Christianity. The Indians of North America had created for themselves a synthetic religion with which they hoped, like the defenders of Canudos, to hold the civilisation of the White Man at bay.

We have seen that it is risky to generalise about the Indians of America. If the Red Man of the Americas once had a culture and a common tongue, it was at a remote period. There is no doubt, of course, that the Indians are a race in the bio-logical sense: with their lack of facial and body hair, their slit eyes and high cheekbones, they are certainly an offshoot of the Mongoloid peoples of Eastern and Central Asia. But that does not take us very far. For the Indians known to history are so remote from one another linguistically and geographically that to point to an "Indian personality" must seem a questionable enterprise. Yet, as we have seen, it is some variant of this Indian culture that forms the cultural subsoil of the greater part of the continent. What the contribution of these sub-cultures will be in the future it is impossible to say. All we can say is that beneath the topsoil of Iberian Catholic culture there lurk forms which, though too weak to reject its domination, have subtly modified it in the past, and will do so in the future. That the results of this cultural confrontation have been largely negative is as clear from Ramos's *Man and Culture in Mexico* or *The People of Aritama* as from da Cunha's book. Indeed, these authors are discussing what is at bottom the same phenomenon: the failure of the European and the Indian culture to merge in a fruitful symbiosis, to form what da Cunha—referring to his mixed-blood *sertanejos*—liked to call "a strong race".

It was a Tupi tribe, migrating from the Brazilian coast to the rim of the Amazonian forest, that brought the Spaniards tidings of an Eldorado in the Amazonian hinterland. But such migra-tions were nothing new. For centuries there had been Tupi migrations from the interior to the coast. These migrations seem to have been due not to any search for gold, but to fear of a swiftly approaching apocalypse. These Tupi tribes, when they found no evidence of their "land of immortality and perpetual rest" on the Pacific coast of America, often made their way back

to the Atlantic seaboard. Where that land might be found was
as little known to the Indians as to the Europeans who were to
follow in their footsteps. Did it lie to the West, among the fastnesses of the Andes or in the depths of the Amazonian forest?
Or did it lie to the east, on some lost Atlantis across the ocean?
The Guarani, related to the Tupi, and once the objects of the
Jesuits' missionary efforts in Paraguay, had the same millenarian urge. The first mention of a migration occurs in 1515. But
it appears that these movements continued down the centuries.
As late as 1921 a French anthropologist found these tribes still
dominated by the same fears of the destruction of the world,
and by the same restless search for an earthly paradise. Some
of these Tupi tribes on the coast of Brazil had evidently not yet
given up hope of crossing and finding that Great Good
Place their ancestors had sought. Pathetically, they still performed incantations and ritual dances designed to rid their
bodies of weight so they might fly across the Atlantic in search
of that paradise.

That these millenarian migrations pre-dated the Iberian
intrusion is certain. But it is no less certain that this intrusion
gave them new impetus and significance. Thus we read of a
Guarani rising in 1579 that is uncannily similar to the events
described by da Cunha.

> A prophet named Obera founded a cult in which the pagan
> elements were blended with elements of Christian teaching; but
> his leadership soon instigated a rebellion openly intended to
> destroy all Christians. . . . The ritual of this sect consisted of
> dancing and singing, avoiding any kind of work, and in the
> glorification of his own person. Proclaiming himself the liberator
> of the Guarani tribes, Son of God, born of a Virgin. . . . Obera
> claimed to have captured a comet which at that time appeared in
> the sky and to have sealed it in a jar ready to be used against the
> Spaniards. . . . Obera's own following became increasingly a
> menace to the Spaniards in Paraguay; finally . . . the Spaniards
> resorted to arms and brought about a battle . . . which put an
> end to Obera and his cult.

All the symptoms are there: the fear and hatred of the White
Man, the assimilation of elements in his religion to ancient,
aboriginal beliefs and practices; the rebellion; the inexorable
destruction of the backlands heretics by the guns of the ortho-

dox. The conclusion, as in da Cunha, is tragic. And tragic, not for the aborigines alone, but also for the invader. For the White Americans inherited the same geography, the same climate, the same frustrations and aspirations. And to it all they added their own Christian-Iberian millenarianism. At the *conquista*, as we have seen, the mystical, crusading energies of Castile—and of Portugal—were directed towards an enterprise which was partly a recapitulation of the *reconquista*, and partly something new. Might not this New World bring forth a new, regenerate man, free from Adam's sin? Whether in More's *Utopia* or in the writings of the Inca Garcilaso or in Voltaire's *Candide*, the legend never died. Somewhere, somehow, this world-without-evil, this best-of-all-possible-worlds, must have its location. The deepest meaning of da Cunha's epic is neither political nor sociological nor historical: it is that the quest is a delusion. There is no New World, no earthly paradise. Man cannot escape from his destiny, which is always and everywhere tragic, for man creates only to destroy. The Noble Savage is no more free of Adam's sin that the White invader. Utopia is not to be found in the high Andes, or in the jungles of Paraguay, or in the treasure-towns of Potosi or Ouro Preto or Manaus. Utopia does not belie its name: Utopia is no-place.

ACKNOWLEDGEMENTS AND INDEX

ACKNOWLEDGEMENTS

Borges, G. L., "Referring to the Death of Col. F. Borges (1835–75)", in *Dream Tigers*, University of Texas Press, 1964.
——*Ficciones*, Weidenfeld & Nicolson, London, 1962; Grove Press, New York, 1962.

Brenan, Gerald, *Literature of the Spanish People*, Cambridge University Press, London, 1951.

Conrad, Joseph, *Nostromo*, Dent, London, 1905, by courtesy of Trustees of Joseph Conrad Estate.

Cuevas, Jose, *Cuevas por Cuevas*, Ediciones Era, Mexico City, 1965.

da Cunha, Euclides, *Rebellion in the Backlands*, Gollancz, London, 1958; University of Chicago Press, 1958.

Diaz, Bernal, *The Conquest of New Spain*, translated by J. M. Cohen, Penguin, London and New York, 1963.

Encina, Francisco, *Historia de Chile*, Empresa Edit. Zig-Zag, Santiago, 1964.

Ferlinghetti, Lawrence, "One Thousand Fearful Words for Fidel Castro", in *Starting From San Francisco*, New Directions, New York, 1961.

Finer, S. E., *The Man on Horseback*, Pall Mall Press, London, 1962; Frederick A. Praeger, New York, 1962.

Freyre, Gilberto, *Brazil: An Introduction*, Knopf, New York, 1945.

Hyams, Edward, *The Last of the Incas*, Longmans, Green, London, 1963; Simon & Schuster, New York, 1963.

Isherwood, Christopher, *The Condor and the Cows*, Methuen, London, 1949 and Author.

de Jesus, Carolina Maria, *Beyond All Pity*, Souvenir Press, London, 1962.

Lévi-Strauss, Claude, *A World on the Wane*, translated by John Russell, Hutchinson, London, 1959; Atheneum, New York, 1964.

Lévi-Strauss, Claude, *Tristes Tropiques*, new translation in process, Cape, London.

Madariaga, Salvador, *Latin America between the Eagle and the Bear*, Hollis & Carter, London, 1962; Praeger, New York, 1962.

Neruda, Pablo, *The Heights of Machu Picchu*, Cape, London, 1966; Grove Press, New York, 1962.

Paz, Octavio, *The Labyrinth of Solitude*, Penguin, London, 1967; Grove Press, New York, 1961.

Rahv, Philip, "Paleface and Redskin", in *Image and Idea*, Weidenfeld & Nicolson, London, 1957; New Directions, New York.

Ramos, Samuel, *Profile of Man and Culture in Mexico*, McGraw-Hill, New York, 1962.

Reichel-Dolmatoff, G. and A., *The People of Aritama*, Routledge & Kegan Paul, London, 1961; University of Chicago Press, 1961.

Sarmiento, D. F., *Life in the Argentine Republic in the Days of the Tyrants*, Macmillan, New York, 1961.

Soustelle, Jacques, *The Daily Life of the Aztecs*, Weidenfeld & Nicolson, London, 1961; Hachette.

INDEX

INDEX